The book reflects an extraordinary innovative, integrative effort. It gracefully bridges the yawning divide between cognitive, social, and psychodynamic approaches to depression and presents a crystal clear, novel, and immediately practically helpful approach to support clinical work with some of the most challenging clients. Potentially a massive contribution to the work of clinicians, from the most experienced to novice therapists. It should be on the shelf of every clinical psychologist.

—**Peter Fonagy, PhD,** Executive Clinical Director, UCLPartners Mental Health Programme, London, England; Chief Executive, Anna Freud National Centre for Children & Families, London, England

Only Golan Shahar could write this unique book, courageously drawing upon his own family history. He is very knowledgeable about psychoanalysis and does not hesitate to revise its formulations. His vast experience in empirical research into depression and suicidality is utilized to develop innovative psychotherapeutic strategies.

—**Emanuel Berman, PhD,** Professor Emeritus of Psychology, University of Haifa, Haifa, Israel

Golan Shahar has one of the best integrative minds in contemporary psychoanalysis. He weaves together a potent brew of approaches to address one of the most intractable disorders extant—complex depression. With his ecodynamics theory, he breaks fresh ground in the expansion and deepening of integrative psychoanalysis so it embraces the developmental, relational, and social-cultural dimensions of complex depression often overlooked by conventional formulations. For an innovative, methodical, and notably personal integrative inquiry, I can think of few rivals.

—**Kirk J. Schneider, PhD,** editor of *Existential-Integrative Psychotherapy: Guideposts to the Core of Practice,* coauthor of *Existential–Humanistic Therapy, Second Edition* (with Orah T. Krug), and author of *Life-Enhancing Anxiety: Key to a Sane World*

Complex Depression addresses a huge public health problem: People with depression are not getting better despite 60 years of antidepressant availability. It offers an alternative perspective to reductionistic models, such as the NIMH RDOC Initiative, that focus primarily on aspects of depression that can be studied in animals. Instead, it brings the same scientific rigor to a reconsideration of the complexity of the people who experience depression and offers informed stratagems for intervention. Reading this book reminded me, once again, that to treat depression most effectively, you need to deeply understand the person experiencing this symptom and their social context.

—**John H. Krystal, MD,** Robert L. McNeil, Jr., Professor of Translational Research; Professor of Psychiatry, Neuroscience, and Psychology; Chair, Department of Psychiatry, Yale School of Medicine, New Haven, CT, United States

---

In this dense volume, Golan Shahar draws on extensive research and clinical experience to help clinicians and researchers understand and focus on patient and systematic aspects that complicate and sustain complex depression. Invaluable insights for clinicians and depression researchers alike.

—**Allan Abbass, MD, FRCPC,** author of *Reaching Through Resistance: Advanced Psychotherapy Techniques*; Professor of Psychiatry and Psychology, Dalhousie University, Halifax, Nova Scotia, Canada

COMPLEX DEPRESSION

COMPLEX DEPRESSION
The Role of Personality Dynamics and Social Ecology
GOLAN SHAHAR

 AMERICAN PSYCHOLOGICAL ASSOCIATION

Copyright © 2024 by the American Psychological Association. All rights reserved. Except as permitted under the United States Copyright Act of 1976, no part of this publication may be reproduced or distributed in any form or by any means, including, but not limited to, the process of scanning and digitization, or stored in a database or retrieval system, without the prior written permission of the publisher.

The opinions and statements published are the responsibility of the authors, and such opinions and statements do not necessarily represent the policies of the American Psychological Association.

Published by
American Psychological Association
750 First Street, NE
Washington, DC 20002
https://www.apa.org

Order Department
https://www.apa.org/pubs/books
order@apa.org

Typeset in Charter and Interstate by Circle Graphics, Inc., Reisterstown, MD

Printer: Gasch Printing, Odenton, MD
Cover Designer: Craig Davidson, Civic Design, Minneapolis, MN

Library of Congress Cataloging-in-Publication Data

Names: Shahar, Golan, author.
Title: Complex depression : the role of personality dynamics and social ecology / Golan Shahar.
Description: Washington, DC : American Psychological Association, [2024] | Includes bibliographical references and index.
Identifiers: LCCN 2023018353 (print) | LCCN 2023018354 (ebook) | ISBN 9781433836077 (paperback) | ISBN 9781433836084 (ebook)
Subjects: LCSH: Personality. | Depression, Mental. | Social ecology. | BISAC: PSYCHOLOGY / Psychopathology / Depression | PSYCHOLOGY / Clinical Psychology
Classification: LCC BF698 .S433 2024 (print) | LCC BF698 (ebook) | DDC 158--dc23/eng/20230722
LC record available at https://lccn.loc.gov/2023018353
LC ebook record available at https://lccn.loc.gov/2023018354

https://doi.org/10.1037/0000377-000

Printed in the United States of America

10 9 8 7 6 5 4 3 2 1

This book is dedicated to my late mother, Yaffa Lavie, who served as my constant source of inspiration for my life's work in the battle against depression.

Contents

Foreword—Thomas Joiner — ix
Acknowledgments — xiii

    An Introduction to the Personality and Social Dynamics of Complex Depression — 3

I. DEPRESSION AND PERSONALITY — 11

    1. The Complications of Depression — 13
    2. The Role of Personality in Complex Depression — 35

II. PSYCHODYNAMICS AND ECODYNAMICS — 57

    3. Reformulating Object Relations Theory and the Depressive Position — 59
    4. Human Ecology and Development Within Social Contexts: Ecodynamics Theory — 81

III. THE ECODYNAMICS OF COMPLEX DEPRESSION — 97

    5. Applying the Reformulated Depressive Position and Ecodynamics to Complex Depression — 99
    6. Suicidal Depression: A Case Study of Complex Depression's Most Severe Consequence — 123

7. Practical Implications for Assessment: Evaluating Complex Depression Through the Reformulated Depressive Position and Ecodynamics   137

8. Practical Implications for Psychotherapy: Specific Interventions for Treating Complex Depression   151

Epilogue: Afterthoughts and Looking to the Future   173

References   *183*
Index   *239*
About the Author   *249*

Foreword

THOMAS JOINER

I have often been rather hard on "psychoanalysis," one of my charges being incoherence. It is an easy target—a strawperson, one might say—in that a juggernaut-like "psychoanalysis" does not really exist (which is the reason for the quotation marks) and so, of course, there is incoherence virtually by definition. As in most domains, once one gets more specific, some specifications are more coherent and more persuasive than others. Golan Shahar gets specific in this book, to all our benefit, more on which soon.

I must admit a kind of contradiction in my views, in that in print I have decried "psychoanalysis," and yet I am the therapist I am today in part because of a graduate training that was heavily psychodynamic. I do not mean to convey that today I practice anything remotely psychodynamic—with every passing decade, I have become more and more convinced that two clinical leverage points tower above all others. One is biology, which our friends and colleagues in psychiatry and specialties like primary care target imperfectly yet to considerable value. The other is behavior—including, of course, social and interpersonal behavior—which we behavior therapists target less imperfectly and to at least as much value. I am especially a fan, in most cases, of the concurrent targeting of these two leverage points.

And yet, lest I stray too extremely in those directions, Golan Shahar's calm, focused, and convincing insistence that there is more sways me. In the way that I relate to patients, to clinical supervisees, and to people in general, my early psychodynamic experience has proved invaluable, as have role models who regard psychodynamic approaches with openness and interest. When

I reflect back on clinicians whom I personally knew and who have had the most effect on me, two immediately spring to mind—and a third deserves note as well.

One was the late, great Paul Meehl, and the second was my major professor, Jerry Metalsky. It might surprise readers to hear of psychologists Meehl and Metalsky described as "clinicians," as I refer to them above, but Meehl most certainly was and Metalsky most certainly is, and ones of great insight to boot. To be sure, they were not only clinicians; they were scientists and scholars, too, and in the latter roles, shared the ability, among many others, to articulate rich and testable theoretical statements. Meehl practiced psychotherapy throughout his professional career, and it will definitely surprise some readers that Meehl—a seminal pioneer in scientific psychology—was highly psychoanalytic early in his professional life. He wrote that with each passing decade, he came to believe less and less of it, but his belief in its clinical utility never reached nil. Much the same with Metalsky. In conversations with him in which I would air some of the antipsychoanalytic rhetoric that would appear in my later books, I vividly recall his pained expression and tone with which he would reply, "I know, I know . . . and yet, there's something useful there."

Indeed, there is something there, which brings me to the third clinician who has influenced me. In my view, anyone with the scientific credentials and integrity of Meehl and Metalsky deserves a hearing, even when they are alluding to the virtues and, indeed, power of a psychoanalytic approach. Like them, Golan Shahar exudes scientific integrity and excellence, and like them, he deserves a hearing—deserves more than that, actually—given the many years he has devoted to a specific, principled, and coherent psychodynamic perspective that is truly accessible to a wide audience, genuinely based on sound scientific psychology, and very amenable to scientific testing. On this latter point, Shahar shares Meehl's and Metalsky's gift for the rare combination of elegant theorizing and clinical incisiveness.

When psychodynamic concepts leap into my head during the course of my own clinical work these days, I have a knee-jerk reaction to banish them. I have learned to tame this instinct; and to do so, Metalsky's "and yet there's something useful there" recurs in my memory, as does Meehl's retention over the course of his career of at least some psychoanalytic faith and as do my respect, admiration, and fondness for Shahar, to my mind a unique exemplar of the systematizing and the translating of psychoanalytic zeal into a clear, scientifically supportable, and clinically useful framework. In this book, Shahar applies this framework to elucidating how personality processes, particularly affect and its regulation juxtaposed against mental representations of self with others, predispose individuals to shape a social context that ultimately not only leads to depression but also complicates it considerably. I am heartened by the way Shahar utilizes the social-cognitive nomenclature for the purpose of reformulating key psychoanalytic theories, primarily object relations theory, and then builds on this reformulation to explain how individuals' mental maps lead to the very interpersonal environment that is maladaptive. As someone who dedicated my life's work to understanding the role of interpersonal processes in psychopathology in general, and in depression and suicidality in particular, I find this integrative endeavor by Shahar absolutely fascinating.

While Shahar applies his perspective to depression and its various complications, I encourage readers to ponder its relevance beyond those specific phenomena to other clinical conditions as well, and indeed to the human condition itself. Readers, read on. What is in store is illumination—illumination of depression, suicidality, character, psychotherapy, and human nature.

Acknowledgments

I thank Ben-Gurion University of the Negev, particularly the Department of Psychology, for being the best academic home for me and for providing me with all of the resources needed to write this treatise. I extend special thanks to Provost Prof. Haim Hames for years of friendship and support.

I also thank my colleagues in Israel and abroad for reading and commenting on earlier drafts of this manuscript (in alphabetical order):

Dana Amir, PhD, Psychoanalytic Institute, Jerusalem, Israel
Emanuel Berman, PhD, Psychoanalytic Institute, Jerusalem, Israel
Richard Chefetz, MD, private practice, Washington, DC, United States
Jeremy Clark, PhD, Tavistock and Portman Charity, London, United Kingdom
Nir Dudek, PhD, private practice, Gizmu, Israel
Zvi Fireman, MA, Ben-Gurion University of the Negev, Beersheba, Israel
Eva Gilboa-Schechtman, PhD, Bar-Ilan University, Ramat-Gan, Israel
Aner Govrin, PhD, Tel Aviv Institute of Contemporary Psychoanalysis, Tel Aviv, Israel, and Bar-Ilan University, Ramat-Gan, Israel
Thomas Joiner, PhD, Florida State University, Tallahassee, FL, United States
Nirit Soffer-Dudek, PhD, Ben-Gurion University of the Negev, Beersheba, Israel
Liat Tikotzky, PhD, Ben-Gurion University of the Negev, Beersheba, Israel
Paul Wachtel, PhD, City University of New York, New York, NY, United States
Sharon Ziv-Beiman, PhD, Academic College of Tel Aviv–Yaffo, Tel Aviv–Yaffo, Israel

My graduate students, Raz Bauminger and Yarin Szachter, have also read the manuscript and provided invaluable comments. I also give very special thanks to my spouse, Pnina Amor, for readily assuming the role of the light of my life.

Last but certainly not least, I express profound gratitude to my patients: You have bestowed on me the knowledge conferred in these pages and given me the privilege of accompanying you in your journey. Invariably, you have given me more that you have received.

COMPLEX DEPRESSION

AN INTRODUCTION TO THE PERSONALITY AND SOCIAL DYNAMICS OF COMPLEX DEPRESSION

By March 2020, the world had been officially "COVID-ized." I am referring, of course, to the COVID-19 pandemic that began in Wuhan, China, in November 2019, and spread rapidly worldwide, taking lives, mounting disabilities, and ruining economies. When I began writing this Introduction at the end of September 2020, Israel was suffering a second COVID-19 wave. Four additional waves ensued in the country, delivering devastating blows to individuals, families, and Israeli society as a whole (Shahar et al., 2022). Yet the development of effective vaccines and their circulation worldwide has largely turned the tide against COVID-19. Individuals, families, and societies are bouncing back, only to find that the real pandemic is here to stay. I am referring, of course, to unipolar depression.

Volumes have been written on unipolar depression in scientific and clinical outlets and likely no less than that by numerous novelists and journalists (Rottenberg, 2014; A. Solomon, 2015; Styron, 1992), illuminating important personal and public points of view. Nevertheless, this disorder is far from being understood and/or properly treated. What do I have to add to this respectable literature? Two things, I submit. First, depression, similar to other noxious viruses, tends to create complications. These complications challenge

https://doi.org/10.1037/0000377-001
Complex Depression: The Role of Personality Dynamics and Social Ecology, by G. Shahar
Copyright © 2024 by the American Psychological Association. All rights reserved.

many of our life domains, making depression particularly difficult to diagnose, prevent, and *contain* (an epidemiological term that has thus far not been used with respect to depression but should be). One such complication—suicidality—is well known. Other complications are a heterogeneous manifestation of the symptoms and depression comorbidity (manifestation of at least one additional psychiatric disorder alongside depression). When I refer to these complications in this book, I also highlight less well-known complications such as physical health and illness, delinquency, violence, and crime. Second, I contend that underlying complex forms of depression are specific personality dynamics that interact with the social context in predictable—and treatable—ways. This active transaction between individuals' personality and their social ecology is what I refer to as an *ecodynamics* perspective on complex depression, which is the foundation of this book's approach.

To illustrate how severe the consequences of complex depression can be, I present the story of my stepfather, Zvika. His lifelong struggle with depression culminated in suicide, which left an indelible mark on my work and strongly influenced my ecodynamics theory.

CASE EXAMPLE OF THE CONSEQUENCES OF COMPLEX DEPRESSION: ZVIKA'S SUICIDAL DEPRESSION

Golan Shalom.

This is a farewell letter.

I made a final decision to end this life cycle. I ran out of steam.

Till this very moment, I am confused by your attitude towards me and I also do not know to what extent, if any, you have an attitude towards me.

The only thing that I know is that I miss you. I was hoping that we would succeed in bridging the rift between us.

I am neither angry nor insulted. I forgive you for whatever you think is deserving of my forgiveness.

I am asking for your forgiveness for any wrongdoing I have committed to you, if I have.

I wish you happiness and long, good years with Rachel.

Love,

Zvika

Zvika was my stepfather and more: He raised me as a father would and was the person I called "Dad" until I turned 10. He died by suicide in Israel in 2002. I was then 31 years old and in the process of transitioning from a postdoctoral position to an assistant professorship in the Yale University Department of Psychiatry. At that time, my (now ex-)wife, Rachel, was more than 6 months pregnant with Lielle, our oldest daughter. I learned the sad news about Zvika via a telephone call from my older brother, Harel. His voice was characteristically steady and quiet as he spoke these very words: "I have very bad news to give you. Zvika killed himself." My reaction: "I told you he would."

And I did. I have witnesses to testify to this, especially Rachel. Six months before Zvika died by suicide, we learned that he had threatened to kill himself. He made this threat in the context of marital turmoil, which will be discussed in Chapter 6. At the time, I was establishing a career as a depression researcher (Shahar, 2001) and studying with Professor Sidney Blatt, a legendary figure in depression research, at Yale University. I was also profoundly influenced by the research and writings of Thomas Joiner, who was already a leading figure in the fields of depression and suicidality. In 1999, Joiner and colleagues published an article that provided scientifically informed guidelines for suicide risk assessment. I read and reread it, deemed it the most useful article I had read on the topic, and began using the guidelines in my clinical practice. When I learned about Zvika's suicide threat, I thought of the work by Joiner et al. (1999) and conducted a suicide risk assessment, which indicated my stepfather's high-risk status. I told my family in Israel that Zvika would very likely kill himself. I was ridiculed for being overly anxious and dramatic, which, indeed, I am at times. But in this case, I was correct in my prediction.

Zvika died by suicide, but from depression. Suicidality, I am convinced, is a major—perhaps the most ominous—complication of what appears to be the greatest pandemic of our time: unipolar depression. There are also other, profoundly problematic complications of depression, and they encompass all of our life domains. I am referring specifically to the heterogenous—sometimes bizarre—manifestation of depression, depression chronicity and comorbidity, and effects of depression on physical health and illness (including somatization and chronic physical illness), delinquency, violence, and crime. The central premise of this book is that one important common denominator of the complications of depression is an individual's personality.

REFORMULATED OBJECT RELATIONS THEORY AND ECODYNAMICS

Since the beginning of my research career, my primary research focus has been the role of personality in psychopathology, with an emphasis on depressive disorders. Proudly wearing the title of a "Blatt student," I worked from his grand theory of personality, development, and psychopathy (Blatt, 2004, 2008). However, I was incorrigibly rebellious and began to challenge Blatt's teachings and modify his theory—a process that reached its peak with the publication of *Erosion*, my book on self-criticism (Shahar, 2015a).

Subsequent to publishing this book, I continued to study clinical depression, and my theoretical, empirical, and clinical work all converged into a novel iteration, which I call the *reformulated object relations theory* (RORT). A derivative of the RORT is the reformulated depressive position, which is described extensively in Chapter 3. Although the precursors of the RORT and the reformulated depressive position were established in three previous publications (Shahar, 2018, 2021b; Shahar & Schiller, 2016b), this book constitutes the most extensive and important exposition of this novel iteration.

This book goes beyond the RORT by situating it within an overarching framework that reconciles internal mental processes and the social environment. More specifically, I have always been intrigued by the numerous ways in which our internal processes are intertwined with the way we actually interact with people and social systems in our lives. I have, therefore, drawn consistently from social-ecological and ecodevelopmental theories that describe interactions between person and context (Bronfenbrenner, 1977, 1979, 1994; G. W. Brown, 1985; Markus & Kitayama, 1991; Wachtel, 1997, 2014). By integrating the RORT with these social-ecological perspectives, I arrive at a novel theory of (the depressive) personality that I refer to as *ecodynamics*.

This book applies ecodynamics to complex manifestations of depression. It is predicated on the following premises:

1. Personality pertains, first and foremost, to an amalgamated cluster of cognitions and emotions that form an internal structure (Block, 2002). This internal structure functions as a mental map for individuals' sense of subjectivity (self) and intersubjectivity (relationships). Because the field of personality is governed by trait approaches that do not focus on such a structure (e.g., the five-factor personality model; Costa & McCrae, 1998), I use the acronym SAPS for *subjective–agentic personality sector* (Shahar, 2020). Works pertinent to the SAPS within personality and clinical psychology comprise the empirical versions of object relations theory (Blatt et al., 1997; Kernberg, 1995; Westen, 1991, 1998), the social-cognitive tradition in personality psychology (Bandura, 1977; Cervone et al., 2001; Mischel & Shoda, 1995), and narrative personality psychology, most identified with the writings of McAdams (2015).

2. Personality (defined as the SAPS) is one of the central causal forces propelling psychopathology. Specifically, the most important path through

which personality impacts psychopathology involves creating a social environment that is marred with risk factors (e.g., stress) and lacks protective factors (e.g., social support), culminating in mental health disorders.

3. Epitomizing the SAPS, RORT consists of three elements: schemas and/or scripts of the self-with-others, affect (broadly defined), and affect regulatory procedures (defense mechanisms, coping strategies, and motivational regulation). These three elements are cocausative, forming an amalgamated whole. They pertain to all three tenses: past, present, and future. The future, in particular, is highly pertinent to the understanding of psychopathology because it regulates goal-directed behaviors.

4. Individuals' personalities (particularly as defined by the RORT) seek an optimal congruence between their inner world and their social environment. They attain such congruence in multiple ways, including interpreting events in a manner consistent with their inner world, navigating in social environments compatible with their inner world, and/or actively shaping the social environment for compatibility with their inner world.

5. The ecodynamics of depression is governed by the *theme of criticism*. Depression-prone individuals are characterized by mental representations of self-with-others that are marred by criticism (self and other criticizing self and other), an affective tone that highlights criticism-based emotions (e.g., shame, anger, contempt and disgust), and ineffective regulatory mechanisms that attempt to minimize criticism but ultimately fail. Such failure is a driving force behind the multiple complications of depression, with heterogeneric manifestation, chronicity, comorbidity, and suicidality as well as physical health and illness, delinquency, violence, and crime.

OVERVIEW OF THE BOOK'S STRUCTURE

This book is composed of three parts.

Part I, an exposition, presents the various complications of depression (Chapter 1) and describes the role of personality, broadly defined, in depression (Chapter 2).

Part II is the theoretical core of this book. It first construes personality in terms of my newly developed RORT and rewrites Melanie Klein's depressive position on the basis of this reformulation (i.e., the reformulated depressive position; Chapter 3). Then, a conceptual position concerning the social context is presented and patterns of person–context transactions are described, culminating in the ecodynamics of depression (Chapter 4). Although there are eight ecodynamic patterns, the chapter focuses primarily on three that are specifically useful for understanding complex depression: action, immersion, and extraction. The others are only briefly described.

Part III describes the ecodynamics of complex depression in depth. First, the RORT and the ecodynamics theory are applied to nearly all manifestations of complex depression (Chapter 5). Then, special attention is given to suicidal depression, complex depression's most severe manifestation (Chapter 6). Finally, practical implications of this theoretical position are discussed, touching on clinical assessment and psychotherapy (Chapters 7 and 8, respectively), with a particular focus on assessing and treating outpatients.

In Chapter 7, I review what I believe to be the best practices to assess the three principal components of the theory advanced here: complex manifestations of depression, personality dynamics, and person–context exchanges. I also present versions of three measures I developed—the Depression Complexity Scale (DCS), the Reformulated Depressive Position Inventory (ReDPI), and the Ecodynamics Questionnaire (EDQ)—that aim to assess the three aforementioned components. While I am only beginning to test the psychometric properties of these measures, feedback from clinicians in Israel who have used them is highly favorable. I decided to publish the early versions in this book so that researchers may join me in testing and improving on them. The fight against complex depression is urgent, and expeditious, collaborative, and international efforts are needed to understand, assess, and treat it.

Indeed, Chapter 8 focuses on psychological treatment, and I espouse an integrative psychotherapeutic perspective drawing primarily from three sources: psychodynamic, existential, and cognitive. More specifically, I describe four integrative interventions that I deem essential in psychotherapy for complex depression: (a) providing psychoeducation (informing patients about the nature of complex depression); (b) neutralizing demoralization (ensuing from past therapeutic failures), followed by instilling hope; (c) diffusing toxic patient–context exchanges (depressive ecodynamics patterns described in Chapter 4); and, most principally, (d) attending to the reformulated depressive position described in Chapter 3. The book ends with a brief Epilogue that reflects on the theory advanced here and summarizes future research and clinical directions.

THE BOOK'S INTELLECTUAL TONE, TEMPERAMENT, AND TARGET AUDIENCE

Consistent with the main credo of American Psychological Association Division 1 (Society for General Psychology) (in particular, see Dewsbury, 2009; Teo, 2017), I strive to synthesize the various strands of scientific psychology (primarily clinical, health, personality, social, developmental, and cultural psychology). I also aim to go beyond such "ingroup" synthesis by conversing with other disciplines, such as medical sociology and anthropology, psychiatric epidemiology, and public health (e.g., see Snow, 1959).

A major aim of this book is to bridge science and clinical psychological practice (Beutler et al., 1995; Shahar, 2010). This is done in three ways. First, I link the scientific evidence reviewed here with clinical experience, mine and others. Thus, numerous case examples are presented throughout the book. Patients linked with these examples provided informed consent after reading the entire manuscript. Descriptions are thoroughly disguised in terms of demographics and other potentially identifying details, but I am convinced that the "clinical truth" is strongly upheld. That all of these patients are Israeli is manifested by the specific nature of the struggles they bring to the clinic, such as military hostilities and Jewish identity. Nevertheless, I believe that the deep clinical structure underlying these issues is universal.

Second, consistent with the mission of the Society for the Exploration of Psychotherapy Integration (2023), I seek to integrate various theoretical schools of thought within psychology, psychiatry, and psychotherapy. Primarily, I am integrating theories from the psychodynamic, cognitive, and existential schools, while also reformulating various strands of these theories. Thus, by expanding on my previous theoretical work, here I am reformulating psychoanalytic object relations theory in a way that sheds light on depression research and treatment.

Third, and this point is worth emphasizing, I go beyond data and integrative theory and offer my own theory of how complex depression develops. The reason I think this point merits emphasis is straightforward: If extant data and theory were adequate, unipolar depression would not be deemed as a pandemic. It is precisely because of their limitations that a fresh theoretical perspective is sorely needed, and I try to provide it here. At the same time, I acknowledge that this book leaves room for future exploration, scientific and clinical alike, to answer questions like these: What about the developmental trajectories of ecodynamics? What about the neurobiological underpinnings? What are the public health implications? I address these and other questions, albeit briefly, in the Epilogue.

The target audience of this book comprises clinicians (primarily psychologists but also psychiatrists and social workers), researchers, and policy makers. In particular, I am appealing to members of these disciplines who share my sense of urgency concerning the need to prevent and avert the calamitous consequences of depression, and who share my conviction that the sound knowledge required to address these consequences must be gained by developing novel and fresh perspectives that will govern innovating research and practice.

PART I DEPRESSION AND PERSONALITY

1 THE COMPLICATIONS OF DEPRESSION

Simply put, the conditions that bring on a first episode of depression may differ in kind or arrangement from those that bring on subsequent episodes: It suggests that the neurobiology of affective disorder is a moving target and changes as a function of the longitudinal course of illness.

—R. M. Post, 1992, p. 1005

"With respect to depression, Connie, I think we nailed it," I said to the woman sitting in front of me. The woman was Constance Hammen, a professor of clinical psychology at the University of California, Los Angeles, and a world leader in depression research. The place was the lobby of the Prudential Hotel in Boston, where the American Psychological Association annual convention was held. The date was very long ago: 1998. I went to the meeting primarily to meet Connie, in an attempt to persuade her to accept me as her postdoctoral trainee. Connie was gracious enough to spare me about 2 hours of her time, and I reveled in every minute. Ultimately, I took my postdoctoral training with Sidney Blatt at Yale University, but I adopted Connie as my long-distance mentor. I was careful to keep in touch with her and solicit her advice over the years. Through then-graduate student Moran Schiller,

---

https://doi.org/10.1037/0000377-002
Complex Depression: The Role of Personality Dynamics and Social Ecology, by G. Shahar
Copyright © 2024 by the American Psychological Association. All rights reserved.

I even collaborated with Connie on two research articles that examined the associations of stress with self-concept and psychological symptoms (Schiller et al., 2016, 2019).[1] I feel very fortunate and privileged to have Connie as a mentor and colleague.

When I told Connie that we had "nailed depression," I was referring to my conviction that the groundbreaking theoretical and empirical work done by her, Sidney Blatt, David Zuroff, Aaron Beck, James Coyne, and Thomas Joiner had provided sufficient insight into the psychological makeup of unipolar, rather than bipolar, depression. Enough insight, I thought, so as to deem this disorder well understood and competently treated. I, of course, was gravely wrong in this naïve comment. Staggering insights have been mined by the luminaries just mentioned and other researchers, and they are highly useful; I wouldn't be able to write this book if it were not for them. But depression is far from being nailed. To the contrary, depression remains elusive in its presentation (e.g., Coyne, 1986; Monroe & Anderson, 2015), comes and goes (remitting-relapsing) in a ninja-like manner (Buckman et al., 2018), inflicts unfathomable damage (World Health Organization, 2012), and, in this sense, is actually nailing us all.

Unipolar depression is a pandemic. This was acknowledged more than a decade ago by the World Health Organization (2012) in its report on depression as a global public health concern:

> Depression is a significant contributor to the global burden of disease and affects people in all communities across the world. Today, depression is estimated to affect 350 million people. The World Mental Health Survey conducted in 17 countries found that on average about 1 in 20 people reported having an episode of depression in the previous year. Depressive disorders often start at a young age; they reduce people's functioning and often are recurring. For these reasons, depression is the leading cause of disability worldwide in terms of total years lost due to disability. The demand for curbing depression and other mental health conditions is on the rise globally. (p. 6)

Over the last decade, the situation has not improved. In fact, it has worsened. Rates of depression were increasing even before the COVID-19 pandemic (Herrman et al., 2019) and they have continued to soar globally (Ayuso-Mateos et al., 2021; Chadi et al., 2022; Ettman et al., 2020; Gozansky et al., 2021; Hao et al., 2020; Islam et al., 2021; Latoo et al., 2021; Lorenzo-Luaces, 2015; Moreno-Agostino et al., 2021). Recent evidence suggests that rates of depression continue to increase even though the COVID-19 pandemic

---

[1]This investigation was funded by the University of California, Los Angeles and Ben Gurion University Joint Research Mechanism (principal investigators: Golan Shahar, PhD, and Constance Hammen, PhD).

has largely subsided (Daniali et al., 2023). Despite the downward trend in COVID-19 infection rates, devastating effects of the pandemic remain. For example, one study reported that individuals who had a history of psychiatric disorders had increased mortality risk for mortality after SARS-CoV-2 infection (Li et al., 2020).

As the prevalence of depression has soared, so too have other clinical, health, and societal outcomes that may be driven by depression (as discussed later). In 2020, evidence began to accumulate regarding increased depression comorbidity subsequent to COVID-19 (e.g., with posttraumatic stress disorder [PTSD]; see Karatzias et al., 2020) and a strong link between depression and physical illness (Sayeed et al., 2020). Another indication was the alarming increase in domestic and intimate partner violence following the start of the pandemic, with repeated lockdowns implicated as a contributing factor (A. R. Piquero et al., 2021). It is possible that at least some of the increase in domestic violence rates is attributable to the rise in depression. Indeed, it is because unipolar depression becomes complicated that we are far from nailing it, and much more research on the impact of massive public health crises like COVID-19 is needed. I will, however, risk a prediction (or an educated guess): The COVID-19 pandemic may turn out to be a natural experiment attesting to the horrendous consequences of an increase in the prevalence of depression, both noncomplex ("simple") and complex.

There are two questions we must ask at this point: What? and Why? Namely, what are the ways in which depression becomes complicated, and why does this happen? This chapter addresses the what, and Chapters 2 through 4 address the why. Chapters 5 through 8 target the question stemming from the latter two: So what? Or, what can mental health professionals do to understand, assess, and treat depression?

COMPLEX AND NONCOMPLEX MANIFESTATIONS OF UNIPOLAR DEPRESSION

First, it is important to realize that even noncomplex unipolar depression is not that simple. Although unipolar depression may be measured with adequate reliability and validity (and norms may be extracted from these measures), even the "simplest" forms of unipolar depression are quite multifaceted. This is best gleaned from (a) the symptom structure of depression and (b) the various diagnostic categories to which it pertains.

As shown in Figure 1.1, unipolar depression is composed of four symptom clusters: emotional, cognitive, motivational, and physical/vegetative (e.g., Coyne, 1986). The *emotional cluster* comprises both the presence of negative

FIGURE 1.1. The Symptoms of Unipolar Depression

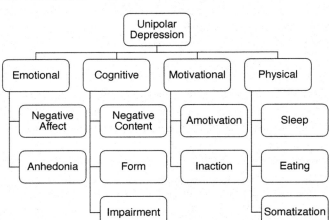

affect (e.g., sadness, anxiety, irritability, and more) and the absence of positive affect, also known as anhedonia (see Chapter 3, this volume; Iqbal & Dar, 2015; Loas, 1996). The *cognitive cluster* consists of three components: negative content of cognitions (e.g., a negative view of one's future, hopelessness; Abramson et al., 1989); repetitive, escalating cognitions (e.g., ruminations, catastrophizing; Ehring & Watkins, 2008); and impairment of basic cognitive faculties (e.g., biased autobiographical memory or derailed executive function; see Perini et al., 2019). The *motivational cluster* comprises amotivation, referring to the lack of motivation to execute behaviors formerly deemed desirable (also called avolition), and inaction (also called psychomotor retardation). Both amotivation and inaction are transdiagnostic, in that they feature in other disorders (e.g., schizophrenia; Park et al., 2017) besides unipolar depression. Finally, the *physical/vegetative cluster* consists of dysfunctional sleeping and eating habits as well as somatic symptoms unexplained by another physical or mental condition (Høstmælingen et al., 2022).

These four symptom clusters make for an already complex picture, but it is possible that even this does not capture the nature of depression at its roots. Thus, Ballard et al. (2018) conducted an exploratory factor analysis on data collected from 76 inpatients with unipolar depression and 43 patients with bipolar depression who completed established measures of depression. The investigators identified eight factors that underlie the variability in these data: depressed mood, tension, negative cognition, impaired sleep, suicidal thoughts, reduced appetite, anhedonia, and amotivation. These eight factors evinced different reactions to a trial of ketamine administration, suggesting that they convey more information than that provided by the established measures used (Ballard et al., 2018).

Whether four clusters or eight factors are identified, it is clear that the manifestation of unipolar depression is inherently heterogenous, even for its less complicated forms (Coyne, 1986; Monroe & Anderson, 2015). Indeed, as Monroe and Anderson (2015) noted, "According to current practices, two people can be diagnosed with an episode of major depression without sharing a single syndrome" (p. 227).

The second aspect complicating even noncomplicated depression is the large number of depressive disorder diagnoses offered in the literature. Here, the term *literature* first and foremost refers to the two central psychiatric classification systems: the *Diagnostic and Statistical Manual of Mental Disorders, Fifth Edition, Text Revision* (*DSM-5-TR*; American Psychiatric Association, 2022),[2] and the *International Classification of Diseases, 11th Revision* (*ICD-11*; World Health Organization, 2018).

Table 1.1 presents a list of depressive conditions, their definition, whether they appear in the *DSM* and/or *ICD*, and—by way of alluding to their impact—whether they incur functional disability and predict suicidality. Table 1.1 is conservative in that it refers only to conditions that, once diagnosed, are likely to lead to treatment. For instance, unspecified diagnoses are not listed, nor is the newly stipulated disruptive mood dysregulation disorder, which pertains to children and for which a diagnosis can be made in the absence of either depressive mood or anhedonia (hence, its relationship with depression is unclear). Moreover, Table 1.1 does not pertain to the various *DSM* and *ICD* specifiers, which comprise different manifestations of depression. Such specifiers are addressed later when I shift gears and describe really complex depression. This conservative approach culminates in seven depressive conditions: (a) nonchronic major depressive disorder (MDD), (b) chronic MDD, (c) dysthymic disorder, (d) mixed depressive and anxiety disorder, (e) adjustment disorder, (f) depressive personality disorder, and (g) subsyndromal depression.

Several caveats must be highlighted with respect to Table 1.1. First, of the seven conditions listed, the first five "find a home" in either the *DSM* or *ICD*, despite the differences between these classification systems. Of the two conditions not listed individually in the *DSM* or *ICD*, subsyndromal depression is located as *depressive disorder with insufficient symptoms* in the "other specified depressive disorders" section of the *DSM-5-TR*. Only depressive personality disorder has been removed altogether. This despite

---

[2]The differences between the *DSM-5* and the *DSM-5-TR* with respect to depressive disorders are very small and have no bearing on this book (see Bradley et al., 2023).

18 • Complex Depression

TABLE 1.1. Conditions and Diagnoses of Unipolar Depression

Condition or diagnosis	Description	Present in *DSM-5-TR*?	Present in *ICD-11*?	Predicts functional disability?	Predicts suicidality?
Nonchronic major depressive disorder	An acute depressive condition lasting 2 or more weeks with a clear onset	Yes, single and recurrent	Yes, single and recurrent	Yes (Hong et al., 2017)	Yes (Ösby et al., 2001)
Chronic major depressive disorder	Symptoms of a major depressive episode lasting for 2 years	Yes, within the persistent depressive disorder category	No	Yes (Iancu et al., 2020)	Yes (Bergfeld et al., 2018)
Dysthymic disorder	A mild, chronic form of depression (2 years or more)	Yes, within the persistent depressive disorder category	Yes	Yes (Devanand, 2014)	Yes (Moitra et al., 2021)
Mixed depressive and anxiety disorder	Symptoms of both depression and anxiety not high enough to meet criteria for another diagnosis	No, but there is a specifier for major depressive disorder with anxious distress	Yes	Yes (Shevlin et al., 2022)	Yes (Bjerkeset et al., 2008)[a]
Adjustment disorder	Emotional distress in the face of a stressful situation	Yes, within the adjustment disorder modality (with depressed mood)	Yes, within the stress-response syndrome modality	Yes (Casey & Bailey, 2011)	Yes (Casey & Bailey, 2011)

Depressive personality disorder	A pervasive pattern of depressive cognitions and behaviors beginning by early adulthood and present in a variety of contexts (from *DSM-IV-TR*; American Psychiatric Association, 2000)	No	Yes (McDermut et al., 2003)	Yes (McDermut et al., 2003)
Subsyndromal depression	Symptoms of depression not meeting criteria for the above diagnoses	Yes, in the "other specified depressive disorders" category of the *DSM-5-TR* (American Psychiatric Association, 2022) as depressive disorder with insufficient symptoms	No	Yes (Lyness et al., 1999)	Yes (Sadek & Bona, 2000)

[a] Assessed via the Hospital Anxiety and Depression Scale (Zigmond & Snaith, 1983).

its inclusion in the *DSM-IV-TR* appendix (American Psychiatric Association, 2000) as "worthy of future study" and research noting strong construct and criterion validity for this condition (Table 1.1 and Chapter 2, this volume; Huprich, 2012; Shahar, 2015a). Taken together, these observations suggest that despite their acknowledged flaws, the *DSM* and the *ICD* cover the majority of the depression diagnosis universe (leaving out the question of whether they do this well).

Second, Table 1.1 suggests that there are many alternatives for receiving a medical-clinical diagnosis of depression, even if the same diagnosis is addressed by an identical pharmacological and/or psychotherapeutic treatment. This gap between many diagnoses and few treatments is disconcerting and provides a clue to the reasons why treatment is unsatisfactory (it also solidifies the rationale for this book).

Third, the gap between many diagnoses and few treatments is even more concerning, given the last two columns of Table 1.1 that attest to the fact that all diagnoses predict functional disability and suicidality. Put simply and bluntly, unless and until we fill this gap with a novel perspective that sheds light on depression, people will continue to become functionally impaired and will continue to die as a result of suicidal depression.

Fourth, Table 1.1 falls short of doing justice to the complexity of noncomplex depression, by (intentionally) not differentiating between single-episode nonchronic MDD and recurrent nonchronic MDD. When acute MDD recurs, even without making the predicament chronic, the "rules of the game" are changed. Every recurrence increases the likelihood of an ensuing subsequent episode, which by definition virtually reduces the likelihood of treatment success and increases personal and public health burdens (Kessler, 2002). Such recurrence is extremely prevalent: About 60% of individuals who experience one depressive episode will experience another, and 70% of those who experience two episodes will have a third (Monroe & Harkness, 2005; D. A. Solomon et al., 2000). According to Post's (1992) kindling hypothesis, with each depressive episode, the contribution of identified life stress to subsequent episodes diminishes, making the impression that these subsequent episodes "occur autonomously" (as cited in Monroe & Harkness, 2005, p. 1001).

For those of us confronting depression in the clinic, the consequences to our patients—and to our effectiveness as therapists—of even a single recurrence of MDD is poignant. I refer to one such consequence, a description of which I could not locate in the extant literature (scientific or clinical), as the *dread of recurrence*, as discussed in Box 1.1.[3]

---

[3]The case example of Dan has been modified to disguise the patient's identity and protect their confidentiality.

BOX 1.1
CASE EXAMPLE OF DREAD OF RECURRENT MAJOR DEPRESSIVE DISORDER

Dan, a 33-year-old male lawyer, approached me for treatment of major depression. This was his second MDD episode. His first episode transpired during law school, in which Dan negatively compared himself to several classmates he had befriended whom he deemed much more accomplished than him. Regardless of this negative social comparison and the ensuing depression, Dan experienced spontaneous remission without any treatment, graduated from law school with flying colors, and landed several jobs quickly after graduating. One job was difficult for Dan to maintain because of what he perceived as the futility, insensibility, and downright injustice of his bosses around their relationship with him and his work. Although his bosses attempted to keep him, Dan quit that job and traveled abroad. Upon his return, he developed a months-long MDD episode and sought therapy with me. About 6 months into therapy, he was no longer depressed. There were also notable improvements in his social situation, and he demonstrated an impressive ability to handle stressful medical and financial situations occurring with his loved ones. However, Dan became stuck occupationally, and he refused to "step out into the world" by assuming another job or going to graduate school (a possibility he had been harboring for years). He was also passive about forming a romantic relationship despite expressing interest in doing so. In sessions, Dan eloquently alluded to the principal reason he avoided stepping out: He found the prospect of experiencing another depressive episode—even one that might happen years from now—unfathomably terrifying. Without assurances that such a recurrence was avoidable, he felt that the best way to handle the threat was by refraining from serious occupational and romantic commitments, so as "not to shutter by stepping out what I have already built."

Finally, Table 1.1 also describes subsyndromal depression. I find this disorder as mysterious as I find it ominous. The fact that many people do not meet criteria for the many depressive diagnoses and conditions in the *DSM* and the *ICD* but nevertheless suffer crippling functional disability due to depression is well documented in research (Judd et al., 1997; Lewinsohn et al., 1995, 2004) and provides a bewildering reflection of the limitations of our understanding of and ability to measure unipolar depression. That some of these individuals may actually be at risk for suicidality is downright alarming, and I frequently encounter this situation in my practice with young people.

WHAT FEATURES MAKE DEPRESSION COMPLEX?

The flowchart in Figure 1.2 differentiates moderately complex unipolar depression from highly complex unipolar depression and stipulates the ways in which highly complex depression is expressed. For example, *moderately complex unipolar depression* refers to depression that is episodic, albeit heterogeneous, and may be recurrent (but not chronic, as discussed later). Moderately complex depression may thus be differentiated from *uncomplicated depression*, which conforms to the way depression is stereotyped (e.g., depressed mood, lethargy, or anhedonia) and/or assumes a single-episode

FIGURE 1.2. The Complexities of Unipolar Depression

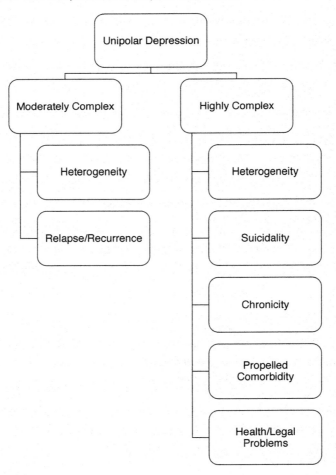

course. Indeed, research suggests that uncomplicated depression exists, although its prevalence is not as high as one might expect (Parker, 2014; Wakefield, 2015, 2016; Wakefield & Schmitz, 2014). For instance, using a large sample of adults ($N = 27{,}609$), Wakefield and Schmitz (2014) examined the 3-year longitudinal course of major depression. They focused on what they referred to as *uncomplicated MDD*: a single episode remitting within 6 months and lacking severe impairment, psychotic or suicidal ideation, psychomotor retardation, and feelings of worthlessness. Wakefield and Schmitz found that 6.1% of their sample evinced such a course. In terms of psychosocial variables, the group with uncomplicated MDD did not differ from the group with no MDD history. The authors concluded that single-episode uncomplicated MDD was a benign subtype of the disorder.

Figure 1.2 highlights the following points. *Highly complex unipolar depression* (a) may be manifested via symptomatic presentations that are nontypical, and this presentation is highly heterogeneous; (b) may spiral into severe suicidal ideation, plans and preparations, suicidal attempts, and (in the most extreme situations) completed suicide; (c) is likely to assume a chronic course, in turn inflicting a severe functional impairment; (d) drives psychiatric comorbidity (i.e., depression leading to another psychiatric condition); and (e) leads to or complicates health problems (e.g., chronic illness, medically unexplained physical symptoms) and/or legal problems (e.g., delinquency, violence, crime). I now explain each in turn.

Complex Depression Has Heterogeneous Manifestations

The typical notion of depression includes a predominant sad mood, physical weakness, lethargy, dependency ("femininity"), and depletion (Blatt & Zuroff, 1992; Cox et al., 2012; Landrine, 1988). However, unipolar depression may manifest differently, as acknowledged in both the *DSM* and *ICD* via their various specifiers or qualifiers of depressive diagnoses. Taking the *DSM-5-TR* (American Psychiatric Association, 2022) as an example, several highly confusing associated features and specifiers of MDD are as follows:

- **Melancholic features:** mood that is regularly worse in the morning; early morning awakening; marked psychomotor retardation or agitation; loss of appetite or unplanned weight loss; excessive or inappropriate guilt; and inability to feel better in the face of a positive event.
- **Atypical features:** mood reactivity (a person's mood brightens in response to positive events); significant weight gain or increase in appetite; hypersomnia (sleeping excessively); leaden paralysis (a heavy, leaden feeling

in the arms or legs); and a long-standing pattern of being highly sensitive to interpersonal rejection.

- **Mixed features:** elevated, expansive mood; grandiosity; talkativeness; racing thoughts; increased energy and/or goal directedness; excessive involvement in potentially painful activities; and decreased need for sleep.

- **Psychotic features:** depression with psychotic symptoms such as hallucinations and delusions, which might be either mood congruent (reflective of a depressed mood) or mood incongruent (incompatible with a depressed mood).

- **Catatonia:** motoric immobility or excessive movement; extreme negativism; posturing (taking up inappropriate or bizarre body positions and holding them for periods of time); stereotyped movements (repeating behaviors over and over); prominent grimacing; and/or the compulsive repetition of someone else's words or movements.

Clearly, these manifestations of depression go beyond the typical (albeit quite complex) heterogeneity of unipolar depression. They can markedly derail diagnosis and treatment—both psychotherapeutic and pharmacological. For instance, atypical and psychotic depression may be highly unrecognized (Dubovsky et al., 2021). Conversely, identification of atypical and/or psychotic features in unipolar depression requires the prescribing physician to consider a mood stabilizer and/or neuroleptic agent. In the context of psychotherapy, the deliberation over a diagnosis of atypical depression or depression with mixed features (both are considered to border on bipolar disorder) may lead to related deliberation of interpersonal psychotherapy for unipolar depression (Klerman & Weissman, 1994) versus interpersonal and social rhythm psychotherapy for bipolar conditions (Frank, 2005).

Another issue closely tied to the manifestation of depression, but not yet recognized by the *DSM* or *ICD*, is the unique manifestation of depression in men (Addis, 2008; Ogrodniczuk & Oliffe, 2011). As noted previously, the stereotypical notion that depression is feminine (i.e., lethargic, dependent). Men, however, appear to manifest depression in ways that are not consistent with female stereotypes. For instance, the pressure to "be a real man" may lead to the tendency to hide mellow emotions, which in turn contributes to centralized anger, agitation, and somatization at the expense of sadness. Social isolation is also likely to characterize male depression, often at the expense of help-seeking (e.g., Addis & Mahalik, 2003). With increased understanding of the differences between men and women in terms of how depression manifests, the U.S. National Institute of Mental Health (NIMH) undertook the "Real Men. Real Depression" public health campaign from 2003 to 2005, to increase awareness of male depression. Results of this campaign appear promising in that they suggest that the information conveyed as part of the campaign has been viewed favorably, leading to increased awareness of the particular nature of male depression (Rochlen et al., 2006).

Complex Depression Kills by Suicide

The most formidable of all complications of depression is suicidality (i.e., ideation, preparation, attempts, and eventually completion). While most people with unipolar depressive disorders will not attempt to end their lives and many fewer will actually kill themselves, the majority of people who die by suicide suffered from depression before their death (Alqueza et al., 2023; Hawton et al., 2013; Miret et al., 2013). In fact, as stated by Miret et al. (2013):

> The most important risk factor for lifetime suicide attempt is depression, with a population attributable risk proportion of around 28%. This implies that the lifetime prevalence of suicide attempts could be reduced significantly by preventing depression . . . and by recognizing and adequately treating it. (p. 2372)

What distinguishes suicidal depression from nonsuicidal depression? To date, there is no definitive answer, although there are some very promising clues. Risk factors for suicidal depression have been documented in neurobiological, epidemiological, and psychological research. Although an exhaustive discussion of this topic is outside the scope of this book, I do have a special interest in the characterization of suicidal depression. Hence, I briefly highlight the following risk factors and discuss them further in Chapter 5: depression severity and chronicity, hyperarousal (e.g., agitation, irritation, insomnia), lack of cognitive control (e.g., problems with executive function, negative repetitive thought patterns), trait and state self-criticism, and interpersonal difficulties (particularly perceived burdensomeness and thwarted belongingness, as identified by Joiner et al. in the interpersonal-psychological theory of suicide; Chu et al., 2017; Joiner, 2005; Van Orden et al., 2010).

For now, two highly disconcerting facts concerning suicidal depression are important to note. First, although there is a long and impressive list of evidence-based psychotherapies for unipolar depressive disorders, the majority of randomized clinical trials (RCTs) testing the efficacy and effectiveness of these psychotherapies have excluded suicidal patients with depression because of their suicidality (Sander et al., 2020). This constitutes a major limitation in our knowledge base for how to treat unipolar depression in "real life" (i.e., with so many depressed individuals who are suicidal). To be sure, things have markedly improved over the last two decades, with some highly salient RCTs for depression including suicidal patients (e.g., Goodyer et al., 2011; Klomek et al., 2021). However, because this progress is recent, decades of additional research will be needed to develop a comprehensive understanding of the impact of these and other RCTs on suicidal depression.

Second, there is an emerging realization in suicidology (the scientific study of suicide) that, particularly in the affective disorder, risk of suicide may surge dramatically within days and even hours. This realization has led to proposals for inclusion of distinct diagnostic categories concerning such acute suicidal risk (e.g., M. L. Rogers et al., 2019). This means that people with affective disorders, including depressive disorders, who appear to have low risk at intake, during treatment, or at discharge from inpatient care may descend into suicidality very quickly and "under clinicians' radar" (Joiner et al., 2018). This terrifying possibility underscores the dramatic need to understand the differences between suicidal and nonsuicidal depression. In the context of this book, I aim to show that what appears to be an acute, state-like crisis is actually driven by deep-seated personality processes, interacting with the social context.

Complex Depression Tends to Be Chronic

Depression is chronic for a substantial number of patients (20%–30%; Angst et al., 2009; Murphy & Byrne, 2012; Pettit & Joiner, 2006; Schramm et al., 2020). Various chronic forms include (a) pure dysthymic disorder (a "mild" form of depression composed primarily of depressed mood for an extended period of time [i.e., at least 2 years for adults and 1 year for children and adolescents]), (b) chronic major depression (symptoms meeting criteria for MDD for at least 2 years), (c) double depression (a major depressive episode superimposed on dysthymia), (d) recurrent brief depression (depressed mood and at least four other symptoms of depression for at least 2–13 days per month for at least 12 consecutive months), (e) MDD with partial remission, and (f) recurrent MDD without full recovery between episodes. The literature compellingly suggests that the impairment and functional disability incurred by these forms of chronic depression is substantial (Hung et al., 2019; Schramm et al., 2020). Moreover, one form of chronic depression is likely to evolve into another (Schramm et al., 2020). Finally, the risk for suicidality implicated in chronic depression is sizeable (Table 1.1) (Joiner, 2005; Pettit & Joiner, 2006).

From a clinical practice point of view, the primary damage that chronic depression inflicts is patient demoralization (Clarke & Kissane, 2002; Costanza et al., 2022; de Figueiredo, 1993). Jerome D. Frank (1974), a renowned psychotherapy thinker and researcher, introduced the term *demoralization* to the psychiatric literature (see Costanza et al., 2022). Frank (1974) defined it as follows:

> persistent failure to cope with internally or externally induced stresses that the person and those close to him expect him to handle. Its characteristic features, not all of which need to be present in any one person, are feelings of impotence, isolation, and despair. (p. 2)

Demoralization appears to be distinct from depression, leads to various forms of psychopathology and to suicidality, and severely derails the therapeutic alliance, treatment compliance, and, by extension, the outcome of both pharmacological and psychotherapeutic treatment (Shahar & Ziv-Beiman, 2020). Arguably, this is the reason why chronic depression is often equated with the term *treatment-resistant depression*. According to Schramm et al. (2020), this conflation is as incorrect as it is confusing because treatment-resistant depression—also an elusive and controversial term—can also ensue from nonchronic depression. Nevertheless, even those authors acknowledged the relatively scarce therapeutic success for chronic depression.

As one patient with chronic major depression once told me during intake: "You can't treat me. I know that something in me is fundamentally sick." Such a pretreatment attitude not only limits patients' active involvement in the treatment process, but it also gives rise to *negative transference* that evokes hostile countertransferential reactions. As I illustrated using multiple cases in my book on self-criticism (Shahar, 2015a), patients often actively, albeit inadvertently, seek to reaffirm their conviction that they are untreatable by undermining the therapist. In Chapter 8, I address this problem explicitly and intensively.

Complex Depression Is Comorbid With Other Mental Health Disorders

In psychopathology, comorbidity—the mutual presentation of numerous disorders—is the rule rather than the exception (Plana-Ripoll et al., 2019). As in the case of chronicity, psychiatric comorbidity is predictive of particularly high levels of functional disability and suicidality (Chang et al., 2021; McKay et al., 2018). Within the range of comorbid psychopathological manifestations, depression leads the way (ter Meulen et al., 2021), co-occurring with a long list of mental disorders, the most prevalent of which are the anxiety and stress/trauma-related disorders but also eating, conduct, dissociative, and somatic disorders (comorbidity with personality disorder is discussed later).

I suggest herein that there are three forms of depressive comorbidity: Types A, B, and C. Type A pertains to depression as an epiphenomenon of another disorder. Type B refers to depression as secondary to another disorder. Finally, Type C—the most pertinent here—refers to another disorder being propelled by depression.

Depressive Comorbidity Type A: Depression as an Epiphenomenon
An epiphenomenon pertains to the possibility that depression is manifested alongside another disorder simply by virtue of its similarity to the symptoms of the comorbid disorder. For instance, both generalized anxiety disorder and complex PTSD include symptoms that strongly overlap with depression (somatic/vegetative symptoms and low self-worth, respectively). It is possible that among some people diagnosed with comorbid unipolar depression and generalized anxiety disorder or complex PTSD, depression actually does not exist in its own right. Although this possibility is fascinating, it is outside the scope of this book and is not discussed further (but see Döpfner et al., 2009).

Depressive Comorbidity Type B: Secondary Depression
The second pattern of comorbid depression—namely, depression secondary to another mental disorder—has been recognized for decades (Clayton & Lewis, 1981; Costello & Scott, 1991; Meier et al., 2015). Anxiety, stress-related, and obsessive-compulsive disorders most commonly manifest with secondary depression, although other mental disorders (e.g., eating, conduct, psychotic, and substance use disorders) have also shown an appreciable comorbidity with depression that appears to be secondary to these disorders (e.g., Tibi et al., 2017). How do we know that depression is secondary to another disorder (as opposed to being an epiphenomenon)? We know this from research performed with prospective-longitudinal designs, in which both disorders are assessed at least twice and an association is demonstrated between the disorder at Time 1 and depression at Time 1+ after statistically controlling for depression at Time 1 and for a host of other potentially confounding factors (e.g., gender or biological sex, genetic makeup, or a third disorder; Tibi et al., 2017). Such prospective-longitudinal studies are far from perfect, but they are considered the best method for studying causal relationships in fields not amenable to experimental research designs.

As for the question of why depression would emanate from another disorder, the answer seems to be straightforward. Any and all mental disorders constitute overwhelming stress, burdening individuals' biological, psychological, and social resources and altering their lives. Stress, particularly major stress, is likely to lead to depression (G. W. Brown & Harris, 1978; Monroe,

2008), thereby shedding light on the phenomenon of secondary depression (Clayton & Lewis, 1981; Costello & Scott, 1991; Meier et al., 2015).

Depressive Comorbidity Type C: When Depression Propels Another Disorder

The third form of comorbidity—depression bringing about another mental disorder—is particularly pertinent to this book. It has been relatively understudied, although extant research renders it quite viable. In my research program, I used the prospective-longitudinal research designs discussed earlier and found that depressive symptoms prospectively predicted an increase in PTSD symptoms in the general population (Schindel-Allon et al., 2010) and in first-time mothers (Shahar et al., 2015). Interestingly, in these studies, PTSD did not prospectively predict depression (but see Aderka et al., 2013).

Substance use disorders constitute another example of Type C depressive comorbidity. Terms such as *self-medicating* and *drinking to cope* were developed in particular to understand the ramifications of failure to tolerate distress in general, and depressive distress in particular, and the resultant use of substances as a way to deal with such distress (N. L. Taylor et al., 2022; Wallis et al., 2022). Because substance use disorders propel individuals toward functional disability and suicidality (e.g., Compton & Han, 2022), the effect of depression on substance use is noteworthy.

Why would depression lead to other mental disorders? The answer to this question is much less straightforward than the answer to why secondary depression occurs. In fact, it is quite likely that the effect of depression on other mental disorders is disorder specific. Thus, in previous studies, my colleagues and I suggested that depression may bring about PTSD symptoms through several mechanisms. First, depression includes negative cognitions about the self, which have been shown to prospectively predict PTSD (Shahar et al., 2013). Second, depression includes anhedonia and amotivation, which interfere with the fear extinction needed to regulate response to trauma-related stimuli (Bonanno, 2004; Guthrie & Bryant, 2006). Finally, depression may impede self-efficacy beliefs, in turn increasing cognitive and behavioral avoidance in dealing with trauma-related reminders that are crucial for recovery (Samuelson et al., 2017).

Complex Depression Leads to Physical, Medical, and/or Legal Problems

Suffering from a debilitating, painful, and/or life-threatening medical condition constitutes a major stress; as such, it is highly likely to lead to depression (Cocksedge et al., 2014; Shahar et al., 2014). Indeed, the prevalence of depression in chronic physical illness—a major challenge in modern medicine—is staggering (e.g., 20%; National Institute for Health and Care Excellence, 2009a, 2009b). Although it is recognized that treating and/or managing chronic physical illness co-occurring with depression is much more difficult that doing so with the same illness without it (e.g., in adult diabetes; Lustman et al., 2007), the realization that such depression is not a "passive victim" of the physical illness, but rather a risk factor (an epidemiological alias to cause) of the putative physical illness, has slowly surfaced over the last three decades. Arguably, the most dramatic illustration of this effect of depression on physical illness comes from research on cardiovascular disease (K. W. Davidson, 2012; Dhar & Barton, 2016; Hare et al., 2014). As indicated by Karina Davidson (2012), a leader in this line of research, "Whether diagnosed or simply self-reported, depression continues to mark very high risk for a recurrent acute coronary syndrome or for death in patients with coronary heart disease" (p. 1). In fact, a *JAMA* study by Harshfield et al. (2020) reported that in a large sample assessed as part of the Emerging Risk Factors Collaboration ($N = 162,036$) and the U.K. Biobank ($N = 401,219$) studies, "baseline depressive symptoms were associated with CVD [cardiovascular disease] incidence, including at symptom levels lower than the threshold indicative of a depressive disorder. However, the magnitude of associations was modest" (p. 2403).

A similar pattern has been surfacing with respect to other chronic physical illnesses. Consider chronic physical pain, one of the most treatment-resistant medical conditions today. That depression (and anxiety) is highly likely to co-occur with pain has been well known for decades, and the majority opinion in pain research and treatment is that pain serves as a risk factor for depression (and anxiety) (see Banks & Kerns, 1996; Hendler, 1984; Max et al., 2006; Orhurhu et al., 2019). However, the possibility of an inverse effect—that depression brings about and/or exacerbates pain—has long been recognized and has received empirical support in studies of various populations across the life span (Lerman et al., 2015; Lv et al., 2023; Magni et al., 1994; Patton et al., 2021; Sachs-Ericsson et al., 2017; Woo, 2010).

To be clear, here I emphasize that findings attesting to the effects of depression on chronic physical illness do not nullify findings on the effects of chronic physical illness on depression. I simply deem the latter findings straightforward, almost trivial scientifically (not clinically), whereas the former findings provide powerful testimony of how depression may spiral into other very serious problems. In fact, within the physical and medical realm, depression is likely to derail health in ways other than leading to chronic physical illness. Specifically, depression has been shown in both healthy and ill individuals to predict "medically unexplained symptoms" (Katon et al., 2001; R. C. Smith, 2020); to result in risky sexual behavior (Ghobadzadeh et al., 2019); to seriously interfere with healthy eating habits, ultimately leading to obesity (Konttinen, 2020); and to derail individuals' ability to incorporate physical activity and exercise into their routine (Brunet et al., 2014) and engage in basic self-care activities (Blazer et al., 1994; Gonzalez et al., 2007).

Forensic and legal outcomes comprise another realm in which depression seems to complicate matters. Specifically, researchers have prospectively predicted aggressive, violent, and otherwise delinquent/criminal behavior among patients with depression (Anderson et al., 2015; Ehrensaft et al., 2006; Fazel et al., 2015; Ozkan et al., 2019). This line of research is focal to work conducted in my laboratory; my graduate student, Ofek Vardimon, is leading a review followed by a meta-analysis on the role of depression in forensic outcomes (forensic depression).

Several issues must be emphasized with respect to research on forensic depression. First, research in this field, especially that based on prospective-longitudinal designs, is far from being voluminous. Much more research is needed. Second, inconsistent findings (e.g., showing no effects of depression on forensic outcomes) have also been reported in leading publications (B. K. Kim et al., 2019).

The question of why depression might propel forensic outcomes is highly underdeveloped. At a theoretical level, there is a dearth of models conceptualizing the potential mechanisms through which depression may confer its forensic effect (see N. L. Piquero & Sealock, 2004, who utilized general strain theory but did not find a link between depression and delinquency or crime). Similarly, very few studies targeting statistical mediators (i.e., variables statistically accounting for a demonstrated effect of depression on forensic outcomes) have been published. In the available studies, the mediators considered were self-control, anger, and hostility, and findings concerning these few mediators were either inconclusive or weak (Koh et al., 2002; Ozkan et al., 2019). Third, research on forensic depression overlaps, by definition, with research on depression comorbidity (discussed earlier), because at least two psychiatric diagnoses (conduct disorder and antisocial personality disorder) are of a forensic nature. Here, too, alongside findings consistent with the prospective effect of depression on these two diagnoses (Cerdá et al., 2011; Measelle et al., 2006), studies reporting null findings also exist (McDonough-Caplan et al., 2018; Skodol et al., 1999).

WHY DOES DEPRESSION BECOME COMPLICATED?

Figure 1.2, which charting the ways in which unipolar depression becomes complicated, is, in my opinion, breathtaking. With the exception of the mild (benign) form or course of depression identified by Wakefield and

Schmitz (2014), unipolar depression is already complex; even moderately complex depression is difficult to understand (see Figure 1.2) and hence difficult to treat. Highly complex depression is really complex, very difficult to treat, and (as studies attest) appears to be prevalent. For instance, in a study conducted in Chile, Vitriol et al. (2021) collected clinical and functional data from 297 patients with depression treated at a public health care facility. The investigators used latent class analysis (Hagenaars & McCutcheon, 2009), a statistical technique that aims to differentiate subtypes within large populations. Latent class analysis yielded a three-class solution. The first (largest) class (58% of the sample) was complex depression, characterized by recurrence and a high probability of psychiatric comorbidity, history of suicide attempts, and interpersonal and social difficulties. Next in size was the recurrent depression class (34% of the sample), characterized by recurrence, a high probability of psychiatric comorbidity and social and interpersonal difficulties, and a low probability of suicide attempts. The smallest class (8%) was single-episode depression, characterized by a single episode and low probability of psychiatric comorbidity, history of suicide attempts, and personal and social difficulties. Next, Vitriol et al. (2021) predicted membership of each class from numerous stress and trauma variables, and they found that members of the complex depression class reported more childhood trauma and intimate partner violence events than each of the two other clusters.

Why is this? Why does depression, once construed as the "common cold" of mental disorders (Lorenzo-Luaces, 2015), constantly mutate? To address this question, two issues must be realized. First, although it is likely that each type of depression complication may be caused by factors specific to this type (e.g., depression leading to crime may pertain to causes different from those involved in depression exacerbating chronic physical illness), it is still highly likely that there are common processes facilitating the so-called mutation of depression.

Second, by now it is clear that neither the *DSM* nor the *ICD* sheds light on the nature of complex depression. Put differently, these two seminal classification systems appear to be the problem, rather than the solution, in solving the depression puzzle. This is so for two related reasons. First, the *DSM* and the *ICD* are richly descriptive, and they thus contribute to the numerous ways in which depression may be diagnosed. Second, the *DSM* and the *ICD* are extensively atheoretical; hence, they are not causative. That is, nothing in these classification systems hints at the origins of even noncomplex depression, let alone complex depression.

To address this problem, NIMH took the bold step of offering the Research Domain Criteria (RDOC) as an alternative to the *DSM/ICD* (Cuthbert & Insel,

2013; National Institute of Mental Health, n.d., 2008; Peters et al., 2018). The NIMH criteria seek to define psychopathology in terms of science-based processes leading to the symptoms observed. Three concepts comprise the RDOC: domains, constructs, and units of analysis. *Domains* pertain to the various arenas of human functioning, and the RDOC focuses on six: negative valence system, positive valence system, cognitive systems, systems for social processes, arousal/regulatory systems, and sensorimotor systems. Within each domain, there are several behavioral elements and processes that are pertinent to the disorder. These are too numerous to specify here but, by way of illustration, the *constructs* of the negative valence system are acute threat (fear), potential threat (anxiety), sustained threat, loss, and frustrative nonreward. Finally, measurement of these constructs occurs using several *units of analysis*: genes, molecules, cells, circuits, physiology, behavior, self-report, and paradigm. Taken together, the three RDOC concepts enable a three-dimensional matrix that may characterize various disorders, including depression (e.g., Woody & Gibb, 2015).

Let me emphasize that this is not an ode to the RDOC. The RDOC has, in my opinion, severe flaws, the worst of which is an overemphasis on (and a downright bias toward) biology, neuroscience, and neuroimaging. Each of these disciplines is paramount for understanding the human mind and of mental disorders; yet as a staunch advocate of the biopsychosocial perspective (Engel, 1977), I see the merits of these disciplines as contingent on profound psychological and sociocultural understanding. The RDOC does acknowledge psychological processes and even addresses social ones. However, these criteria emphasize lower-level cognitive variables that are usually conducive for measuring neuropsychological processes. In addition, the social/interpersonal dimension of human functioning is (I believe) underdeveloped in the RDOC, and its treatment of personality in psychopathology is almost nonexistent.

Nevertheless, I do believe that the RDOC constitutes a major epistemological step forward in psychopathology research, because it goes beyond mere identification of symptoms and seeks to identify the root causes of mental disorders. I enthusiastically endorse this progress. Indeed, this book theorizes about potential root causes of depression and how it becomes complicated. In contrast with the RDOC, the root causes of depression—simple and complex—are (in my opinion) located in the interface between personality and the social context. The remaining chapters further describe personality and the social context (or social ecology) as fundamental factors in depression. By way of a primer, however, I offer the following exposition.

My point of departure is ecological biology. Depression happens to living organisms (my focus is on humans, so I do not discuss depression in animals).

According to Lewontin (2000), active organism–environmental transactions constitute the most basic feature of life. Consistent with this view, Dunbar (1998) posited that the human brain has evolved because of the need to compete for social skills for the purpose of outsmarting others (see also Brothers, 1990). Also consistent with this position is the notion of gene–environment correlations (to be distinguished from gene–environment interactions), according to which our genetic makeup shapes the environments we select (Rutter et al., 1997).

This notion leads to a theoretical next step: an emphasis on active interactions between humans and their physical and social environment. Such emphasis draws from transactional, ecological, and action theories in development, social, and clinical psychology as well as from seminal notions developed in the context of social-cognitive theory: principally, Albert Bandura's seminal notion of reciprocal determinism (for reviews, see Shahar, 2006a, 2015a, 2016) and Mischel and Shoda's (1995) notion of personality signature. Applied to unipolar depression, I argue that this disorder is primarily, fundamentally transactional: It evolves within and, as a consequence of, active person–context exchanges.

This is far from being an original statement. I am simply standing on the shoulder of giants such as Blatt (1974, 2004), Coyne (1976a, 1976b), Depue and Monroe (1986), Hammen (1991, 2006), Joiner (1994, 2000a), Klerman and Weissmans (1994), Wachtel (1994), and others who have identified the predominantly interpersonal nature of depression. People with depression become depressed and maintain their depression in the midst of interpersonal strife and loss, and effective treatment of depression must short-circuit vicious interpersonal processes propelling such strife and loss.

People with depression are not just dealing with strife and loss. Drawing from a rich psychodynamic/psychoanalytic tradition, particularly one filtered through the scrutiny of empirical science (e.g., Blatt et al., 1997; Shahar, 2015a; Wachtel, 1994; Westen, 1991, 1998), I posit that people with depression deal with the strife and loss that they create, albeit inadvertently (Shahar, 2006a, 2015a). They create this strife and loss because of their personality, an obscure construct that applies to many definitions. Herein, *personality* is defined primarily in terms of individuals' mental maps of social interactions: their perception, and representations, of themselves and others with whom they relate and toward whom they have feelings. And this, in a nutshell, is the story of complex depression. It is now incumbent on me to explicate this story in the chapters that follow.

2 THE ROLE OF PERSONALITY IN COMPLEX DEPRESSION

From the perspective of personality psychology, one way to describe the changing psychoanalytic landscape is to suggest that psychoanalytic theory is increasingly catching up with its clinical practice in recognizing the extent to which personality lies in person-by-situation interactions. Personality is not something people carry with them and express elsewhere; rather, personality processes are essentially if-then contingencies (Kammrath et al., 2005; Mischel & Shoda, 1995).

—Westen et al., 2008, p. 78

Voluminous research attests to the important role of personality in mental disorders and related problems (Kotov et al., 2010; Krueger et al., 2012; Wilson & Olino, 2021). Arguably, depression research and treatment is spearheading interest in the role of personality in psychopathology (Bagby et al., 2008; Blatt, 2004; Enns & Cox, 1997; Fu et al., 2021; D. N. Klein et al., 2011; M. H. Klein et al., 1993). The association between personality and depression dates back to ancient times and has origins in Hippocrates' four humors (bodily fluids): blood, phlegm, yellow bile, and black bile,

https://doi.org/10.1037/0000377-003
Complex Depression: The Role of Personality Dynamics and Social Ecology, by G. Shahar
Copyright © 2024 by the American Psychological Association. All rights reserved.

with the latter serving as the precursor of melancholic temperament and culminating in depression (for a historical account of depression, see Horwitz et al., 2016).

Although many researchers define personality via trait-based models, I contend that this approach is fundamentally flawed for numerous reasons discussed in detail later in this chapter. Subjective–agentic models, which I refer to as the subjective–agentic personality sector (SAPS), are more useful for conceptualizing personality, owing to their emphasis on self-concepts and interpersonal schemas, which offer a more nuanced understanding of an individual within their social context. This understanding, in turn, can help explain the roots of that individual's complex depression. Before we arrive at a more precise definition of personality, it is important to understand the various theoretical and empirical models of the role of depression in personality.

A REVIEW OF FOUR MODELS OF PERSONALITY AND DEPRESSION FOCUSING ON SELF-CRITICISM

I posit that the link between personality and depression can be captured by four empirical patterns, or models: overlap, passive vulnerability, active vulnerability, and scarring. Passive vulnerability can be subdivided into two patterns: stress–diathesis and dual/rival vulnerability. Table 2.1 summarizes these patterns and cites studies supporting each model. These studies have a notable common denominator: The personality factor investigated is the stable dimension of *self-criticism*. Defined as the tendency to set unrealistically high self-standards and to adopt a punitive stance toward the self once these standards are not met (Shahar, 2015a), self-criticism is considered an ominous dimension of personality vulnerability, primarily to depression but also to a host of other psychopathologies (Werner et al., 2019). The four empirical models are discussed next.

The Overlap Model

The *overlap model* posits that personality and depression overlap both conceptually (i.e., in the way they are defined) and assessment-wise (i.e., in the content of their measures). Understanding the overlap model is quite straightforward when one considers it in the context of self-criticism. Negative cognitions, including those directed toward the self, have been conceptualized as an inherent component of unipolar depression (A. T. Beck, 1983). Indeed, the definitions of depression in the *Diagnostic and Statistical Manual of Mental*

TABLE 2.1. Leading Models of Personality and Depression

Model	Description	Illustrative references[a]
Overlap	Aspects of personality and depression overlap in content and measurement	J. D. Brown and Silberschatz (1989); Coyne and Whiffen (1995); and Whiffen and Sasseville (1991)
Passive vulnerability	Personality leads to depression under specific conditions that are not associated with personality itself	See below
Stress–diathesis	External stress, unrelated to personality, activates the latter's effect on depression	Abela et al. (2006) and Shahar, Joiner, et al. (2004)
Dual/rival vulnerability	External stress, unrelated to personality, competes with the latter over their effect on depression	Kopala-Sibley et al. (2017) and Shahar and Henrich (2019)
Active vulnerability	Personality leads to environmental conditions (e.g., stress) that, in turn, lead to depression	Mandel et al. (2018); Shahar (2015a); and Shahar, Joiner, et al. (2004)
Scarring	Depression leads to personality dysfunction	Shahar and Henrich (2019) and Shahar, Blatt, Zuroff, Kuperminck, & Leadbeater (2004)

[a]All of the cited sources investigate self-criticism as a common factor across the four models.

Disorders, Fifth Edition, Text Revision (*DSM-5-TR*; American Psychiatric Association, 2022), *International Classification of Diseases, 11th Revision* (World Health Organization, 2018), and Research Domain Criteria (National Institute of Mental Health, n.d., 2008) all include criteria pertaining to a negative self-concept. Empirically, measures of self-criticism, particularly the extensively used Depressive Experiences Questionnaire (DEQ; Blatt et al., 1976), correlate relatively strongly with self-report measures of depression.

Coyne and Whiffen (1995) published the most comprehensive—and, in my opinion, clever—critique of research on personality and depression to date. They noted that the zero-order correlation between DEQ self-criticism and measures of depression was as high as .70 in college students and .65 in clinical samples (see J. Brown & Silberschatz, 1989; Whiffen & Sasseville, 1991, cited in Coyne & Whiffen, 1995). Coyne and Whiffen opined the following:

> It may seem paradoxical, but the ideal measure of vulnerability to depression should show a low or even nonsignificant correlation with the current level of depression in a representative nonclinical sample. First, a strong correlation weakens the claim that the diathesis is distinct from its manifestation in

depression. Second, a large correlation reduces the amount of variance in personality available to be related to subsequent depression and independent of initial depression. The majority of people who are vulnerable do not spend most of their life in an episode of depression. Therefore, at any moment in time, the co-occurrence of a common vulnerability factor and the less prevalent depression should be relatively low. Furthermore, diathesis models assume that a diathesis itself is insufficient to produce depression, so concordance of a high score on a measure of the diathesis and an episode of depression should be limited to times when there has been a recent severe life event to provide the link. Thus, the correlation between personality and depression should be relatively low, even when a valid diathesis has been identified. Theoretically and practically speaking, too strong a cross-sectional correlation between a measure of personality and depressive symptoms argues against the personality measure being able to serve as a useful measure of vulnerability. (p. 363)

To the extent that it is accurate, this statement by Coyne and Whiffen (1995) essentially disqualifies self-criticism as a dimension of vulnerability to depression. This is exactly what overlap models do: They disqualify personality as a vulnerability to psychopathology. If the former is indistinguishable from the latter, there is no logical rationale to speak of vulnerability. However, despite being cogent, Coyne and Whiffen's statement is inaccurate. To understand why, let us unpack it. Then, I strongly encourage you to consult the wonderful rejoinder to Coyne and Whiffen by Zuroff et al. (2004a), then a response by Coyne et al. (2004), and, finally, the reply by Zuroff et al. (2004b). I find this exchange to be one of the most inspiring and informative debates in the fields of psychology and psychiatry.

Coyne and Whiffen (1995) posited that the correlation between the vulnerability factor (diathesis) and depression should be quite low (even statistically nonsignificant) because a large correlation (a) suggests that the diathesis is indistinguishable from depression; (b) hinders the prediction of subsequent depression by personality (due to its collinearity with baseline depression); (c) violates the assumption that, more often than not, people with depression are not actually depressed; and (d) violates the assumption of diathesis models whereby the diathesis itself is insufficient to produce depression.

Clearly, a correlation between a personality factor (self-criticism) and depression that approaches unity indicates that the two are indistinguishable. However, how much further from unity (namely, $r = 1.00$) must the correlation be for it to be considered "not large"? While Coyne and Whiffen (1995) did not specify this, Watson (2001) proposed that the cutoff for prohibitive correlations was .85. None of the correlations cited by Coyne and Whiffen (1995) even got close to this magnitude. Soffer-Dudek and Shahar (2009) proposed an alternative cutoff of .70, which implied approximately

50% of shared variance, suggesting that the constructs were as distinct as they were indistinguishable. In the correlations cited by Coyne and Whiffen (1995), only one instance was detected with an *r* of .70 and only for college students. Correlations in clinical samples were lower.

With regard to the allegation that large correlations between personality and depression hinder the ability of personality to predict subsequent depression, this is true, but it is also a good thing. Personality factors that meet this criterion, such as self-criticism, are deemed robust, as attested to by numerous meta-analyses of research on both clinical and nonclinical samples, including treated patients (e.g., Löw et al., 2020; M. M. Smith et al., 2016).

Next, Coyne and Whiffen (1995) claimed that a particularly strong correlation between diathesis and depression would hinder the prediction of subsequent depression by personality because, more often than not, people with diathesis are not actually depressed. This is incorrect (as may be gleaned from Chapter 1 of this volume) because research has shown that what we refer to as simple depression is actually less prevalent than we might expect. Specifically, depression is continuous rather than binary, as demonstrated by extensive taxometric research (for a review, see Pettit & Joiner, 2006; Schmidt et al., 2004) as well as by the subsyndromal depression category reviewed in Chapter 1. In this respect, as my friend and mentor David Zuroff once told me: "You would be hard-pressed to find a happy self-critic."

Finally, the statement that diathesis is insufficient to produce depression is grossly erroneous. Any factor can lead to any outcome directly (as a main effect) and by interacting with other factors. Put differently, additive and interactive effects are not mutually exclusive; in the case of self-criticism and depression, both additive and interactive effects are operative, as shown in Table 2.1.

The Passive Vulnerability Model

Next is the *passive vulnerability model,* in which personality interacts with other factors (usually social-environmental) to produce depression. I refer to this model as passive because it is contingent on the assumption that personality is not associated with these social-environmental factors. Passive vulnerability models are further divided into stress–diathesis and dual/rival vulnerability subtypes. *Stress–diathesis* is arguably the most extensively studied model in psychopathology (Monroe & Simons, 1991); it posits that diathesis (e.g., personality) leads to psychopathology (e.g., depression) under conditions of life stress. As presented in Table 2.1, self-criticism indeed interacts with stressful events in predicting depression.

The second subtype is known as *dual vulnerability* (Kushner, 2015) and is somewhat counterintuitive. According to this model, the diathesis and the stress (or environmental risk factor) do not augment each other in leading to the outcome. Rather, the two compete to impact the outcome, such that psychopathology results from either the diathesis or the stress. The origins of this model can be traced to research on hyperactivity and aggression in children, which yielded results whereby biological (e.g., genetic) vulnerability predicted these outcomes more strongly under favorable social conditions than under unfavorable ones (i.e., social path model; Raine, 2002). Because of this competition between diathesis and stress to impact outcomes, Chris Henrich and I prefer the term *rival vulnerability* (Shahar & Henrich, 2019). Currently, there are only two studies with findings consistent with the dual/rival vulnerability model for self-criticism (Kopala-Sibley et al., 2017; Shahar & Henrich, 2019). Kopala-Sibley et al. (2017) reported that among female adolescents assessed three times separated by 9-month intervals, self-criticism predicted the first onset of nearly all depressive and anxiety disorders under low (but not high) levels of life stress. Similarly, Henrich and I previously reported that among Israeli adolescent girls and boys routinely exposed to missile attacks, self-criticism prospectively predicted depression when missile exposure was low compared with high (Shahar & Henrich, 2019).

The Active Vulnerability Model

The third model of personality and depression is *active vulnerability* (Table 2.1). This model contrasts with the former two passive vulnerability subtypes (stress–diathesis and dual/rival vulnerability) in that personality is directly associated with the stress or the social-environmental risk factor. In fact, under the active vulnerability model, personality is not just associated with the stress, but it actually leads to the stress. In turn, stress leads to depression. The origins of this model are a group of broad theories of human behavior referred to as *action/transactional theories* (for a review, see Shahar, 2006a, 2015b; Shahar, Cross, & Henrich, 2004), which emphasize the active contribution of children, adolescents, and adults to their development and well-being. Within depression research, there is a steady slew of theoretical and empirical works highlighting the effect of depression and related factors on life stress (particularly interpersonal stressful events), low levels of social support, and low levels of positive, enjoyable life events, all of which lead to depressive symptoms. Among these factors, self-criticism has shown remarkable predictive power vis-à-vis these social-environmental factors, thereby providing strong support for the active vulnerability model (Shahar, 2015a).

The Scarring Model

The fourth and final model of the role of personality in depression is *scarring*. According to Lewinsohn et al. (1981), depression might generate changes in cognitions, self-concept, and personality, similar to how a wound leaves a physical scar on the skin. Early research on scarring mainly yielded null findings (e.g., Lewinsohn et al., 1981; Rohde et al., 1990; Zeiss & Lewinsohn, 1988). However, my colleagues and I reported findings supportive of scarring when depression was assessed as a continuous variable and when the personality outcome was the self-concept (Schiller et al., 2016, 2019; Shahar & Henrich, 2019; Shahar, Blatt, Zuroff, Krupnick, & Sotsky, 2004). I elaborate on these studies later in this chapter.

With these four models and two subtypes in mind, let us now consider various definitions of personality and their role in depression.

WHAT IS PERSONALITY? TRAIT VERSUS SUBJECTIVE-AGENTIC MODELS

Let us distinguish the trait models of personality and psychopathology from the subjective–agentic (self-related) models (Shahar, 2020). Traits are dimensions that describe stable behavioral tendencies, whereas the SAPS targets the way we experience, learn, and narrate ourselves (i.e., our self-schema). By far, trait models predominate personality psychology and, by extension, the field of personality and psychopathology, despite ongoing criticism leveled toward these models (e.g., Block, 1995, 2001; Boyle, 2008; McAdams, 1992; Westen, 1995, 1996).

Common Personality Trait Models

Trait models are so prominent that a relatively small segment of traits are often equated with personality. This is particularly pertinent to the five-factor personality model (FFPM; Costa & McCrae, 1998). The FFPM focuses on only five traits that can be summarized using the OCEAN acronym: *openness* to experience (curiosity, intellectualism, and artistic interests), *conscientiousness* (discipline and order), *extroversion* (tendency to socialize and experience positive affect), *agreeableness* (warmth and kindness), and, last but not least, *neuroticism* (tendency to experience negative affect). The FFPM-guided research suggests that elevated neuroticism is causally implicated in psychopathology in general and in depressive disorders in particular (Lahey, 2009), with low extroversion also adding to the prediction of depression (D. N. Klein et al., 2011).

Two other influential trait models of personality that have a strong association with depression are the behavioral inhibition/activation systems (BIS/BAS) model (Carver & White, 1994; Gray, 1987) and the Cloninger temperament and character model (TCM; e.g., Cloninger et al., 1993; De Fruyt et al., 2000). The BIS/BAS model was formulated using an elaborate neurobiological theory of personality that identifies various phenotypes that drive behavior inhibition and activation, each in turn contributing to different mood and anxiety disorders. The TCM distinguishes biologically based traits such as temperament (i.e., novelty seeking, harm avoidance, reward dependence, and persistence) from more transcendental/experiential traits like character (i.e., self-directedness, cooperativeness, and self-transcendence). Cloninger and Svrakic (1997) proposed that these seven dimensions can inform the etiology and classification of psychopathology as well as case formulation and treatment planning.

Trait models of personality and psychopathology are intimately tied to research on personality disorders and their role in depression. Specifically, the *DSM-5-TR* classifies 10 personality disorders as belonging to three clusters: Cluster A (odd: paranoid, schizoid, and schizotypal), Cluster B (dramatic: antisocial, borderline, histrionic, and narcissistic), and Cluster C (anxious: avoidant, dependent, and obsessive-compulsive) (American Psychiatric Association, 2022). Virtually all 10 personality disorders are associated with unipolar depression, although some studies suggest a stronger link between Cluster B personality disorders and depression (e.g., Sedlinská et al., 2021). Unlike its predecessors, the *DSM-5-TR* also recognizes a dimensional conceptualization of personality disorders via its maladaptive personality traits model and the Personality Inventory for *DSM-5* (Krueger et al., 2012). Research links the dimensional *DSM-5* model with FFPM traits (e.g., Trull & Widiger, 2013), suggesting that all 10 personality disorders could be derived from extreme levels of the OCEAN traits (e.g., Samuel et al., 2010).

Another important development emanating from the link between trait personality theory and personality disorder research is the hierarchical taxonomy of psychopathology (HiTOP; Kotov et al., 2017). The HiTOP aims to transform categorical classifications of psychopathology into dimensional ones, and it does so via a hierarchical structure. At the top of the structure is a general psychopathology factor. Next, there are broad domains of internalizing, externalizing, and thought disorders. Further down are six domains: internalizing, thought disorders, disinhibited externalizing, antagonistic externalizing, detachment, and (provisionally) the somatoform. The first five domains are strongly linked to the FFPM OCEAN traits (Widiger et al., 2019). Interestingly, Widiger et al. (2019; see Table 1) simply labeled the FFPM OCEAN criteria as "personality."

Critiques of Personality Trait Models

Despite the dominance of trait models and their numerous variations, powerful opposition remains. I refer to this opposition as the SAPS because it comprises a group of theories that highlight subjective (self-related) processes and goal-directed action. Before I describe these theories, however, it is important to explain my three major objections to trait models of personality: (a) trait models do not describe personality, (b) trait models are built on the wrong data, and (c) neuroticism is tautological with depression. I explain each next.

Trait Models Do Not Describe Personality

Here, I am not arguing that trait models are not useful. Rather, what they all describe, in my opinion, is a set of behavioral vectors (see Westen, 1995, 1996): that is, patterns of behaviors that are characteristics of the person, particularly in social-emotional arenas.

To gain a better appreciation of this statement, consider the link between intelligence and the brain. Arguably, we may be able to know a lot about a person if we know their "level of intelligence," assuming we agree on what that is. Yet how much does this knowledge of a person's intelligence tell us about their brain anatomy and/or neural connectivity? Not a lot. To learn more about this person's brain anatomy (structure) and neural connectivity (process, dynamics), we need to observe subtypes of the brain and how they correspond with each other. This is exactly what the fields of neurology and neuroscience do. Because the brain is a body part (i.e., is a concrete, tangible object), it is easier to observe its structure and function than that of the abstract entity we refer to as personality. Moreover, advances in technology have further bolstered neuroscientists and neurologists' ability to observe brain structure and processes, and these advances are absent from personality psychology (but see the Epilogue of this volume regarding future directions in research).

Dan McAdams, one of the leading theorists within the SAPS, considers the FFPM a level 1 description of personality, which is conducive to an initial acquaintance with the person (McAdams, 1992, 1995). Faithful to the earlier intelligence analogy, I take a stronger position. I acknowledge that the FFPM is highly conducive to predicting a person's behavior and is less but still conducive for knowing the person (albeit superficially); nevertheless, the FFPM does not address personality per se because it cannot provide information about structure and process. The same criticism holds, I maintain, for other trait theories.

Trait Models Are Built on the Wrong Data

Previously, thinkers more senior than I alluded to the strange nature of the data on which FFPM is built (Block, 1995). Here is what Drew Westen (1996) had to say about these data:

> The constructs that dominate contemporary personality psychology emerged from the study of the dictionary. The products of that lexical quest have often been remarkably fruitful, especially in their contribution to our understanding of the heritability and continuity of personality over time. Yet if I were an alien trying to understand personality (just a hypothetical example—unconscious processes are as far as I go), I doubt I would begin by abducting *Webster's Unabridged*. Indeed, the dictionary is probably not among the first two or three hundred places I would look (unless I was confused about the spelling of *extroversion*, which happens with some regularity). I suspect, instead, I would begin by talking to people and watching them behave in their natural environments. And I believe that is where we should begin. (p. 400)

Similar criticisms could (and should) be leveled toward biologically based trait theories such as the BIS/BAS and TCM. These theories offer self-report measures that assess behaviors stemming from neurobiological and neurochemical processes. Obviously, people's reports on their behavior constitute a very distal proxy of neurobiological and neurochemical processes, and a theory predicated on biology and/or chemistry should be tested using biochemical data. I can accept the position that self-report measures constitute an intermediate phase for such theories, which should later be replaced with collection of biochemical data. But until and unless such data are collected, the validity of such theories cannot be genuinely evaluated.

Neuroticism Is Tautological With Depression

I now turn to an objection that targets only one of the traits described by these theories: *neuroticism*, which is sometimes referred to as emotional instability or negative emotionality. Decades of research have attested to the predictive utility of neuroticism in myriad mental and physical health problems and it is most pronounced in depression and anxiety. Indeed, in an extensively cited article, Lahey (2009) declared neuroticism to constitute a serious public health problem.

Lahey (2009) did not cite a previous (and in my mind, very incisive) article by Johan Ormel, Judith Rosemalen, and Ann Farmer (2004), titled, "Neuroticism: A Non-informative Marker of Vulnerability to Psychopathology." This article is particularly intriguing because Ormel and colleagues also published studies focusing on the adverse effect of neuroticism (Ormel & Wohlfarth, 1991). In their 2004 article, Ormel et al. took a very critical stance toward neuroticism, leveling caveats with which I completely agree.

Specifically, the authors argued that the associations between neuroticism and psychopathology are not informative because of the following:

> neuroticism reflect[s] a person's characteristic (or mean) level of distress over a protracted period of time. In this perspective, even prospective associations of neuroticism with mental health outcomes are basically futile, and largely tautological since scores on any characteristic with substantial within-subject stability will predict, by definition, that characteristic and related variables at later points in time. This situation will not change until knowledge becomes available about: (i) the mechanisms that produce high neuroticism scores (and psychopathology) and (ii) its neurobiological substrate. Only then might we understand why neuroticism appears to "predict" the outcomes it predicts. Until recently, the efforts to demonstrate the neurobiological basis for neuroticism and the mechanisms involved have been surprisingly few (e.g., Gray, 1981) and not very successful (Claridge & Davis, 2001). (p. 907)

I am in full agreement with this statement, except that I am less optimistic than Ormel et al. (2004) about the utility of neuroticism. Namely, I do not believe that it is useful to investigate the mechanisms that produce high neuroticism and/or its neurobiological basis before neuroticism is shown to be any different from chronic depression and/or anxiety. Nor do I believe that the latter will ever be demonstrated. In the absence of a clear indication of the distinct nature of neuroticism, I posit that a focus on chronic distress (depression and anxiety; see Chapter 1) should replace the focus on a (presumed) trait such as neuroticism.

Self-Concept and the Subjective-Agentic Models of Personality

The point of departure between the SAPS and trait models is the centrality of the self-concept in psychological science at large (e.g., Markus & Wurf, 1987). Thus, in cognitive psychology, the self-concept has been found to regulate memory, attention, and learning (e.g., Kim et al., 2022). Relatedly, in neuropsychology, the self-concept is theorized—and empirically demonstrated—to play a major role in neural connectivity (Northoff, 2011). In social psychology, the self-concept has been repeatedly reaffirmed to formidably propel emotion and interpersonal behavior (Frijda, 2001; Swann et al., 1992). In developmental psychology, the self-concept is considered a cornerstone of identity formation (Harter, 1990). In personality psychology, alongside and despite the dominance of trait theories, there is a steady stream of research on individual differences in the numerous self-concept dimensions—such as self-esteem, self-criticism, self-efficacy (domain-specific and generalized), and self-concept clarity—across the life span. This line of inquiry is closely tied to research on psychopathology and psychotherapy (e.g., Löw et al., 2020; Rieger et al., 2016).

The self, however, is never alone. It is invariably relational: People experience, collect information about, and narrate themselves in relation to others (Andersen & Chen, 2002; Baldwin, 1992; Mischel & Shoda, 1995), and self-schema is inexorably linked to schemas and scripts of other people. Indeed, schemas and scripts of self-with-others could be seen as the most fundamental units of personality. Put differently, personality structure and dynamics evolve around subjective (self-related) and intersubjective (self-other relations) processes (Shahar, 2020).

Within subjective and intersubjective processes, the role of human agency is paramount:

> Rather than being static, interpersonal relationships are dynamic and transactional, in that persons and social contexts are co-causative. This dictum is strongly emphasized in Bandura's (1978) well-known reciprocal determinism principle, although it had already appeared in Heinz Hartmann's psychoanalytic writings, albeit in German (Hartmann, 1957). Many theorists in personality, developmental, and clinical psychology have reiterated and elaborated upon this transactional nature of the human situation (e.g., McAdams, 2013; Sameroff, 2009; Shahar, 2015). Agency, described as individuals' belief that their actions are relevant to attaining their goals (Bandura, 1997), is built into the co-causative nature of person-context exchanges: People act upon each other in order to realize goals (Buss, 1987). To do that, they must expect themselves to be able to influence others, i.e., they must be agentic (Shahar, 2015). (Shahar, 2020, p. 3; note that Shahar, 2015, in this quotation is Shahar, 2015a, cited in this volume.)

Thus, the SAPS theory amounts to the view that personality is composed of subjectivity, intersubjectivity, and agency. Four broad psychological theories address these three components: social-cognitive (formerly social-learning) theory, psychoanalytic object relations theory (reformulated), attachment theory, and McAdams's identity theory. The overlap among these theories is vast (Shahar, 2021b). Social-cognitive theory is most associated with the works of Bandura and Mischel and has evolved as a reaction to radical behaviorism, which deemed mental processes as belonging to a "black box." Over the years, the writings of Bandura, Mischel, and their colleagues have gravitated toward a focus on the agentic nature of the self (i.e., self-efficacy) and the link between the self-concept and representations of other people (i.e., interpersonal schemas; see Baldwin, 1992; Cervone et al., 2001; Dweck & Leggett, 1988). This is very strongly manifested in clinical psychology through the development of cognitive-integrative forms of treatment for complex clinical conditions, such as schema therapy (E. Rafaeli et al., 2011). In a manner reminiscent of a medical miracle, psychoanalytic object relations theory has been gradually extracted from the antiscientific psychoanalytic establishment and has been reformulated by giants such as Sidney Blatt, Peter Fonagy, Otto Kernberg, Drew Westen, and others using social-cognitive and cognitive-developmental jargon and drawing from empirical research that they and others have conducted (Blatt et al., 1997; Fonagy, 1993; Kernberg et al., 2008; Westen, 1991, 1998). So convincing is the rapprochement of social-cognitive and object relations theory that, as I have repeatedly argued, they can now be seen as corresponding to a single theoretical approach, differentiated only by nuances (Shahar, 2016, 2018, 2021b; Shahar, Cross, & Henrich, 2004; Shahar et al., 2023).

Next is Dan McAdams's identity theory, which builds on earlier contributions by Erikson (1968) but at the same time extends these by (a) highlighting the narrated (story-like) nature of self-others representations, (b) describing specific developmental pathways of such narratives (McAdams, 2013), and (c) grounding these developmental pathways in the humanities, particularly political theory and psychobiography (McAdams & Ochberg, 1988). Finally, attachment theory (see Bowlby, 1969; then Ainsworth & Bell, 1970; Main et al., 1985) ascended in both developmental and social psychology by shedding light on the understanding of actual (as opposed to fantasized) relational patterns (internal working models), primarily in parent–child, romantic, and other close relationships (Bartholomew & Horowitz, 1991; Fonagy & Luyten, 2018; Mikulincer & Shaver, 2016).

This, I believe, is a paradigmatic shift in the field of personality and psychopathology. As in other instances, depression research spearheads this paradigmatic shift. Let us now turn to describing how several converging SAPS theories of the depressive personality—those of Sidney Blatt, Aaron Beck, and later of Paul Gilbert—have been doing this over the last 5 decades.

RELATEDNESS, SELF-DEFINITION, AND THE DEPRESSIVE PERSONALITY: THE PIONEERING WORKS OF BLATT, BECK, AND GILBERT

Since the 1970s, the theories of Blatt (1974, 2004, 2008) and A. T. Beck (1983, 1996) have featured prominently in depression research and treatment. The two theories converge conceptually in identifying personality structures that confer risk for unipolar depression. Namely, in both theories, one structure pertains to a coherent, essentially positive, self-definition, whereas the other structure pertains to an ability to attain stable and nurturing relationships (Blatt et al., 2001). Both Blatt and Beck argued that failure in securing each of these structures results in two specific constellations of depression-related, as well as other forms of, psychopathologies. Blatt and colleagues labeled the first personality/psychopathology constellation as *introjective/self-critical*, pertaining to obsessive preoccupation with success and fear of failure. In contrast, Beck called it *autonomous*, referring also to fear of failure but more strongly to defensive separation from others (Robins et al., 1994). Furthermore, Blatt labeled the second personality/psychopathology constellation as *anaclitic/dependent*, pertaining to chronic loneliness and a sense of "object loss," whereas Beck called it *sociotropic*, carrying a similar meaning. The introjective/self-critical and autonomous constellation purports to lead to introjective (guilt-ridden) depression and to obsessive and paranoid psychopathologies that highlight the need for control. The anaclitic/dependent and sociotropic constellation is hypothesized to lead to anaclitic (dependent) depression as well as to relational psychopathologies like dependent and borderline personality disorders (Blatt et al., 2001; Blatt & Zuroff, 1992; Luyten & Blatt, 2011, 2013).

The two theories were revived and elaborated on in P. Gilbert's (1995, 2005) cognitive-evolutionary model, which stipulated that two central, evolutionary-based *social mentalities* (caregiving and social rank) regulate our cognition and behavior. The *caregiving mentality* is governed by oxytocin and targets affiliative behavior; it is tantamount to Blatt's anaclitic dependency and Beck's sociotropy theories. Similarly, the *social-rank mentality* is governed by dopamine and is reward based, targeting achievement; this mentality is tantamount to Blatt's introjective–self-criticism and to Beck's autonomy theories. Similar to Blatt and Beck's theories, Gilbert posited that an overdominance of one mentality at the expense of the other is bound to lead to psychopathology, primarily to depression and suicidality. However, Gilbert went beyond Blatt and Beck by identifying two forms of self-criticism: one that centers on a sense of inadequacy and another on self-hate (P. Gilbert et al., 2004). Another very important theoretical advancement of Gilbert and colleagues is their assumption that self-compassion is a positive self-stance that might ameliorate the deleterious effects of self-criticism. Consequently, P. Gilbert (2009) developed a cognitive form of brief therapy that assists self-critical individuals in developing self-compassion.

Although the theories of Blatt, Beck, and Gilbert converge conceptually, measures of self-criticism and autonomy do not appear to converge empirically. More accurately, whereas Blatt's dependency and Beck's sociotropy theories converge, Blatt's self-criticism and Beck's autonomy theories evince very weak correlations (Coyne & Whiffen, 1995). Another major problem with both theories is the unequal vulnerability status shown for dependency/sociotropy and self-criticism/autonomy. To understand this unequal status, one needs to consider theory and research focusing on personality by life stress interactions.

As indicated in Table 2.1, the stress–diathesis model is a leading conceptualization within psychopathology research. In the context of Blatt and Beck's theories, a particularly nuanced version of the stress–diathesis model was formed, called the *congruency hypothesis* (Hammen et al., 1985; Zuroff & Mongrain, 1987). According to this hypothesis, individuals with extreme dependency tendencies experience depressive symptoms only when their pivotal concerns (e.g., maintaining close and protective interpersonal relations) are threatened by stressful interpersonal events (e.g., rejection, confrontation, abandonment, loss). Those with extremely high self-criticism or autonomy levels experience depressive symptoms only when their principal concerns (e.g., achievement) are threatened by failure-related events (e.g., failing an exam or being laid-off). While this is a robust, clear-cut, empirically testable hypothesis, empirical research putting it to the test yielded largely disappointing results: Dependent individuals appeared to experience depressive symptoms in the face of interpersonal stressful events (Priel & Shahar, 2000; Shahar, Joiner, et al., 2004), whereas self-critical people reacted with depressive symptoms to both interpersonal and achievement-related life stress (Coyne & Whiffen, 1995). Thus, the vulnerability implicated in self-criticism was more pervasive than that implicated in dependency (Shahar, 2015a; see also Table 2.1).

When this pattern is juxtaposed against findings concerning zero-order correlations between dependency/sociotropy and self-criticism/autonomy on the one hand and depressive symptoms and diagnosis on the other, an unequal vulnerability status is further revealed. As noted previously, the correlation between self-criticism and depression (broadly defined) is strong but, as I argued earlier, not prohibitively so. The correlation between dependency and depression is much weaker, and that involving sociotropy and depression is somewhere in the middle between dependency and self-criticism. Correlations involving autonomy and depression appear to be the weakest (Shahar, 2015a).[1] This pattern becomes even more revealing

---

[1] Clive Robins and colleagues developed the Personal Style Inventory (PSI), which is an improved measure of sociotropy and autonomy (Robins et al., 1994). In the PSI, sociotropy and autonomy are assessed via three dimensions each. Sociotropy is assessed via need for approval, appeasing others, and dependency; autonomy is assessed via defensive separation, need for control, and self-criticism/perfectionism. Obviously, because it includes a subscale tapping self-criticism, PSI-autonomy correlates with DEQ self-criticism more strongly than previous autonomy measures do. Nevertheless, I previously showed that PSI–self-criticism/perfectionism is best construed as a dimension independent of both PSI-sociotropy and PSI-autonomy (Shahar, 2006b).

when longitudinal associations between these personality dimensions and depression are examined. Longitudinal associations pertain to the correlation between personality at Time t and depression at a subsequent measurement ($t + 1$), after partialing out the shared variance between personality at Time t and depression at $t + 1$ that is related to depression at Time t (i.e., baseline depression). When this is done, self-criticism prevails by a knockout: Its longitudinal association with depression is strong, statistically significant, and highly consistent (for reviews, see Blatt, 2004; Shahar, 2015a; Werner et al., 2019; Zuroff et al., 2004a, 2004b). What is even more impressive is the pattern whereby this longitudinal association between self-criticism and depression remains even after statistically controlling for a host of other potentially confounding factors, including neuroticism (Shahar, 2015a; M. M. Smith et al., 2016; Werner et al., 2019). The fact that the effect of self-criticism on subsequent depression survives even after controlling for neuroticism is (in my opinion) no less than astonishing. Recall the redundancy of neuroticism and depression, and the claim by Ormel et al. (2004) that neuroticism is likely to simply represent stable (mean) levels of individuals' distress. If so, then the fact that self-criticism predicts depression even after controlling for neuroticism suggests that self-criticism is such a powerful predictor that it is able to detect even *slight* fluctuations around the mean of a person's depression (!).[2]

But research on the role of self-criticism in depression gets even more dramatic. Work inspired by the previously noted action/transactional models (for reviews, see Shahar, 2006a, 2015b; Shahar, Joiner, et al., 2004) led to examination of an alternative, active vulnerability perspective. Such examination, propelled first by Zuroff (1992) and carried out primarily, concurrently, and independently by his former student David Dunkley and colleagues as well as me and others, has led to a crystal-clear pattern: Self-criticism predicts life stress (both interpersonal and achievement related), which in turn predicts symptoms of not only depression but also anxiety (e.g., Shahar & Priel, 2003). In fact, self-criticism predicts other environmental factors such as low perceived social support, low level of satisfaction with social relations, dyadic difficulties, and low levels of positive life events (for review, see Shahar, 2015a). These effects are demonstrated both within and outside

---

[2]Related to footnote 1, there is confusion in the literature with regard to the distinction between self-criticism and perfectionism. This confusion is fostered by some of the most illustrious investigators in the field, including my mentor, Blatt (1995). Because this issue is discussed at length in *Erosion* (Shahar, 2015a), I provide the gist of my position here, which (in my opinion) is consistent with the empirical literature: Perfectionism, in and of itself, is benign when it does not include self-critical (harsh, punitive) aspects.

psychotherapy, and they portray self-criticism not only as a powerful dimension of vulnerability but also as a dimension of vulnerability characterized by an interpersonal mechanism: Self-critics are depressed because they appear to sabotage their social environment. In contrast, active vulnerability research on dependency evinces a markedly different pattern: While dependency does appear to generate life stress, it also generates high levels of protective factors such as perceived social support and positive life events. Dependency is thus depicted as a complex personality dimension, one that comprises both risk and resilience (Bornstein, 1998; Shahar, 2008, 2015a).[3]

To complete the picture implicating self-criticism as a chief villain, mounting evidence has shown that this dimension is longitudinally associated with other forms of psychopathology beyond depression, including anxiety, bipolar, somatic, and substance use disorders; in addition, self-criticism is reported to be a strong predictor of suicidal thoughts, suicide attempts, and nonsuicidal self-injury (for a review, see Shahar et al., 2020). In most studies, the associations between self-criticism and self-injurious thoughts and behaviors are significant, even after controlling for depressive symptoms. Although most of this body of research is cross-sectional, thereby seriously limiting causal inference, several studies are based on longitudinal designs. Arguably, the most rigorous study is that of R. C. O'Connor and Noyce (2008), who assessed 232 healthy adults twice over a period of 3 months. They found that, controlling for depression, Time 1 self-criticism predicted a rank-order increase in suicidal ideation, and this effect was fully mediated by Time 1 ruminative brooding, reflecting passive comparison of and perseveration about one's current situation with some unachieved standard (Treynor et al., 2003).

But what about the other two models of personality vulnerability that are included in Table 2.1: namely, dual/rival vulnerability and scarring? As for the former model, I have already mentioned the only two studies showing findings consistent with dual/rival vulnerability (Kopala-Sibley et al., 2017; Shahar & Henrich, 2019). In both studies, dual/rival vulnerability was shown for both self-criticism and dependency. Both studies appear to be very robust methodologically. It should be noted, however, that these two supportive studies out of dozens that tested personality by stress interactions constitute a minority. Hence, the jury is still out with respect to the prominence of dual/rival vulnerability in the context of personality and depression.

And what about the scarring model? Results concerning this model, strongly converging with my clinical experience, gave rise to this book.

---

[3]PSI-sociotropy (see footnote 1) reflects some serious vulnerability features (e.g., Shahar et al., 2018), although overall its vulnerability status lags behind self-criticism. With regard to PSI-autonomy, without the self-criticism/perfectionism subscale, it actually emerges as a dimension of resilience.

SELF-CRITICISM AND DEPRESSIVE SCARRING: JUST THE BEGINNING?

Earlier, I noted that the scarring hypothesis (Lewinsohn et al., 1981) posits that depression might generate changes in cognitions, self-concept, and personality, similar to the way a wound leaves a physical scar on the skin. I also noted that although initial scarring research mainly yielded null findings (e.g., Lewinsohn et al., 1981; Rohde et al., 1990; Zeiss & Lewinsohn, 1988), supportive findings exist as well (e.g., Coyne et al., 1998; Shahar & Davidson, 2003; Shahar & Henrich, 2010). More specifically, Chris Henrich and I (Shahar & Henrich, 2010) proposed that because of the self's heightened sensitivity to mood states (e.g., Frijda, 2001), it might be the most suitable candidate for the examination of depressive scarring. Consistent with this view, my colleagues and I have repeatedly shown scarring effects involving low self-esteem (Schiller & Shahar, 2013; Shahar & Davidson, 2003; Shahar & Henrich, 2010; Weinberg et al., 2012), self-criticism (Shahar, Blatt, Zuroff, Kuperminck, & Leadbeater, 2004), self-concept clarity and generalized self-efficacy (Schiller et al., 2019), and other self-related constructs (Shahar & Henrich, 2019; Shahar et al., 2008, 2013). In fact, Moran Schiller and I have shown that scarring may ensue from a host of psychopathological symptoms (e.g., anxiety, somatization, etc.), not just from depressive symptoms (Schiller & Shahar, 2013; Schiller et al., 2016, 2019).[4]

Of the various self-concept dimensions affected by psychopathology, self-criticism seems to me to be the most noteworthy. This is because of the previously described, formidable effect of self-criticism on psychopathology, and the findings whereby this vulnerability effect of self-criticism is mediated through the social context (active vulnerability). In three published studies, my colleagues and I demonstrated self-critical scarring alongside self-critical vulnerability. In the first (Shahar, Blatt, Zuroff, Kuperminck, & Leadbeater, 2004), we examined the longitudinal, year-long association involving depressive symptoms (assessed via the Beck Depression Inventory) and depressive vulnerability (dependency and self-criticism, measured via the DEQ) in young US adolescents. Two assessment waves were implemented, at the beginning

---

[4] An independent group of illustrious investigators focusing on the longitudinal associations between depression and self-esteem have consistently demonstrated findings concerning low self-esteem vulnerability. However, they did not seem to obtain findings consistent with scarring, even though the research designs, measures, and analytic strategies they used were very similar to mine (with the exception that their samples were much larger; for review, see Schiller et al., 2016, citing Orth and numerous colleagues; see also Orth et al., 2021). I am at a loss as to why this is the case, and I hope that we will be able to clarify this in the future.

and end of the school year. Whereas no longitudinal associations were found for dependency and depression, clear longitudinal associations were revealed for self-criticism and depression: Both predicted each other over time, evincing almost the same magnitude (standardized regression coefficients of .23 and .22 for vulnerability and scarring effects, respectively).

In the second study (Schiller et al., 2016), we examined the longitudinal association between a host of psychopathology symptoms (assessed via the Brief Symptom Inventory; Derogatis, 1982) and five self-concept domains: self-esteem, generalized self-efficacy, self-concept clarity, self-criticism, and self-concept reassurance. Interestingly, self-criticism was measured via three instruments: the six-item version of self-criticism from the DEQ, the Self-Inadequacy subscale of the Forms of Self-Criticizing/Attacking and Self-Reassuring Scale (FSCRS; P. Gilbert et al., 2004), and the Hated-Self subscale of the FSCRS. Participants were Israeli first-year undergraduates ($N = 170$; $M_{age} = 23.19$ years). Three assessment waves were employed: at the beginning, midway through, and at the end of the academic year. Both acute and chronic stressful circumstances were assessed at Wave 2 with the University of California, Los Angeles Stress Interview. Psychopathological symptoms predicted all self-concept dimensions, including the three self-criticism scales, with the exception of self-concept clarity. However, a serious military escalation between Israel and Gaza erupted 2 years later when participants were in their last year of college. These participants, studying at Ben-Gurion University of the Negev nearby, were exposed to ongoing, life-threatening missile attacks. We reassessed participants after the escalation and found that Wave 1 distress predicted an increase in all self-concept dimensions, including self-concept clarity and again the three self-criticism subscales (Schiller et al., 2019).

The third study (Shahar & Henrich, 2019) was described earlier in this chapter. In a manner consistent with dual/rival vulnerability (see Table 2.1), among Israeli adolescent girls and boys routinely exposed to missile attacks, self-criticism prospectively predicted depression when missile exposure was low compared with high (Shahar & Henrich, 2019). Yet, in a manner consistent with scarring, we also found that when missile exposure was low, depressive symptoms also predicted an increase in self-criticism among these participants.

In *Erosion* (Shahar, 2015a), I reported being very impressed by scarring effects that surfaced on top of active vulnerability, so much so that I charted a self-critical cascade whereby self-critics create a negative social environment that leads to their distress. This distress, in turn, feeds back to their self-concept, enhancing self-criticism (see Figure 1.5 in Shahar, 2015a; see also Shahar, 2016). At that time, I only had the 2004 study to rely on (Shahar, Blatt, Zuroff, Kuperminck, & Leadbeater, 2004). The studies that I summarized earlier subsequently accumulated (Schiller et al., 2016, 2019; Shahar & Henrich, 2019), and they conversed loudly with my clinical practice.

THE SELF-CRITICAL CASCADE: QUESTIONING THEORY THROUGH RESEARCH DATA AND CLINICAL EXPERIENCES

In the preface for *Erosion*, I alluded to my passion concerning the integration of research and practice and how I toil to apply this integration in my own life's work (Shahar, 2015a). A very illuminating illustration of the power of such integration is my unmediated clinical encounter with self-critical scarring, nested within the self-critical cascade. As you may have probably guessed by now, my clinical load is largely composed of patients presenting with complex, treatment-resistant psychopathology, and many of these individuals present with the complex depression manifestations described in Chapter 1. One of the (many) things I have learned from these patients is the following vicissitude: Patients already arrive to treatment highly depressed, and their social environment is in havoc. As weeks and months in treatment go by, I see patients' active vulnerability, or what Wachtel (1997, 2014) called *cyclical psychodynamics*: Patients' personality, particularly their mental representations of self and others, propels them to behave in a way that evokes rejections, confrontations, and loss; prevents positive experiences (life events); and derails social support. All of this, of course, increases patients' symptoms. Then, with my own eyes, I see how these depressive (and anxious) symptoms activate the most noxious mental representations of self and others. What is particularly stunning is that this often happens very quickly (i.e., within days or even hours).[5]

These clinical encounters, which I process through the lenses of the previously reviewed research, had me thinking intensely about the link between personality and depression. In *Erosion*, my major conclusion was that self-criticism is a personality virus of sorts, a principal villain that must be stopped in order to prevent or reduce psychopathology (Shahar, 2015a). But the

---

[5]Wachtel's cyclical psychodynamics theory is strongly echoed by developments within personality disorder theory and research, particularly as manifested by contemporary integrative interpersonal theory (Pincus & Ansell, 2013; Wright et al., 2023). Drawing from the previously described HiTOP, the contemporary integrative interpersonal theory emphasizes the impact of personality pathology on interpersonal relationships, thus echoing active vulnerability models within depression research and treatment.

more I witnessed the self-critical cascade, the more I considered the possibility that self-criticism was only the tip of the iceberg. What was really operating, and very fast and powerfully so, was an entire system of factors encompassing symptoms, mental representations of self and others (not just self-representations), a specific kind of affect (criticism based), and a specific way that this affect is (mis)regulated, ultimately leading to exacerbation of the depressive picture. It was then that I realized that, 2 decades ago, as a graduate student, I had learned about such a system of variables operating in the context of depression: Melanie Klein's depressive position, nested within psychoanalytic object relations theory. This presented me with a problem.

I am thoroughly psychoanalytically trained and informed, and I have always considered psychoanalytic object relations theory to be a useful resource of clinical wisdom, provided that it is tallied with extant empirical research. It was Melanie Klein's work that I really disliked. The graphic, esoteric jargon; the condescending, often melodramatic writing style; and the brutal therapeutic style (e.g., telling patients what their presumably "deepest" anxieties are) strongly alienated me. My preference was the softer and much clearer (even if still poetic) writing of psychoanalytic scholars such as Donald Winnicott, Michael Balint, Harry Guntrip, Ronald Fairbairn, and, of course, John Bowlby. However, the research that I produced and consumed and my clinical experience left me no choice but to reconsider Melanie Klein's theory.

So I did what is often done in clinical theory (including psychoanalysis) when one is ambivalent about a theory: I rewrote Klein's object relations theory to fit my sensibilities. The diplomatic among us would call it a "reformulation," which I discuss next in greater detail in Chapter 3.

PART II PSYCHODYNAMICS AND ECODYNAMICS

3 REFORMULATING OBJECT RELATIONS THEORY AND THE DEPRESSIVE POSITION

With the changes in the relation to the object, new anxiety-contents make their appearance and a change takes place in the mechanisms of defence.
—M. Klein, 1935, p. 146

This chapter aims to briefly present psychoanalytic object relations theory (ORT) as a focal personality theory that bears particular relevance to the understanding of complex depression. To that aim, I will

- present ORT with a focus on the version developed by Melanie Klein that advances the notion of position, pertaining to an amalgamation of various personality processes that lead to psychopathology. In particular, the depressive position is posited by Klein and her followers to account for vulnerability to depression.

- present a reformulated object relations theory (RORT) and a reformulated depressive position that bridge Klein's work with later interdisciplinary research.

- relate the reformulated versions to depression research and treatment.

https://doi.org/10.1037/0000377-004
Complex Depression: The Role of Personality Dynamics and Social Ecology, by G. Shahar
Copyright © 2024 by the American Psychological Association. All rights reserved.

Psychoanalysis is characterized as having numerous strands (e.g., Ghent, 1989), which tend to deem each other "non-psychoanalytic" (Blass, 2010). For the sake of this discussion, let us assume that the largest strands of psychoanalysis are (a) drive-focused classical or Freudian psychoanalysis, (b) psychoanalytic ego psychology, (c) ORT, (d) psychoanalytic self-psychology, and (e) interpersonal/relational psychoanalysis. Interestingly, all five strands have abundant research support, although reviewing such support is outside the scope of this work. Nevertheless, I contend that the most prominent strand in psychoanalysis, and the one that is also most promising in terms of conversing with academic psychology, is ORT.

The rationale for my selection is this: From a philosophical or metapsychological perspective, ORT constitutes the most comprehensive theoretical statement of psychoanalysis, one that subsumes the other four strands and lends itself most easily to clinical practice that is conversant with non-psychoanalytic schools. Specifically, ORT recognizes biological drives as central to human psychology and action, although the theory (drawing primarily from Melanie Klein) highlights that drives are invariably directed toward human figures. In addition, ORT acknowledges the principal role of the ego as a self-sector responsible for regulating thought, affect, and behavior. ORT, however, construes the ego as always located in a self-in-relationships context. ORT can easily incorporate psychoanalytic self-psychology by acknowledging the latter's ability to elucidate unfolding of narcissistic phenomena (Blass & Blatt, 1992). Finally, as extensively argued by Mitchell (1995a) and others, the interpersonal/relational psychoanalytic strand, as adept as it is in describing interpersonal behavior, stands on the ORT description of mental representations of the self and others (for a comprehensive treatment of the role of ORT in the history of psychoanalysis, see Ogden, 1992; and J. R. Greenberg & Mitchell, 1983).

Inspired by mentors and role models such as Blatt, Westen, Fonagy, and others, I have embarked on a journey to align ORT further with academic psychology (e.g., Shahar, 2001, 2004, 2006a, 2010, 2011, 2012, 2015a, 2015b, 2016, 2018; Shahar & Davidson, 2009; Shahar, Cross, & Henrich, 2004; Shahar & Henrich, 2010). As noted previously, central to this journey is my effort to reformulate Melanie Klein's (1928, 1935, 1940, 1945) notion of the positions.

OVERVIEW OF KLEIN'S OBJECT RELATIONS THEORY

Those of you versed in psychoanalytic writings hardly require explanation of the Kleinian positions. This book, however, seeks to reach out beyond this respectable readership; hence, I offer a relatively brief, yet hopefully informative, exposition. Before I discuss the positions, the intellectual and historical context serving as a platform to Klein's work should be presented. To put it simply (and somewhat provocatively), Melanie Klein was one of the greatest dissidents of psychoanalysis. However, her revolt was not directed at the progenitor of psychoanalysis, Sigmund Freud, but rather at one of his most central followers: his daughter, Anna. Both Klein and Anna Freud were working in London during the 1950s and 1960s, and the two strong-willed women disagreed about virtually everything. Anna Freud accepted as a given her father's portrayal of psychological development (the psycho-sexual theory), whereas Klein challenged this stage-based theory, proposing instead a theory of positions (discussed later) that not only ensue but also solidify over the first year of life. As one of the leaders of psychoanalytic ego psychology, Anna Freud placed marked emphasis on the ego, the psychic entity in charge of adaptation. In contrast, Klein, being "more Freudian than Freud," held firmly onto traditional emphasis on the id and instinctual drives, although she modified Sigmund Freud's theory by highlighting the fact that drives are invariably directed toward an object (e.g., a human being; J. R. Greenberg & Mitchell, 1983). Relatedly, Anna Freud emphasized the impact of the social environment on the ego and, consequently, was a staunch supporter of the healing power of education. In contrast, Klein elevated constitutional forces, was suspicious of the possibility that the social environment can "correct" the ego, and sought direct contact with the ego instead, primarily via play (for children) and deep-seated interpretations of fantasy and anxiety (for both children and adults). It is, therefore, not surprising that whereas Anna Freud continued her father's focus on the "neurosis," Klein broke new ground in clinical psychoanalysis by applying her theory to the treatment of young children and of individuals with severe (primitive) psychopathology (see Holder, 2005; Viner, 1996).

Klein's Position: Anxiety, Defenses, and Object Relations

According to Klein (1935), a *position* is a system of personality processes working in tandem to produce a coherent experience of the self, the world, and the self within the world. Klein's positions comprise three processes: anxiety, defense mechanisms, and object relations.

Anxiety
Anxiety has been the emotion of focus for other psychoanalytic thinkers as well. Klein, in this sense, is similar to Sigmund Freud in positing that the entire dynamics of personality is propelled by the psyche's attempt to

deal with anxiety. Unlike her predecessors, Sigmund Freud included, Klein (1928) distinguished between two forms of anxiety: paranoid-schizoid and depressive. *Paranoid-schizoid anxiety* is primitive (surfaces during the first months of life), dramatic, and all encompassing. It centers on a fear of overwhelming aggression that threatens to annihilate all that is good. The engulfing nature of this persecutory anxiety awards it the *paranoid* adjective. The *schizoid* adjective pertains to the basic way of handling this persecutory anxiety—namely, distancing all that is good from all that is perceived as potentially bad.

In contrast, *depressive anxiety* recognizes the inevitable proximity of good and bad: they often dwell next to each other. Consequently, the bad cannot simply be exiled from the good. Rather, it must be managed. Within this context, the focal apprehension is this: "I will not succeed in managing the bad, and it will eventually harm the good." Such anxiety is mellower and more nuanced than paranoid-schizoid anxiety because it acknowledges the difficulty in distinguishing between good and bad and includes culpability ("I am in charge of managing the bad").

Defense Mechanisms
The stark difference between paranoid-schizoid and depressive anxiety is also reflected in how the self defends against them. In psychoanalysis, defense mechanisms are cognitive-affective maneuvers that aim to distort incoming information so as to maintain a positive sense of self and the world, one that enables functioning. These mechanisms are unconscious and automatic. Whereas Sigmund Freud and his daughter, Anna, laid the foundation for understanding of defense mechanisms (A. Freud, 1946), Melanie Klein broke new ground in defense mechanism theory, which was strongly manifested in her notion of the paranoid-schizoid position. This requires some explanation.

The defense mechanisms described by Sigmund and Anna Freud are circumscribed in terms of the information that is distorted. A certain aspect of the self and/or the world is being denied awareness, invariably in the form of *repression*. The theory behind repression is that threatening content is subjectively experienced as forgotten, although it is actually relegated to the unconscious. Sometimes, repression works alone. Other times, additional defense mechanisms join repression in distorting information. In *displacement*, after a person "forgets" (represses) threatening mental content, their attention is directed toward other content (internal or external) that bears such symbolic semblance to the forgotten content. The prototypic example is anger toward authority figures (e.g., father, boss). Because these figures are (by definition) more powerful than us, we perceive the prospect of getting angry at them as potentially dangerous. The psychic apparatus thus forgets that we are angry at these figures, and we instead displace our anger to another person ("object") with whom we can be angry without imperiling ourselves.

In the classic theory of Sigmund and Anna Freud, this repression-displacement combination is joined by several others. For instance, the repression-isolation combination amounts to relegating only the affective component of the threatening object to the unconscious ("I remember my boss's abusive behavior, but I feel no anger toward them"). Another combination is the repression-reaction formation: The memory of the threatening object is retained, but the emotion is reversed ("I just love my newly born brother. Let me hug him to death"). In the repression-projection combination, the threatening object is a self-aspect. It is repressed, and the individual then assigns it to someone else ("Why are you so envious of me?"). And so on and so forth.

What was Klein's revolutionary modification of defense mechanism theory? She realized that the previously described maneuvers were too tame to explain primitive experiences, such as the ones we see in childhood or in severe psychopathology (e.g., paranoia, schizophrenia, or borderline personality disorder). Such primitive experiences are dichotomous, dramatic, and all encompassing. They are imbued with total conviction, often to the point of compromising basic tests of reality (e.g., hallucinations and delusions, dissociative depersonalization and derealization). Accordingly, the cognitive-affective modification of incoming information is comprehensive: Entire segments of experience are nullified, not just specific aspects of the self and world. However, psychoanalysis (at that time) lacked a dictionary to describe such comprehensive manipulations of information, so Klein had to invent one. This is how she came up with the primitive defenses: primarily, splitting and projective identification.

Splitting. Just as repression serves as the benchmark of all other defenses in the Freudian theory of defense, *splitting* is the benchmark in the Kleinian theory of defense. In splitting, there is only good or bad. When the focus is placed on one, all information concerning the other is nullified. Of course, this means that when all information concerning the good is nullified, a person's experience is engulfed by threatening material (the bad), rendering the experience as absolutely horrific. Conversely, when all information concerning the bad is nullified, the experience is that of supreme content or bliss. But there is always an either/or situation.

How is splitting accomplished? Imagine that you are a reconnaissance soldier operating behind enemy lines. This is a very dangerous situation: If you are captured, you may be tortured, killed, or both. Hence, you must be ultrasensitive to all stimuli and signs that convey potential threats. When you are approached with an ambiguous stimulus (e.g., an unfamiliar noise), you cannot afford to "entertain its complexity." You should be ready for the worst. Therefore, splitting the experience and interpreting all ambiguous stimuli as bad would be highly adaptive. Only after you return from the mission and are in a safe place can you embrace the potential for content and bliss (and, as tragically happens with veterans, be completely unprepared for the "bad among us").

Thus, splitting is for primitive experiences what repression is for the more complex ones. Whereas repression is often joined by other "tame" defenses, splitting is often joined by other primitive ones. The most notable are idealization (magnifying the good by expelling from it all potential bad aspects), denial (of the mere presence of the bad), and projective identification. The latter defense is the peak of Klein's ingenious theoretical imagination; hence, it merits a brief description.

Projective identification. In *projective identification*, individuals (infants, children, adolescents, and adults) who are overwhelmed by internal qualities (thoughts, emotions, drives, wishes, and traits) project these qualities onto another person (parent, spouse, or therapist). The projection process is both internal (i.e., symbolized in fantasy) and external, whereby the person exerts pressure on the recipient to embrace the projected quality. For instance, an infant may exert pressure on their mother to feel the anxiety that the infant projects; a patient may exert pressure on their therapist to experience the anger that the patient feels toward the therapist. The initiator then identifies with the response manifested by the recipient. To the extent that this response is modulated, then a "softer" modality of the projected quality is internalized. Conversely, to the extent that the response is as stormy as (or stormier) than the one projected, this too is internalized, further driving future projective identifications (Bion, 1959; M. Klein, 1935; Ogden, 1982).

Primitive defenses thus regulate persecutory anxiety. What regulates depressive anxiety? Here, Melanie Klein and her followers appear to accept the theoretical position of Sigmund and Anna Freud concerning repression-based defenses, which are also labeled *neurotic defenses*. These defenses are measured, moderate, and nuanced, thereby matching the nature of depressive anxiety in general and the neuroses in particular.

Object Relations

To the extent that there are indeed defensive cognitive-affective maneuvers, who executes them? This question is about personhood and agency, but the answer is unclear from a psychoanalytic perspective. It was Winnicott, succeeding Klein, who dedicated his theory to the explicit identification and understanding of subjective, self-related, and agentic processes. Such processes (I submit) are only suggested in pre-Winnicottian psychoanalysis, including Kleinian psychoanalysis. For didactic purposes, however, let us assume that Klein acknowledged the presence of a self-like entity that regulates anxiety using the previously described defense mechanisms. Yet as the nature of defenses change, so does this mysterious entity.

We are all aware of the saying "extreme situations require extreme measures." To paraphrase, one can argue that extreme measures require extreme operators. Primitive defenses are executed by extreme entities against extreme entities—that is, by an extreme self against an extreme object. Klein very cogently posited that beginning in infancy, the psyche is characterized by ongoing projection and introjection of mental content. In early development, projection and introjection are geared toward distancing good from bad. Any hint of badness within the self is projected outward onto a bad other. Similarly, any good within the other is readily introjected. The end result is what Klein called *part-object relations*. The self and others are either completely good or bad—no in-betweens, no ambivalence, and no complexity.

This likely works well for reconnaissance soldiers during their mission behind enemy lines. But when they return home to their family, they must adopt a more nuanced experience of others. Failing to do so would entail treating spouses and children as either angels or devils, which is a very bad platform for romantic and parental relationships. Instead, recognition of the multiplicity of individuals' traits—of the fact that people almost often imbue benevolence and malevolence as well as aggression and love—is required. So too is recognition of the fact that traits at the forefront of others' behavior are influenced by an individual's behavior: "I can evoke good or bad behavior in people close to me when I change my behavior toward them." This is the foundation of intersubjectivity (Ogden, 1992), which means that the self and others are now "whole" and share a fabric of traits. Of course, such a change in object relations goes hand in hand with changes in affective tone, which include sadness, guilt, and remorse.

The Paranoid-Schizoid Versus Depressive Position

As Klein (1935) posited, "With the changes in the relation to the object, new anxiety-contents make their appearance and a change takes place in the mechanisms of defence" (p. 146). Thus, the personality processes do not just coexist; they bolster and augment each other. Accordingly, the paranoid-schizoid position is composed of persecutory anxiety, splitting-based defense mechanisms, and part-object relations. In contrast, the depressive position consists of depressive (guilt-ridden) anxiety, neurotic defenses (tame and moderate), and whole-object relations. The paranoid-schizoid position develops during the first 6 months of life, primarily as a consequence of strong experiences of pain and pleasure that are felt and dichotomized by the infant. With the increase in biological maturity juxtaposed against a required dominance of positive experiences provided by the mother ("the good breast"), good and bad become less dichotomized, paving the way to the depressive position. Importantly, the advent of the depressive position does not signal the expiration of the paranoid-schizoid one. Rather, both positions continue to occupy the psyche, constantly fighting over dominance.

KLEIN'S POSITIONS IN PERSPECTIVE: PROS AND CONS

As I stated previously (Shahar, 2018), I am awestruck by Klein's idea of positions because it offers profound insights into the human condition.

1. Positions chart psychological development, as characterized by increasing cognitive and affective complexity (e.g., the primitive paranoid-schizoid position is succeeded by the more nuanced depressive position).

2. At the same time, unlike stage theories of development (e.g., from Sigmund Freud and Jean Piaget), the formation of a new position does not nullify the previous one. They coexist, with one position occupying the center of the psyche and the other operating in the background. This coexistence of positions enables understanding of rapid oscillations between diverse levels of personality organization, so rapid that individuals may appear, within hours, as highly unstable and hostile and then collect and composed. Stage-like notions of personality regression and progression do a much worse job accounting for such rapid shifts in personality organization.

3. The notion of positions epitomizes the fact that in human personality, various aspects and processes work in tandem: A unidimensional nature of paranoid anxiety necessitates dramatic defensive measures aimed at keeping the good away from the bad (e.g., splitting), and such dramatic defensive measures can only be executed by a self that is full of conviction as to who is good and who is bad. In contrast, depressive (guilt-ridden)

anxiety inherently recognizes the coexistence of good and bad (Eros and Thanatos) within the self, requiring more circumscribe defensive measures that cloud specific self-aspects (e.g., repression, displacement, reaction formation), as opposed to severing large self-segments.

This notion of various personality processes working in tandem to create a coherent worldview has been incorporated in both psychoanalysis and cognitive theory in the past few decades. Several are akin to Klein's pioneering notion of positions, including Horowitz's (1998, 2014) states of mind, Kernberg's (1984) personality organization, A. T. Beck's (1996) notion of modes, and Mischel and Shoda's (1995) cognitive-affective personality systems. Interestingly, highly controversial novelist and philosopher Ayn Rand (1969) suggested a similar idea in her treatise on esthetics (i.e., the notion of sense of life): "A sense of life is a pre-conceptual equivalent of metaphysics, an emotional, subconsciously integrated appraisal of man and of existence. It sets the nature of a man's emotional responses and the essence of his character" (as cited in Shahar, 2021a, p. 19).

THE POSITIONS REFORMULATED

In considering the pros and cons of Klein's positions, there are two main reasons to reformulate them. First, Klein used jargon (e.g., "good and bad breast" and "projective identification") that virtually alienates scholars outside psychoanalysis and, as I can personally attest, even several scholars within the field. Second and not necessarily unique to the notion of positions, Klein's descriptions are far removed from knowledge accumulated over decades through scientific methodologies—specifically knowledge about emotions, awareness, and the self.

Nuanced Emotions

In most psychoanalytic theories, including Klein's ORT, anxiety epitomizes negative affect. As such, in these theories, anxiety is the emotional state imbuing most, if not all, dynamic consequences. To paraphrase Aristotle, anxiety is the prime mover of the psyche. This, however, is not the way emotions seem to work. The larger category of negative affect is much more nuanced, comprising numerous aversive emotions. The obvious ones are sadness, anger, and guilt, but one can easily add shame, disgust, disappointment, contempt, hostility, and irritability (Watson et al., 1988). Moreover, positive emotions seem to be largely independent of negative emotions, which means that people may experience both negative and positive emotions concurrently (e.g., Tuccitto et al., 2010). For instance, while I write these words, I am both curious and enthusiastic (because I am interested in the topic and aim to decipher it) and nervous and fearful (that I will not do a good job of explaining my ideas). After I complete this work, I will likely feel a measure of pride but also mental exhaustion and some emptiness.

Awareness Is a Continuum

Kleinian psychoanalysis, emanating from Freudian psychoanalysis, rests on the idea of a thick "repressive line" that squarely separates conscious versus unconscious material (Billig, 1999; Fink, 2009). Along what with Ricoeur (1970) called the *hermeneutics of suspicion,* unconscious material is more real and is also much more difficult to access compared with conscious material (see Eagle, 2011).

Interestingly, the hermeneutics of suspicion is starkly inconsistent with research attesting to the ease with which mental material, pushed outside of consciousness because it is threatening, may then be resummoned based on experimental manipulation (e.g., Erdelyi, 2006; Sedikides & Green, 2009; Shahar, 2006b; Tzelgov, 1997). For instance, consider psychological laboratory studies of the *mnegic neglect effect* (e.g., Sedikides & Green, 2004), in which people selectively forget feedback that threatens their self-concept. A simple experimental procedure ("priming") aimed to increase accessibility to self-improvement motives completely erases the mnegic neglect effect (Green et al., 2009).

Such experimental evidence agrees with gradual transformations in psychoanalytic theory, ensuing from Ferenczi, continuing with Balint, Winnicott, Guntrip, and Kohut, and represented contemporaneously by Stolorow et al. (1987), Strenger (1989), Eagle (2011), and others. All of these works eschew this notion of a clear divide between conscious and unconscious material, adopting instead a more continuous, experience-near, phenomenologically based perspective. According to this perspective, material repeatedly, and possibly very rapidly, oscillates between conscious and unconscious levels, often in a manner dependent on patients' central life goals. For instance, in my psychotherapeutic work with first-time-parents, I am impressed by the fact that this role transition summons memories and mental material (often painful) concerning patients' early relationships with their parents. Such material has always been known to first-time-parents, but quite often it has not entered into their center of awareness and was thus left unprocessed. This material becomes highly accessible when patients become parents, arguably because it now has to (mis)guide their central role in their child's development.

Why is it important to replace the thick repressive line perspective on awareness with a continuous, phenomenological, experience-near one? Because the latter provides options to understand the positions. In stress theory and research, there is a traditional distinction between defense mechanisms and coping strategies (Cramer, 2006; Haan, 1977; Vaillant, 2011); this is based on the notion that defense mechanisms are unconscious, whereas coping strategies are conscious. However, adopting a continuous, phenomenological, or experience-near perspective essentially nullifies this distinction, in turn encouraging consideration of both defense mechanisms and coping strategies as (partly conscious) ways to regulate affect. In fact, I posit that the term *affect regulatory strategies* should be used instead of *defense mechanisms* in describing specific positions. I illustrate this later when outlining the depressive position.

A "Projected" Self

The majority of psychoanalytic theorizations of self and objects focus on the impact of the past—particularly early relationships with caregivers—on object relations and on the reactivation of these object relations in the present (i.e., at the interpersonal arena). In contrast, the future tense is quite neglected in psychoanalytic theory. This is as interesting as it is unfortunate, given that a large amount of empirical research amassed over the last 4 decades now clearly points to the centrality of the future in the psyche (Seligman et al., 2013). This centrality is often titled *prospection* (D. T. Gilbert & Wilson, 2007).

Specifically, the following notable research findings support this centrality:

- Mental representations of future goals and "projects" appear to have a profound impact on our behavior (Austin & Vancouver, 1996).

- A form of cognition titled *prospective memory* has been discovered, pertaining to memory for actions planned to be performed in the future (McDaniel & Einstein, 2007). Prospective memory is considered a cognitive faculty that is highly important for everyday life.

- Several brain areas (e.g., Brodmann area 10 of the prefrontal cortex) and processes are considered to be in charge of future planning.

- Theory and research comparing humans with other species suggests that the principal function of the prefrontal cortex, an area largely unique to humans, is to plan for the future (Amati & Shallice, 2007).

- Representations of the self in the future (future self) predict behavior in general, and behavior aimed at influencing the future (e.g., saving for retirement) in particular.

As in the case of awareness, the wealth of empirical research just described is consistent with small, albeit repeated, streams of psychoanalytic theorizing that touch on the role of the future in the psyche (Summers, 2003). Consider, for instance, these words from Sullivan (1953):

> If he is interested in psychiatry, he is almost certain to come to consider the role of foresight in determining the adequacy and appropriateness of the energy transformations, his overt and covert activity, with respect to the actual demands of the situations in which he finds himself involved with significant others. (p. 369)

And later, Sullivan (1953) stated the following:

> I am saying that, circumstances not interfering, man the person lives with his past, the present, and the neighboring future all clearly relevant in explaining his thought and action; and the near future is influential to a degree nowhere else remotely approached among species of living. (p. 369)

In a contribution titled "The Future as Intrinsic to the Psyche and Psychoanalytic Theory," Summers (2003) reviewed the scant treatment of the future in psychoanalysis. For instance, he mentioned Loewald's emphasis on expectations of the superego, Schafer's language of action in which the self-narrative includes future goals, Bolas's notion of destiny (which I believe is similar to humanistic psychologists' notion of self-actualization), and others. In applying this review to the clinical situation, Summers stated the following:

> It follows that the analyst who looks at time in only a linear fashion, in which the past affects the present and future, adopts a simplistic and limited view of temporality that does not fit the lived experience of time. Because the present moment is embedded in and only gains meaning in the projected future, or pluperfect tense, understanding the patient's present requires that the analyst grasp the patient's experience of the future and how the present moment fits into it. The emptiness, passivity, and complacency we see in so many patients reflect their loss of future, an inability to live in the pluperfect tense, and this empty future issues in the bleakness of their present lives. Because the present and past gain their meaning via their relationship to the projected future, or the pluperfect tense, when the future looks dim, the present becomes empty and the past constricting. When the future looks bright, the present shines and the past is viewed as potentially useful, as a way to transform the present. To be sure, we can all look at the past and find reasons why the future looks so bleak and the present empty, but it is equally true that the void in the

future leads to an empty present and a sense of imprisonment in the past. (pp. 139–140)

This relatively recent theoretical focus within psychoanalysis, which is consistent with empirical research, draws psychoanalysis closer to philosophical and psychological existentialism (Cooper, 1999; May, 1958; Shahar, 2010), with its emphasis on authenticity and goal-directed action.

A New Definition for Klein's Positions

Let us integrate these issues for the sake of reformulating Klein's definition of position. Here is my proposed definition: A *position* is an amalgamation of affect, its regulation, and schemas and scripts of self-in relationships, all of which augment each other and form a distinct and coherent experience of the world. Positions are formed throughout childhood and adolescence and are maintained via interpersonal action. They are projected into the future, representing individuals' hopes and fears; as such, they guide further cognition, motivation, emotion, and behavior. Although all positions strive to be confirmed in the interpersonal arena, some occupy a large space in the psyche and are likely to create a maladaptive social environment that culminates in psychopathology.

In breaking down the key segments of this definition, I note the following:

1. Positions are causal systems that include reciprocal influences of affect, its regulation, and schemas and scripts. Put differently, positions epitomize the perspective whereby affect, motivation, and cognition are all cocausative (A. T. Beck, 1996).

2. The evolutionary advantage of positions is the clarity they afford. Humans need a clear worldview so they know how to act (Amati & Shallice, 2007; Shahar, 2015a). The subjective experience of the position is vivid and could be given as follows: "This is what the world looks like, and I should act accordingly."

3. Rather than being merely mentalistic, positions are translated into action, whereby people try to shape reality in accordance with their worldview. Thus, positions that include persecutory features are likely to translate into "making enemies," whereas positions that include optimistic features are likely to lead to positive outcomes. Terms such as *self-fulfilling prophecy*, *vicious and virtuous cycles*, *positive feedback loops*, and *dynamic equilibrium* are all consistent with this characteristic of the positions (in particular, see Wachtel, 1994).

4. Because positions offer clarity and are translated into action, they are projected into the future. The future, therefore, is a good place to start from in an attempt to understand and modify positions (Shahar, 2011, 2012).

5. There are likely many positions in the psyche, much more than the two identified by Melanie Klein (and of these two, at least one [the depressive] needs an extensive reformulation, which I offer later). Thus, I can think of paranoid-schizoid, depressive, obsessive, somatic, dissociative, playful/humoristic, and stress-resisting positions, among others. From an evolutionary point of view, the more the merrier; having many positions increases individuals' repertoire of adaptive behavior, particularly under threat.

6. However, it is possible that some positions "eclipse" others, in that they occupy a disproportionally large segment of the psyche. When this happens, individuals make a concerted, albeit only partially conscious, effort to confirm these positions in the interpersonal arena, and this effort is likely to be successful. When the interpersonal arena is shaped according to the position, psychopathology ensues. The distinct nature of the psychopathology (e.g., anxiety, depressive, and eating disorders as well as somatization and psychosis) "speaks," by means of symptoms, the inner drama of the positions.

The Reformulated Depressive Position

A close reading of Klein's work on depression reveals that, for her, clinical depression was an obscure construct. Klein was at her best describing psychotic-like and other "primitive" psychopathological conditions; her description of depression sometimes gave the impression that, for her, this condition is actually an indication of health. She appeared to merely hint at psychological processes that render individuals vulnerable to depression (e.g., failure in repairing a good object harmed by actions of the self), but rarely (if ever) explained this vulnerability and how it translates into symptoms (see also Ogden, 1992). Indeed, when Klein (1935) wrote about clinical depression, her prose quickly "regressed" into paranoia and/or mania (p. 158).

Yet, when my reformulation of Klein's depressive position is applied to what we know of depression, my sense is that new avenues are opened in understanding of the disorder. I present graphical summaries of the RORT in Figure 3.1 and the reformulated depressive position in Figure 3.2. These summaries go beyond my previous formulation of this position (Shahar, 2018, 2021a; Shahar & Schiller, 2016b).

FIGURE 3.1. Graphical Presentation of Reformulated Object Relations Theory

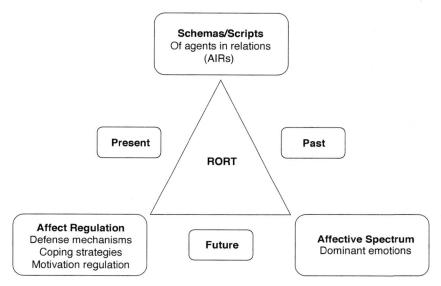

Adapted from "Reformulated Object Relations Theory: A Bridge Between Clinical Psychoanalysis, Psychotherapy Integration, and the Understanding and Treatment of Suicidal Depression," by G. Shahar, 2021, *Frontiers Psychology*, 12, p. 7 (https://doi.org/10.3389/fpsyg.2021.721746). Copyright 2021 by Golan Shahar. Adapted with permission.

The basis for understanding unipolar depression is its profoundly interpersonal nature (Pettit & Joiner, 2006). People actively, if inadvertently, create three interpersonal factors implicated in the onset and maintenance of unipolar depression: (a) life stress (divorce or relationship breakup, job loss, death of a loved one, and other "exit events"; Brown & Harris, 1978; Hammen, 1991; Paykel, 2003), (b) lack of social support (Dew & Bromet, 1991), and (c) lack of positive life events (Bylsma et al., 2011).

As discussed in Chapter 2, research suggests that behind this active maintenance of depression lies the formidable force of self-criticism (for reviews, see Shahar, 2015a, 2016; Shahar et al., 2020; Werner et al., 2019). This effect is demonstrated even after controlling for baseline depression and for neuroticism (Smith et al., 2016, 2021). Self-criticism also appears to beget other psychopathologies and suicidality (R. C. O'Connor, 2007; R. C. O'Connor & Noyce, 2008; O'Neill et al., 2021; Robinson et al., 2022; Shahar, 2015a; Werner et al., 2019). Furthermore, the detrimental effects of self-criticism have been demonstrated in the context of evidence-based treatment for depression (Blatt, 2004; Shahar, 2015a) and eating disorders (Löw et al., 2020). The mechanisms leading from self-criticism to depression

74 • *Complex Depression*

FIGURE 3.2. Graphical Presentation of the Reformulated Depressive Position

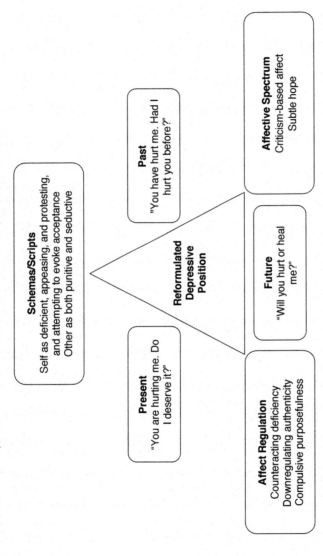

Adapted from "Reformulated Object Relations Theory: A Bridge Between Clinical Psychoanalysis, Psychotherapy Integration, and the Understanding and Treatment of Suicidal Depression," by G. Shahar, 2021, *Frontiers Psychology*, *12*, p. 7 (https://doi.org/10.3389/fpsyg.2021.721746). Copyright 2021 by Golan Shahar. Adapted with permission.

and related psychopathology appear to be largely interpersonal: stress generation and "degeneration" of social support, positive events, and therapeutic relationships. Finally, per the scarring hypothesis, recall that depressive symptoms and related psychopathology might also prospectively predict an increase in self-criticism over time (e.g., Schiller et al., 2016; Shahar & Henrich, 2019; Shahar, Blatt, Zuroff, Kuperminck, & Leadbeater, 2004). As noted in Chapter 2, depressive scarring suggests that self-criticism and depression may be viewed as a segment of a larger system of mutually causative elements characterized by affect and cognition (i.e., the depressive position). I now elaborate on this system.

Research has shown that self-criticism activates a host of other emotions besides sadness, which is prototypic for depression. Shame, anger, and contempt might constitute such affective states (Whelton & Greenberg, 2005). Moreover, self-criticism and painful affect might be reciprocally related through maladaptive defense mechanisms (e.g., acting out, undoing, projection, devaluation, denial, isolation and splitting, and turning against oneself and others) (Besser, 2004) as well as more conscious, maladaptive coping strategies (e.g., venting distress to others without attempting to solve the putative problem) (Dunkley et al., 2003), and highly maladaptive motivational regulative endeavors (namely, attempting to suppress authentic interest in activities) (Shahar, Henrich, Blatt, Ryan, & Little, 2003). Some of these defense mechanisms (e.g., projection, turning against others, and splitting) actually shed light on a very close link, which is also likely to be reciprocal, between self-criticism and representations of other people. Specifically, self-criticism is shown to be strongly associated with the perception of others as harsh, punitive, and judgmental (Mongrain, 1998).

To synthesize this voluminous line of empirical findings, I propose reconfiguring the depressive position to include four components: (a) criticism-based affect, (b) regulatory processes that are aimed at minimizing critical affect but actually reinforce this affect, (c) schemas and scripts of the self and others that are consistent with self-criticism, and (d) a time axis that considers past and present influences as well as projections of the self in the future. The time axis is a higher order component in which the other three are embedded. I also describe interpersonal actions, which are a consequence of the reformulated depressive position that primarily involve externalizing self-criticism. This externalization creates a vicious cycle that reinforces depressive, self-critical feelings.

Affect. The most dominant affect in the reformulated depressive position is neither sadness nor fear but rather a demeaning *criticism-based affect*. It consists of emotions such as anger, shame, guilt, content, disgust, disappointment, hatred, and envy. The overall affective tone is that of putting down (either the self or other) and focusing on deficiencies.

However, I propose that within this toxic emotion, there also exists a positive one: hope. The rationale for this postulate is as follows. Unipolar depression, even of the psychotic form, is not accompanied by a severe impairment in reality testing. Depressed individuals know, at a very basic level, what they and the world are made of. This means that people with depression are aware of their strengths and virtues, even though they focus on their deficiencies. In fact, it is their focus on deficiency alongside individuals' awareness of their strengths that leads to hope: "If I succeed in doing/accomplishing this or that, I will be exempt from feeling so deficient." In a way that complements individuals' reliance on their strengths, they also hold a representation of others as being aware of these strengths and of stirring the very same hope in the person based on them (see the upcoming section, "Schemas and Scripts").

Affect regulation. What defenses, coping strategies, and other regulatory maneuvers are utilized in the depressive position? I propose that the long list of regulatory maneuvers identified by previous research should be grouped into three regulatory clusters: (a) counteracting deficiency, (b) downregulating authenticity, and (c) maintaining hope through "prospection," or compulsive purposefulness.

Counteracting deficiency is straightforward. Experiencing oneself as deficient is incredibly painful, particularly in Western cultures that elevate competence and appearance (hence, the depression-modernity link). Accordingly, a host of maneuvers (defenses, coping strategies) are employed in the service of counteracting deficiency. Some maneuvers are aimed at vindicating the self from deficiency, perhaps through turning attention away from it (displacement) or tying it to others (projection, turning against others; Besser, 2004). Another way to counteract deficiency is to induce guilt in others. This may be done via turning against the self so as to yield reassurance seeking (Joiner, 1994; Joiner et al., 1999); here is where coping strategies such as venting distress manifest (Dunkley et al., 2003). Another way to counteract deficiency is to rule it out, convincing the self and others that one is wonderful and/or seamless. Klein (1940) referred to this maneuver as *manic defenses* (see also Barrett, 2008; Ogden, 1992; Winnicott, 1958) and it consists of denying difficulties and threats, disavowing mellow sentiments such as loneliness, and inflating self-importance while putting others down.

Another set of maneuvers is *downregulating authenticity*. Why would that be important? Because, as compellingly argued by Winnicott (1965) in his treatise on the true self as well as by Carl Rogers (1963a) in his description of organismic valuing, authenticity is inevitably spontaneous, rendering it unpredictable. If individuals' inner world is unpredictable, they cannot prevent a situation where they will be caught defaulting on something. They therefore feel that they should always be prepared, which means that they should beware of *going-on-being* (Winnicott, 1960). When the guns roar, the muses are silent.

My colleagues and I conducted a study on self-criticism and motivation that demonstrated this compellingly, in my opinion (Shahar et al., 2003). We assessed 900 US adolescents for personality, depression, and sources of motivation in both the academic and social domains. We found an unusually strong association between self-criticism and *autonomous motivation* that was negatively directed: Higher scores for self-criticism were associated with lower scores for autonomous motivation. This term was developed within self-determination theory (Ryan & Deci, 2000) and pertains to doing things because one wants to do them (true self, organismic valuing). In previous studies, we observed that this association holds even after controlling for depressive symptoms, and it completely accounts for the adverse effect of self-criticism on positive life events (Shahar & Priel, 2003; Shahar, Henrich, Blatt, Ryan, & Little, 2003; Shulman et al., 2009; see also Clegg et al., 2023).

How is authenticity downregulated? This occurs primarily by selective use of isolation of affect (S. Freud, 1926; Schafer, 1954) directed toward emotions such as joy and enthusiasm. In the cognitive-behavioral world, such a maneuver is referred to as *experimental avoidance*, and research has attested to the link between this construct and self-criticism (Moroz & Dunkley, 2019).

Finally, there is the issue of *maintaining hope*. Someone who suffers from depression may experience a thought pattern such as this:

> How can I keep hope from being annihilated altogether by all these horrible experiences? I can do this by firmly believing that the positive prospect I desire can arrive as a consequence of exact planning and hard work. If I only plan my actions meticulously, I can accomplish enough for others to deem me as nondeficient, hence worthy of love.

Thus, defenses such as intellectualization and rationalization (e.g., Arnold, 2014) are added to the isolation of affect (joy, spontaneity, enthusiasm) and are used in service of what I refer to as *compulsive purposefulness* (Shahar et al., 2020): a constant pursuit of worthy goals. Karen Horney (1950) would call it the tyranny of the "shoulds."

Schemas and scripts. Within an emotional context that highlights deficiency, it is of little wonder that schemas and scripts of the self are characterized by self-criticism (Shahar, 2015a). It is also not surprising that the other toward which the self is attuning is schematized as punitive and judgmental (Mongrain, 1998). Herein, however, I emphasize the issue of *agency* of the self and others. Namely, the self and others are schematized and scripted in the psyche as acting on each other (Shahar, 2004), which I labeled previously as *agents in relations* (AIR; Shahar, 2010; see Figures 3.1 and 3.2). The other conveys judgment and disappointment, and the self is actively attempting to shield against punitive judgment and disappointment in two ways: appeasing the other and protesting against the other. As noted earlier, appeasement is done by way of what Klein called *reparation* (see Thieberger, 1991), in which a fantasy of reconstituting the other as good is accompanied by solicitous behavior. The self is trying to "be good" so that the other deems the self as nondeficient. Protests come to the fore either when the self does not succeed in appeasing the other or by way of a "preemptive strike" (e.g., "Are you mad at me?"). The tone of this question is angry rather than inquisitive: "How dare you be mad at me when I am so good?!"

In addition, there is a subtle experience of the other as seductive, in the evaluative (rather than erotic) sense. The seduction may be represented by the following unsaid words: "If you only accomplish this or that or be this or that, then I will cease judging you and will lovingly accept what you are." Such seduction is, of course, reciprocally related to the hope that I described earlier, which also subtly dwells within the person's affective spectrum. From a psychoanalytic point of view, this aspect of the other (as represented in the mind) agrees with the term *exciting object* coined by Ronald Fairbairn, a Scottish contemporary of Klein and one of the parents of ORT. Fairbairn (1944) developed this term to account for a personality configuration that arises out of emotional deprivation and leads to psychopathology. Specifically, Fairbairn maintained that early emotional deprivation propels the child to create a part-object that leads to excitement within the ego, making the child feel loved and full of hope. The part of the child's *libidinal ego* (i.e., a part of the self that is full of zest and anticipation) becomes attached to this exciting object. Fairbairn and others used this link between libidinal ego and exciting object to understand various psychiatric disorders (e.g., see Celani, 1999), and it is (I submit) useful to understanding the reformulated depressive position.

Time axis. The reformulated depressive position considers the relevance of the past, present, and future. The past produces a wealth of autobiographical memories from which the person draws on the experience of being wronged (maltreated) by the other, but also the possibility of being at least partly responsible for the wrongdoing because the person somehow offended the other (Ferenczi, 1933). Hence, "You have hurt me. Had I hurt you before?"

In the present, there are active exchanges (both internally and externally) between the self and others that revolve around hurt, grievance, and wrongdoing: Someone is always hurting someone else. These schemas and scripts surface from, but are also amalgamated by, the aforementioned regulatory maneuvers shifting blame from the self to other and vice versa. Thus, "You are hurting me. Do I deserve it?"

Following Sullivan (1953) and Summers (2003), however, I highlight the role of the future. This is where both dread and hope lie. The self yearns to experience accepting the other but dreads a scenario in which, despite all efforts, the other will remain judgmental and punitive. The tragedy is that the self, via interpersonal action, actually solidifies this punitive judgment by evoking rejections, confrontations, and interpersonal loss.

Interpersonal action. Interpersonal action is likely the most important in terms of bridging psychoanalytic theory and other psychological disciplines as well as bridging clinical psychoanalysis and other therapeutic schools of thought. It is widely agreed that individuals with depression tend to contribute to interpersonal strife (Coyne, 1976b; Hammen, 1991; Joiner, 2000a; Joiner & Coyne, 1999).

One of the great strengths of psychoanalysis in general, and of ORT in particular, is its ability to give life to interpersonal descriptions by portraying the inner drama that underlies social exchanges (Mitchell, 1995a). Horney (1937) referred to this as *externalization* and thought that it serves as the basis of the vicious cycle. Both externalization and the vicious cycle played a major role in Wachtel's writing about cyclical psychoanalysis. However, most treatments of these concepts have focused on the present, whereas I extend them to the future. Depressed individuals project into their future both their hope for an accepting other and their expectations for a judgmental and punitive one. However, their actions, automated throughout the years, are more consistent with the latter than the former. In a manner consistent with Klein's projective identification but also with Sandler's (1976) *role responsiveness*, the actions of depressed individuals exert pressure on others to react negatively rather than with compassion. This example represents a typical social exchange that highlights both externalization and the vicious cycle: "Are you mad at me?" "No, I am not." "Yes, you are!" "Well, now I am."

AN EXAMPLE OF THE REFORMULATED DEPRESSIVE POSITION: COVID-19 AND THE IMPACT OF SOCIAL FACTORS

Consider the impact of COVID-19 on our deepest psychological layers. The virus has resulted in vast rates of infection and death, crumbling economies, social distancing, and overwhelming restrictions on freedom of movement.

> **BOX 3.1**
> ## CASE EXAMPLE OF THE REFORMULATED DEPRESSIVE POSITION
>
> A 24-year-old female university student was experiencing comorbid depression and posttraumatic stress disorder (PTSD). She had been doing very well in treatment until the COVID-19 outbreak. During the first wave, the patient was thrilled that school was out and very little performance was expected. This sentiment quickly gave way to strong feelings of hopelessness and frustration because she could not meet friends outside her apartment and also could not date. For this young woman, spending time with friends and dating were not leisure activities. They were necessities. She had to engage with these activities in order to battle the interpersonal circumstances leading to the onset of her depression and PTSD. As the spread of COVID-19 in Israel progressed into waves 2 and 3, the patient's hopelessness and frustration quickly spiraled into a depressive relapse. I observed how the previously described depressive position resurfaced: strong criticism-based emotions, unsuccessful attempts to combat these emotions using counteracting deficiency (to counteract her sense of deficiency, the patient needed to be outdoors, applying her interpersonal skills), and eclipsed mental representations of self-and relations ("I can trust no one. Everyone is judging my coping with COVID"). It can be said that COVID-19 and its resultant social restrictions locked this patient, and probably many others, inside a box consisting of her and her reformulated depressive position.

I have learned that the ramifications of COVID-19 are worse than the illness itself, particularly for young adults, largely because of its effects on schemas and scripts of self-in relations. Box 3.1 presents a clinical illustration.[1]

This clinical illustration highlights the power of larger societal circumstances to ignite personality processes that are relevant to depression and related psychopathology. As such, this clinical illustration paves the way for the focus of Chapter 4: the social context.

---

[1] This case example has been modified to disguise the patient's identity and protect their confidentiality.

4 HUMAN ECOLOGY AND DEVELOPMENT WITHIN SOCIAL CONTEXTS
Ecodynamics Theory

An a priori commitment to the view that it is what is "in the head" that is most important—vs. "what the head is in" or how the head is in transaction with the interpersonal world—discourages curiosity about how depressed persons' self-complaints may be functionally related to the demands, criticism, rejection, and emotional invalidation they receive in their significant relationships.
—Coyne, 1994a, p. 403

There is a major fallacy in our field, which I call the *mentalistic fallacy*. This pertains to the belief that psychological processes can be measured in clinically useful ways irrespective of the social context. While I agree that psychometrics can be used to assess deep-seated psychological processes via self-report questionnaires, projective procedures, interviews, or computer tasks (Shahar, 2019), I am highly skeptical of assigning meaning and planning treatment based on such scores in the absence of an assessment of patients' interpersonal relationships and social positions. One of my principal teachers in this respect (albeit informally) is James C. Coyne, particularly his early work on unipolar depression (Coyne, 1976a, 1976b; Coyne & DeLongis, 1986;

https://doi.org/10.1037/0000377-005
Complex Depression: The Role of Personality Dynamics and Social Ecology, by G. Shahar
Copyright © 2024 by the American Psychological Association. All rights reserved.

Coyne & Downey, 1991; Coyne & Whiffen, 1995; Coyne et al., 1987; Joiner & Coyne, 1999; Kaplan et al., 1987) and his later research on couples coping with chronic physical illness (Coyne & Racioppo, 2000; Coyne & Smith, 1991; Coyne et al., 2001). His writing corresponds strongly with theory and research in medical sociology and epidemiology, which highlights the role of social context variables in psychopathology in general and in depression in particular (e.g., G. W. Brown & Harris, 1978; Depue & Monroe, 1986; Dohrenwend et al., 1978; Paykel, 2008).

Coyne's impact on depression research and treatment is twofold. First, drawing on his expertise in strategic family therapy, he reformulated the processes leading to unipolar depression, with an emphasis on interpersonal relationships. Specifically, he argued that depression unfolds as a consequence of the suffering person's need for reassurance from close others (Coyne, 1976b). The pressure exerted on others evokes rejection, in turn leading to depression (Joiner, 1994; Joiner et al., 1999). Coyne also demonstrated experimentally, in a manner eerily consistent with the psychoanalytic notion of projective identification, that a brief interaction with a depressed person produces negative affect and an unwillingness to interact further (Coyne, 1976a; see also Bareket-Bojmel & Shahar, 2011). Second, Coyne leveled unparalleled criticism of cognitive/personality models of depression, especially their emphasis on "what's in the head" (as opposed to "what the head is in") and their attempts to measure this with methods that do not consider the social context (Coyne, 1992, 1994a, 1994b; Coyne & Gotlib, 1983; Coyne & Whiffen, 1995). As an alternative, Coyne and Downey (1991) emphasized the arguably causative role of social-ecological variables such as life stress and social support.

Given that this book focuses on the role of personality (and cognition) in depression, I do not agree with many of Coyne's critical comments (see Zuroff et al., 2004a, 2004b). I do, however, believe that (a) without Coyne's criticism, the field has been going astray for decades and that (b) because of his criticism, the field is currently in a position to offer a sophisticated theoretical account of the interplay between personality and context and its role in the development of depression, both simple and complex. I call this exchange *ecodynamics*.

KEY SOCIAL-ECOLOGICAL VARIABLES IN DEPRESSION

My point of departure is Coyne and Downey's (1991) extensively cited article that implicates two social-ecological variables in unipolar depression: stress and social support. I, and many others, agree with this postulate. In fact, the psychological, psychiatric, and epidemiological literatures suggests that stress and severe acute life events (e.g., transition to parenthood, divorce), traumatic events (e.g., wars, natural disasters), and serious chronic stressful conditions (e.g., childhood maltreatment, marital discord, chronic physical illness) in particular are the most powerful predictors of depression (and many other psychiatric conditions) among all others, psychosocial and biological alike. The pattern of results causally implicating stress in depression has been solidified over the last four decades, with the advent of sophisticated semistructured interviews that assess the impact of life stress over respondents' lives irrespective of their subjective experience of this stress (G. W. Brown & Harris, 1978; Dohrenwend et al., 1978; Hammen, 1980; Monroe, 2008).

My prolonged reading of—and contribution to—the literature has led me to appreciate the antidepressant (protective) effect of *perceived social support* (Cohen, 2004; Cohen & Wills, 1985; Henrich & Shahar, 2008; Shahar & Henrich, 2016; Shahar et al., 2009; Uchino et al., 2012). Perceived social support pertains to individuals' general appraisal of the availability of social support in their social environment. It is distinguished from *received support* (Cohen & Wills, 1985), which refers to the support that individuals actually receive (or at least, the support they report receiving) and demonstrates some depressogenic effects (Barrera, 1986). Although the perception of social support is often marred by subjective (cognitive) processes (Lakey & Orehek, 2011; Sarason et al., 1994), it has also been linked with actual, usually ongoing, qualities of interpersonal relationships (Feeney & Collins, 2015; Lakey & Orehek, 2011; Russell et al., 1997). Perceived social support seems to exert two types of protective effects: (a) a main effect, in which elevated levels of social support are predictive of a prospective decrease in psychological symptoms irrespective of the level of stress experienced by individuals; and (b) a stress-buffering effect, whereby the effect of stress on psychological symptoms is much stronger when stress is high versus low (for a criticism, see Cohen & Wills, 1985; Burton et al., 2004; Lakey & Orehek, 2011). My research on the effect of a major stressor (i.e., exposure to terrorism) on adolescent depression yielded findings consistent with both main and stress-buffering effects of perceived social support (Henrich & Shahar, 2008; Shahar & Henrich, 2016; Shahar et al., 2009). Moreover, satisfaction with naturally occurring social relationships has been shown to predict outcomes in scientifically informed treatment for unipolar depression (e.g., Shahar, Blatt, Zuroff, Krupnick, & Sotsky, 2004).[1]

---

[1] There are also some relatively rare reports of no effect of perceived social support (Burton et al., 2004) and of an adverse effect in some instances (Henrich & Shahar, 2008; Shahar et al., 2009; Wills et al., 2004).

Thus, stress and perceived social support are two social-ecological variables that work in tandem to produce psychopathological outcomes, including unipolar depressive symptoms. There is, however, another very important social-ecological variable that affects unipolar depression: *positive life events*. These events pertain to satisfying social interactions, pleasant activities, and successful performances (Cohen & Hoberman, 1983; Cohen et al., 1984; Shahar & Priel, 2002). Positive life events are conceptualized as protective because they produce positive affect that may dilute negative affect, and also because they can provide relief in the face of life stress and distress (Cohen & Hoberman, 1983; Cohen et al., 1984). Accordingly, and similarly to the dual effect of perceived social support, positive life events have been posited to exert their protective effect either directly (a main effect) or by buffering the adverse effect of stress (Shahar & Priel, 2002). There is now evidence consistent with both effects, among individuals with and without a clinical diagnosis of depression, and across cultures and the lifespan (L. Davidson et al., 2006; Needles & Abramson, 1990; Kleiman et al., 2014; Krause, 1988; Li et al., 2021; Shahar & Priel, 2002; Stallings et al., 1997).

The COVID-19 pandemic is relevant to each and every concept considered in this chapter. Accumulating research demonstrates that the pandemic has created unique stressful life events (e.g., infection, deterioration of economic status), increased distress (e.g., Bareket-Bojmel, Shahar, & Margalit, 2021; Rossi et al., 2021), and decreased positive events, particularly among young people (Klaiber et al., 2021). The pandemic has also highlighted the centrality of social support to adaptation, in particular, perceived support and its main and stress-buffering effects (Bareket-Bojmel, Shahar, Abu-Kaf, & Margalit, 2021; Szkody et al., 2021).

Accordingly, if we wish to obtain a rough map of the social ecology, we could arguably seek to learn more about the three variables just described (stressful events, perceived social support, and positive life events) and, of course, their interaction. The problem, however, is that clinicians need a map that is as detailed and accurate as possible so they can understand the psychopathology and plan treatment accordingly. This is where the plot thickens.

Social-Ecological Variables Nested Within Interpersonal Relationships

One of the wittiest academic articles I have ever read is Steven Hobfoll's (2009) "Social Support: The Movie." Hobfoll, a premier stress researcher and originator of the conservation of resources theory of stress (Hobfoll, 1989), took on the prevalent distinction between perceived and received social support. Perceived support is considered protective (either as a main effect or a stress buffer), whereas received support is viewed as a double-edged sword, often predictive of adverse outcomes. Hobfoll (2009) challenged this distinction by calling attention to the fact that perceived support (and the way it is conceptualized and measured) usually taps into individuals' memory and evaluation of long-term relationships—what Hobfoll (2009) called the "movie." In contrast, received support (and the way it too is conceptualized and measured) almost always taps into brief, circumscribed, and decontextualized interpersonal acts, the meaning of which cannot really be ascertained without prior knowledge of the unfolding of the "film." Thus, Hobfoll (2009) implicated measures of received support as committing the fallacy of a too-brief film clip (p. 97). For instance, in the context of a happy marriage, even small and subtle acts of support (e.g., quietly alleviating spouses of their chore responsibility when they are burdened) contribute greatly to a person's generalized perception of the availability of social support (thus culminating in elevated scores of perceived support), although these acts may be considered low forms of received support.

Moreover, according to Hobfoll (2009), when the full feature film is being viewed, it becomes clear that individuals' perception of the availability of social support is quite accurate (i.e., reality based). This is because such individuals both (a) correctly evaluate the quality of their long-term relationships and (b) behave (propelled by their expectations of others) in a way that actually confirms these expectations, in a manner consistent with a study by Coyne (1976b) and with the notion of projective identification.

Although Hobfoll (2009) called on investigators to recontextualize the measurement of variables such as social support, I think this call was not radical enough. In my opinion, any assessment of variables such as social support, negative life events, and positive life events is doomed to commit the fallacy of a too-brief film clip. The very act of focusing on variables necessitates a highly circumscribed assessment. What, then, is the alternative to focusing on variables? We should focus on both variables and relationships. In addition to focusing on whatever the individual is exposed to (high stress, low support), we can also characterize their relationships. Concepts such as dyadic reciprocity (Chandola et al., 2007; Siegrist et al., 2020), compatibility (Howard, 2020), interpersonal synchrony (Cohen et al., 2021), congruency (Bar-Kalifa & Atzil-Slonim, 2020), power distribution (Lindová et al., 2020), and shared reality (i.e., the experience of having the same thoughts, feelings, and concerns about the world as one's significant other; Bar-Shachar & Bar-Kalifa, 2021; Hardin & Higgins, 1996) all pertain to dyadic (rather than individual) levels of analyses. The dyad could be romantic, friendship based, parental, work related, therapeutic, or another type. Exciting new technological developments, such as voice analysis and digital traces, may now be used to gather information about the lived experiences of dyads (Nasir et al., 2017; A. Rafaeli et al., 2019). These data can be analyzed using recently developed, sophisticated data analytic methods such as dyadic data analysis (Kenny et al., 2020) and generalizability analyses (Lakey & Orehek, 2011). These analyses disentangle the role of individual versus dyadic characteristics in a variety of outcomes, such as depressive symptoms experienced by one or both members of the dyad.

The impact of COVID-19 on dyadic relationships is overwhelming. Even in very early stages of the global pandemic, there were alarming indications of a dramatic increase in family and intimate partner violence (Moreira & Pinto da Costa, 2020; Spiranovic et al., 2021). The pandemic has also influenced the quality of romantic relationships in both negative and positive ways (e.g., more dyadic stress, but also more dyadic intimacy; see Jones et al., 2021). In fact, COVID-19 seems to affect specific dyadic features that lead to relationship satisfaction. Thus, dyadic characteristics such as shared reality (e.g., among health care workers during the pandemic) have been shown to predict perceived support, in turn predicting romantic relationship satisfaction (Enestrom & Lydon, 2021).

It should be noted, however, that even this nuanced account is far from being enough for a thorough understanding of mental processes in general and depression in particular. This is because interpersonal relationships and relationship characteristics are themselves nested within social systems, as discussed next.

Relationships Nested Within Systems

Dyadic relationships are systems, albeit small ones. As such, they are governed by many, if not all, laws and patterns describing systems in general and human systems in particular. What must be considered, however, is that dyadic systems are themselves nested within larger human systems: romantic relationships are nested within relationships among families (e.g., Shakespeare's Romeo and Juliet), parent–child relationships are nested within both nuclear and extended family relations, teacher–pupil relationships are nested within school systems, employer–employee relationships are nested within organizational environments, and so on.

The comprehensive work of Urie Bronfenbrenner (1977, 1979, 1994) inspired psychology in general, and developmental psychology in particular, to embrace a human-systems perspective on psychological phenomena. According to Bronfenbrenner, a child develops within five socioenvironmental systems, which are nested within one another: The *microsystem* pertains to groups and/or institutions that directly affect the child (e.g., families, schools). The *mesosystem* pertains to the links between various microsystems (e.g., parent–teacher relationships). The *exosystem* affects the child from outside their interactions with other systems (e.g., via a parent's stressful job). The *macrosystem* pertains to the norms, expectations, and attitudes of culture and society. Finally, the *chronosystem* relates to changes and transformations experienced by individuals, as well as by cultures and societies, over their life span and/or human history.

In *Erosion* (Shahar, 2015a; see also Shahar, 2016), I applied Bronfenbrenner's perspective to understanding the development of self-criticism over the life span. I now push the envelope further by focusing on all components of the reformulated depressive position presented in Chapter 3: namely, criticism-based, demeaning affective spectrum, affect regulations aimed at diffusing this spectrum, and mental representations of self and others aimed at absolving the self from perceived deficiency and self-hate.

Readers of my previous theoretical works are familiar with my emphasis on authenticity as the hallmark of mental health. In those works, I repeatedly alluded to my acceptance of the notion of a biologically based, evolutionarily informed propensity of humans to become aware of and materialize their talents and proclivities. Here, I enthusiastically draw from psychoanalytic and humanistic–existential thinkers such as Horney, Winnicott, Kohut, Rogers, Maslow, Sullivan, May, and others (see Shahar, 2015a, 2015b, 2016). Herein, let us assume that the child (infant, toddler, baby) is offering an expression of its authentic being, expecting the adult to affirm this venture. The adult either affirms it (which Sullivan would refer to as "empathic linkage," and Kohut as "mirroring"), thereby further reinforcing an expression of authenticity, or disapproves it, which may take many shapes and forms (e.g., overt criticism, neglect, etc.) and is extensively documented in empirical research (Amitay et al., 2008; Koestner et al., 1991; Lassri & Shahar, 2012; Lassri et al., 2016, 2018; Mason et al., 2019; McCranie & Bass, 1984; Nation et al., 2021; Pagura et al., 2006; Soenens et al., 2010; Soffer et al., 2008). It is also possible for the adult to either approve or at least not disapprove the authentic gesture, but for the child to experience the adult's reaction as disapproval.

To the extent that the child feels that their authentic gestures are approved more often than not, they experience themselves as "good enough" (Winnicott, 1973) and are encouraged to base their self-representation on authentic cues (in Rogers's terms, *organismic valuing*; Rogers, 1963a). Others are represented as essentially benevolent and nurturing; the affective spectrum is diverse, multifaceted, and integrated, in which the child learns to accept as given the unfolding of both negative and positive affect, in turn adopting a trusting, curious, and mindful stance toward their inner world (see the discussion of the fully functioning person in Rogers, 1963b). Affect regulation is flexible: It can contain all of the dramatic, reality-distorting maneuvers described in Chapter 3, but these would be used moderately and would be diluted by more mature affect-regulatory maneuvers. In contrast, a proportion tilted toward disapproval (real or imagined) will be internalized by the child (Schafer, 1968). An entire position is internalized: an affective spectrum (in this case, criticism based, demeaning), affect-regulatory maneuvers (counteracting deficiency, downregulating authenticity, compulsive purposefulness), and schemas and/or scripts of self-in relations (self as deficient, appeasing, and protesting; other as both punitive and seductive).

To the extent that this depressive position is internalized, two "vectors" operate to solidify it. First, it is propagated within the couple, in what Wachtel, following Horney, referred to as the *vicious cycle* (described in Chapter 3, this volume). Second, it is further enforced by changing systems exerting force on dyads. Examples of this force are observed in nuclear families via relationships among siblings; in extended families through relationships with grandparents, aunts, or uncles; in schools via relationships with teachers and other school personnel; in friendships and neighborhoods during the shift from childhood to adolescence; in romantic relationships; in mandatory army service (e.g., in Israel) and among colleagues during young adulthood; in workplaces; in marriages and the transition to parenting during adulthood; and again in couples, families, friendships, and workplace or retirement during the "third (or fourth) age."

How do systems exert this force on dyads? This usually occurs by central people in the various systems (e.g., *gatekeepers*) and present expectations for a "good-enough being." Oftentimes dyads and individuals either cannot meet these expectations because they are inconsistent with their authentic being, or they are able to meet these expectations at the cost of sacrificing their authentic being. Examples of this are abundant, and they all show up in my clinic. Three such examples are presented in Box 4.1.[2]

Figure 4.1 depicts the nested structure of social-ecological levels of analyses. The most superficial level of analysis pertains to extensively studied variables such as stressful events, positive life events, and perceived social support. Because these variables are profoundly interpersonal, they are nested

---

[2]All of the case examples in this chapter have been modified to disguise the patients' identities and protect their confidentiality.

BOX 4.1
THREE CASE EXAMPLES OF PARENT-CHILD DYADS

CASE 1

A high school adolescent was feeling compelled to select a math major when he enrolled in college, even though his passion was literature. His father was an outstanding mathematician straggling with his own startup, despite his wife's (the patient's mother) requesting that he leave the startup and "find a stable job." The father declared that without a math major, his son had no occupational future. I protested and provided proof of why this was not the case, but the adolescent told me that he had to select a math major to bolster his father's mood. This made me think that had the father felt more fulfilled in his own career, his son would have been "allowed" to follow his passion for literature.

In this example, the macrosystem (with its emphasis on the importance of a "math major" to the adolescent son's future), the exosystem (with the financial and operational challenges presented for entrepreneurs launching startups in Israel, which is often labeled "the Startup Nation" because of the large number of startups emanating from this country), and the mesosystem (through pressure the patient's mother exerts on his father to leave the startup) all affect the microsystem (i.e., the adolescent-father dyad) and act through it to affect the adolescent's inner work (i.e., the depressive position).

CASE 2

In anticipation of mandatory recruitment to the Israel Defense Forces (IDF), an older Israeli adolescent decided to apply to one of the IDF elite commando units. Admission required outstanding physical shape and stamina, coupled with outstanding intelligence. This adolescent had both. He therefore passed the rigorous admission tests and commenced training. In training, my patient learned that he did not really like the job. He could handle the physical pressure and the intellectual demands, but the unit's culture was coarse, perhaps even vulgar, and the pressure to socialize impinged on his need for solitude (Coplan et al., 2019). He could have easily quit the training and obtained a respectable position elsewhere, but he toughed it out and completed it. Why?

My patient felt that he had to complete the training because this was his ticket to normalcy and respectability. Despite his formidably masculine appearance, he was called a "freak" in childhood and early adolescence

(continues)

BOX 4.1
THREE CASE EXAMPLES OF PARENT-CHILD DYADS (*Continued*)

due to his daydreaming, depth, and sensitive disposition. His family was an Israeli military aristocracy, which meant a great deal in the country. His father, an illustrious retired general, had high expectations and was very proud of his soon-to-be-commando son. The patient's older brother served as an officer in infantry at a prestigious unit, albeit decidedly less prestigious than the commando unit. In a manner similar to the patient in Case 1 who stuck with the math major, this adolescent felt he could not afford to forgo a tribute to his beloved father. And the father could not accept his son dropping out of commando training as an option. So a tacit agreement was sealed and the son completed the training, only to be seriously injured in the process. This injury contributed immensely to the son's complex depression.

This analysis is similar to that in Case 1. Here, the emphasis of the Israeli macrosystem is on illustrious military service. Similar to the way "old money" is transferred from one generation to another, so too is "prestigious military service." The exosystem exerts pressure through compulsory military service that causes many adolescents to feel a need to excel in the army. With respect to the mesosystem, consider the interactions of the father, older brother, and their "brothers in arms," which further apply pressure to the patient to apply to commando service. The chronosystem is also relevant here because the centrality of serving in a prestigious unit diminishes in Israel as time passes, making the other dyadic pressures less ubiquitous today than they were when the patient enlisted.

CASE 3

This generic example pertains to many first-time parents I see in the clinic. The pertinent common denominators are (a) these patients' experiences of estrangement and alienation from their role as parents and (b) the attacks they direct toward themselves in the face of this estrangement and alienation. The phenomenon is neither novel nor overlooked, but I suggest that it is interesting to view it from the vantage point of Jewish-Israeli culture. To say that this culture is encouraging of childbearing would be an understatement: It actually pressures young women and men to have children (and more than two, for that matter). The prospect of leading an adult life without having children has only recently been considered in

BOX 4.1
THREE CASE EXAMPLES OF PARENT-CHILD DYADS (*Continued*)

the Israeli media. Setting aside reasons for this pressure to bear children, my work in the clinic has revealed that young people are overwhelmed by a role they are not sure they actually want, and some couples play the "blame game" as to who is less involved (i.e., more alienated) in their children's lives.

A macrosystemic emphasis on childbearing lures young people into having children without a proper preexamination (and ownership) of parental roles. Exosystemic pressures concerning career development (e.g., Hochschild & Machung, 2003) and financial (in)security (e.g., ever-rising housing prices in Israel) further erode parents' ability to meet stringent parental standards, in turn burdening married life. Without understanding the macrosystemic and exosystemic pressures, can we really appreciate the meaning of both reported satisfaction with romantic relationships among these couples as well as of self-reported social support, stressful events, and positive life events? Finally, and likely most important, the consequences of these pressures on child development are dire.

FIGURE 4.1. Nested Structure of Social-Ecological Levels of Analyses

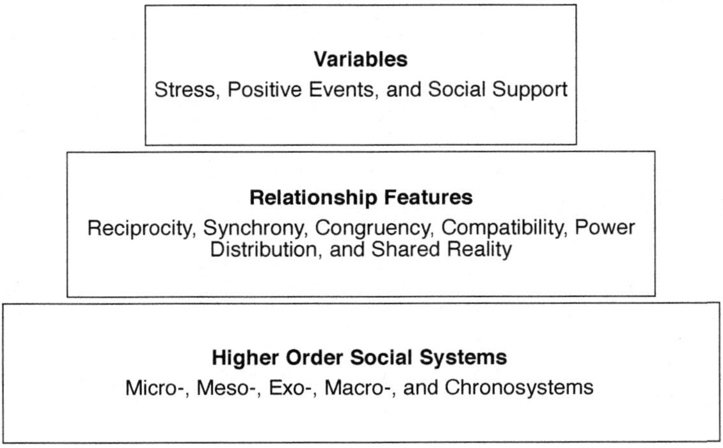

Variables
Stress, Positive Events, and Social Support

Relationship Features
Reciprocity, Synchrony, Congruency, Compatibility, Power Distribution, and Shared Reality

Higher Order Social Systems
Micro-, Meso-, Exo-, Macro-, and Chronosystems

within relationship features (e.g., parent–child, work-related, friendship-based, romantic, or therapeutic relationships), which affect the former variables by virtue of relationship characteristics (e.g., reciprocity, synchrony, congruency, compatibility, power distribution, and shared reality). These characteristics are nested within higher order social systems (e.g., micro-, meso-, exo-, macro-, and chronosystems). To circumvent the mentalistic fallacy noted at the beginning of this chapter, we must consider all three levels of analysis as well as their nested structure.

The impact of COVID-19 on higher order social systems is straightforward. When children are confined to the home and forbidden to play in their neighborhood or visit friends, the impact on the microsystem (families, friends, school) is profoundly adverse. This disconnect spills over to parent–school relationships (i.e., the mesosystem), further eroding both received and perceived support (for more on the effect of mass disasters on social support, see Norris & Kaniasty, 1996). Exosystemic effects are apparent in multiple forms, such as economic crises, health service shortages, barriers to education delivery, and so on. Macrosystemic effects are noticeable via the ascendance of discussions (usually through the media) concerning ties between civilians and governing agencies (e.g., various protests against mask wearing in some parts of U.S. society). Finally, chronosystemic effects are manifested, for example, by the growing presence of long-distance communication (e.g., videoconferencing) during the pandemic spread. On the one hand, this form of communication has enabled learning and commerce to continue, which could not have happened only 2 decades ago. On the other hand, use of these long-distance communication methods could be exhausting (e.g., Zoom fatigue) and fall short in enabling benefits afforded by face-to-face communication.

ECODYNAMICS: EIGHT PATTERNS LINKING PERSONALITY AND SOCIAL ECOLOGY

Table 4.1 presents eight patterns of person–context transactions: collision, action, infatuation, immersion, oppression, exclusion, extraction, and detachment. These patterns are the product of two nested axes: The horizontal axis (rows) refers to the extent to which the individual has power with respect to the social context, as opposed to being powerless in the face of contextual forces. The vertical axis (columns) pertains to the extent to which the social context is altered or not, as a consequence of person–context transactions.

TABLE 4.1. Eight Ecodynamic Patterns

	Social context is altered	Social context is stable
Individual is powerful	**Action**	Collision
	Immersion	Detachment
	Infatuation	
Individual is powerless	**Extraction**	Oppression
		Exclusion

Note. Patterns pertinent to the understanding of complex depression are highlighted in bold.

This 2 × 2 matrix yields four general configurations, each containing specific transactions. The configuration in the upper-left cell links the powerful individuals altering the social context and contains three transactions: action, immersion, and infatuation. The configuration in the upper-right cell links powerful individuals not altering the social ecology (i.e., leaving it stable) and includes two transactions: collision and detachment. The configuration in the lower-left cell links powerless individuals altering the social context and consists of a single transaction: extraction. Finally, the configuration in the lower-right cell links the powerless individuals not altering the social context and consists of two transactions: oppression and exclusion. Next, we examine each of these transactions, beginning with the three most relevant to complex depression: action, immersion, and extraction.

Action

Action corresponds strongly with the literature reviewed in Chapter 3: Individuals' behavior alters their social context. The individual is powerful in the face of the social context, but this power is iatrogenic: The social context is shaped depressogenically. Specifically, a person governed by the reformulated depressive position is haunted by demeaning affect; exercises affect-regulatory maneuvers such as compensating for deficiency, downregulating authenticity, and compulsively seeking purposefulness; and experiences the world via schemas and scripts of a deficient self who is appeasing or protesting against a punitive or seductive other. Therefore, this person is generating a social context consistent with this inner dynamic. This social context would be marred by rejection and loss (generating interpersonal stress) and improvised with respect to nurturing relationships and social arenas (lack of position events and social support). Creation of such a social environment is likely to lead to depressive symptoms, further solidifying the reformulated depressive position.

Immersion

In *immersion*, as in the case of action, individuals are powerful in the face of their social context, but they express their power tacitly. Specifically, they are attracted to context or, in behavioral genetics terms, they select themselves to context. An example is perfectionist, self-critical individuals who self-select a highly perfectionistic and competitive environment. In *Erosion*, I described (hopefully with the right amount of self-humor) how I paved my way to Yale University, only to lament the competitiveness characterizing this academic context (and how a wise therapist helped me recognize the irony of this sentiment; Shahar, 2015a).

Because individuals select themselves into contexts, they in turn alter these contexts through their traits. Thus, competitive individuals select themselves into competitive social environments, in turn maximizing the competitiveness of such environments, which then are even more appealing to competitive individuals. This process epitomizes Bandura's (1978) notion of reciprocal determinism.

Extraction

Extraction is a fascinating pattern that bears considerable relevance to complex depression: The social context actively *extracts* individuals out of their comfort zone by luring them in, often via a subtle and/or indirect force such as persuasive marketing techniques. For instance, shopping malls are physically designed to attract potential shoppers. Another example is the pursuit of human "assets" by military intelligence agencies. In both examples, the social context maps the characteristics of the individuals that are likely to render them getting attracted to the context, and it then plants cues that activate these individual characteristics. Individuals conforming to this pattern are powerless in the face of the social context, although they are not aware that they are. Rather, they experience their attraction to the social context *as their own selection, based on choice*. Bronfenbrenner's theory is highly relevant to understanding this pattern: Some features of the macrosystems, such as norms, values, and ideals (e.g., concerning heroism and patriotism), may lure adventurous individuals into seeking military service in commando units (see Case 2 in Box 4.1). Another example is "pro-ana" (promotion of anorexia) websites that seek adolescents with body image problems (Lamb, 2022; Mento et al., 2021). The social context is altered by developing mechanisms that lure powerless individuals into its midst.

Next, I succinctly describe the remaining five patterns: collision, infatuation, exclusion, oppression, and detachment. Because they are less relevant to complex depression, a more thorough discussion of these patterns is outside the scope of this work.

Collision

The *collision* pattern amounts to action, replicated by both parties. Causality here is reciprocal; therefore, it is very difficult to distinguish the doer from the done-to.

Infatuation

Infatuation is a blissful pattern whereby the individual's personality dynamics are highly compatible with characteristics of the social setting, a scenario described in occupational psychology as *person–environment fit* (Law et al., 1996). Moreover, the person and the social setting seek each other out (i.e., are attracted to each other). Examples include neighborhoods and communities seeking specific types of inhabitants who also seek them (e.g., rural neighborhoods seeking individuals who prefer to live in the periphery). So long as nothing changes in the fundamental makeup of the individual and social setting, the honeymoon persists. Hence, this pattern is not pertinent to psychopathology research and will not be discussed further.

Exclusion

In the *exclusion* pattern, the individual (driven by their personality dynamics) actively seeks a certain social context, but the latter actively and deliberately excludes this individual because of their personal characteristics. The individual is powerless in the face of social exclusion and cannot bear the social context. Ethnic, religious, and sexual minority groups experience such exclusions all the time. While exclusion is frustrating and humiliating, it (by definition) does not involve a long-term relationship between the individual and the social context; hence, it is outside the scope of this discussion.

Oppression

In the extreme *oppression* pattern, the social context exerts pressure on the individual in order to shape them in ways consistent with the context's interests and/or requirements. Dictatorships constitute such contexts, and they are known to create personality dynamics (e.g., see the classic work on authoritarian personality types by Adorno et al., 1950). Other dramatic situations, such as war and mass disasters, may be operative in the sense that social contexts exercise force on individuals' behavior and inner world. Note, however, that in this pattern, individuals' behavioral leverage is quite limited. The context essentially "manufactures" the individual. Because the present discussion highlights the role of goal-directed action and future-oriented thinking (i.e., choice), this pattern is less relevant here.

Detachment

The *detachment* pattern is essentially about no relationship. Aspects of the person's personality dynamics join aspects of the social context in repelling, pushing away, or boring the other. Clearly, this pattern is not relevant to the present discussion.

PART III THE ECODYNAMICS OF COMPLEX DEPRESSION

5 APPLYING THE REFORMULATED DEPRESSIVE POSITION AND ECODYNAMICS TO COMPLEX DEPRESSION

Psychotic depression thus is the outcome of a failure to experience and master the depression inevitable in developmental crisis.
—Zetzel, 1970, p. 88

We do not know ourselves in any deep or meaningful way unless we know and understand our impact on others, nor do we understand very well our impact on others without understanding the affective and motivational wellsprings of the behavior that overtly expresses itself in our daily living. Especially is this the case because the impact of our behavior on others resides not simply in the acts per se but in the subtle qualities of affect and meaning that inevitably accompany them.
—Wachtel, 2009, p. 159

This chapter applies the theoretical framework described in Part II to the problem of complex depression. Specifically, I show how the reformulated depressive position, derived from reformulated object relations theory, in conjunction with ecodynamic patterns described herein form a system that spirals into the complications of depression: chronicity, heterogeneity, comorbidity, health and legal problems, and suicidality.

As described in Chapter 1, Wakefield and Schmitz (2014) and Vitriol et al. (2021) reported that noncomplex depression was present in a small proportion of their study samples (e.g., 6.1% and 8%, respectively). Perhaps understanding why depression does not become complicated can pave the way toward understanding complex depression.

I posit that a relatively "loose" reformulated depressive position underlies noncomplicated depression. Namely, the three components of the reformulated depressive position (affect, affect-regulatory maneuvers, and schemas and scripts of agents in relationships) are not strongly related. To the extent that the reformulated depressive position is loose, it does not lead to a toxic interpersonal environment (in particular, see Joiner, 2000a; Wachtel, 1994).

What solidifies the link between the three components of the depressive position? Although they are involved in reciprocal causality conceptually and realistically, the magnitude (or severity) of the affect component is often experienced by patients and is accessible to clinicians. Specifically, to the extent that criticism-based affect is intense, it cannot be tolerated. Consequently, affect-regulatory maneuvers aimed to diminish such affect are set in motion. These maneuvers are aided by, but they also bolster, schemas and scripts of a self-appeasing judgmental and punitive other. Note, however, that affect-regulatory maneuvers and self-other schemas or scripts are iatrogenic: The more intense and rigid they are, the less the person is able to tolerate criticism-based affect. This is because the three affect-regulatory maneuvers severely distort inner and outer reality: We all have deficiencies that cannot be countered and authenticity resists downregulation, certainly in the long run. In addition, no judgmental and punitive other (i.e., "persecutory introject") can really be appeased. Consequently, as time passes, a person's inability to tolerate criticism-based affect eventually increases its intensity, creating a feedback loop that solidifies the entire depressive position.

I find it striking that the notion of an inability to tolerate criticism-based affect reverberates throughout the various strands of clinical thought. To illustrate, from an early and relatively traditional psychoanalytic perspective, Elizabeth Zetzel (1970) alluded to a pattern in which an inability to tolerate early signs and symptoms of anxiety and depression eventually exacerbates them, ultimately bringing about more severe forms of these conditions (see Zetzel's quote that opens this chapter). Conversely, the ability to tolerate signs and symptoms of anxiety and depression strengthens the ego, in turn preventing more severe manifestations of psychopathology. From a humanistic-phenomenological perspective, Carl Rogers (1963b) repeatedly emphasized that the ability to tolerate affect is the hallmark of psychological health and a major characteristic of the fully functioning person. Conversely, according to Rogers, the inability to do so is the main driver of cognitive distortion (i.e., "defense mechanisms") that eventually leads to any type of psychopathology. Such a Rogerian position underlies brief, increasingly popular, evidence-based, and emotion-focused psychotherapies for individuals and couples (L. S. Greenberg, 2011; Johnson, 2015), which aim to encourage patients to express the hitherto unacknowledged affect. Finally, harnessing the ability to tolerate distress is a central aim of third-wave cognitive behavior therapies such as dialectical behavior therapy (Robins et al., 2018) and acceptance and commitment therapy (Hayes et al., 2012). Moreover, research on evidence-based psychotherapy for unipolar depression and posttraumatic stress disorder (PTSD) suggests that patients who can express elevated symptoms during the first few weeks of psychotherapy experience greater improvement during treatment (Gilboa-Schechtman & Foa, 2001; Gilboa-Schechtman & Shahar, 2006).

Another aspect of the reformulated depressive position that likely complicates depression is the extent to which future representations of the reformulated depressive position dominate the psyche. Recall that in Chapter 3, I added a future-oriented dimension to the reformulated depressive position (prospection) and described how it is projected into the future with both dread and hope. The dread pertains to being hurt by others in the future, and the hope refers to being accepted, validated, and nurtured. Let us rephrase these postulates a bit differently: while hope propels this projection of the position into the future, dread dominates it. Generally speaking, this is unsurprising, given the human tendency to favor the prevention of harm over the attainment of benefit, as reflected in research in behavioral economics (e.g., prospect theory; Kahneman & Tversky, 1979, 2000). This tendency, however, is exacerbated in the reformulated depressive position to the extent that its three components are strongly linked: Dread takes over and launches behaviors that contribute to the toxic environment the patient must navigate. As described in Chapter 4, this occurs via three ecodynamic patterns: action, immersion, and extraction.

THREE ECODYNAMIC PATTERNS THAT MAKE DEPRESSION COMPLICATED

Action

The action ecodynamic pattern is adequately represented in research showing that depression and self-criticism generate negative stressful events and degenerate social support and positive events (for a review, see Shahar, 2015a, 2016). Some of this research has also identified mechanisms implicated in the effects of self-criticism on the social context. Thus, mechanisms, or mediators, of the stress-generating effect of self-criticism have been reported, including controlled motivation (Shahar, Henrich, Blatt, Ryan, & Little, 2003), maladaptive coping (Dunkley & Blankstein, 2000), avoidant coping (Dunkley et al., 2017), hostility and submissiveness (Mongrain et al., 2004), and interpersonal sensitivity (Mandel et al., 2018). Studies show that negative social interactions mediate the degenerating effect of self-criticism on perceived social support (Dunkley et al., 2006, 2009), whereas nonauthentic motivational regulation mediates the degenerating effect of self-criticism on positive life events (Shahar, Henrich, Blatt, Ryan, & Little, 2003).

I posit that both the generation of stress and the degeneration of social support and positive events are driven by a system of variables that I call the reformulated depressive position, rather than merely by self-criticism. Specifically, the three components working in tandem (criticism-based affect, affect-regulatory maneuvers, and mental representations of a self that appeases a punitive other) lead to rejection and confrontation in close relationships (interpersonal stress), social isolation accompanied by low perceived support, and a dearth of enjoyable, uplifting activities (positive life events). These social conditions are likely to produce depressed and anxious mood and other symptoms of depression, which feed back to the inner world sooner or later, solidifying the three components of the depressive position.

Immersion

The immersion ecodynamic pattern pertains to individuals' self-selection to contexts. As I argued earlier, self-critical individuals are likely to self-select a highly perfectionistic and competitive environment (e.g., a top-tier university; see Shahar, 2015a). From this perspective, the agent behind such self-selection is not self-criticism per se but the entire reformulated depressive position. Unfortunately, once individuals characterized by the depressive position self-select to a competitive or perfectionistic environment, they immerse themselves in it and are likely to unscrupulously absorb its culture and values. In my clinical practice, I see this often with my physician-patients.

In a previous work, I shared my perspective on conducting psychotherapy with physicians and described the sordid state of affairs concerning physicians' well-being and mental health (Shahar, 2021a). Specifically, physicians are repeatedly exposed to unique stressors such as morally injurious events and violence from patients and patients' families. For physicians, normative stressors such as marital discord are exacerbated because of their long work hours, contributing to very poor work–life balance. Financial stress is abundant at the beginning of, and sometimes years after and midway through, their career. Therefore, it is unsurprising that physicians frequently report alarmingly high levels of depression, anxiety, burnout, and suicidality. Israeli physicians confront additional dire circumstances, including a highly hierarchical and often oppressive "chain of command" within hospitals, a delay to the start of their medical career (as a result of going to medical school after completing mandatory army service), and repeated exposure to war-related traumatization, both primary and secondary. Of course, challenges posed by epidemics and pandemics such as COVID-19 increase the heavy load on the actualizers of this seemingly impossible profession (for a review, see Shahar, 2021a). The predicaments experienced by physicians and other medical team members are well known and have been movingly narrated in films, novels such as *The House of God* (Shem, 1978) and *This Is Going to Hurt* (Kay, 2018), and television series such as *Grey's Anatomy*. This begs the question of why young people around the world are eagerly applying to medical school with the dream of becoming a physician.

The scientific literature reveals myriad motivations harbored by young people—medical students, interns, and residents—for entering the medical profession. These include interest in helping people, actualizing humanistic values (primarily healing), attaining respect and power, acquiring a vocation, engaging in intellectually stimulating work, and others. In my practice, however, I am learning that these motivations, albeit genuine, are at the surface of physicians' consciousness. Below the surface, many physicians, particularly those prone to depression (and there are many of these), harbor a redemption fantasy: That is, the medical profession will absolve them of their perceived deficiency, first in the eyes of others and then hopefully in their own. This is in strong agreement with the future-oriented component of the reformulated depressive position (see Chapter 3): projecting a hoped-for nurturing object into the future and attempting to appease this object via extraordinary performance, but at the same time fearing that this same object will cause harm and conducting oneself in such a way that (ironically) propagates the hurt.

The most tragic part is that once these self-with-others mental representations are projected into the future through the longed-for field of medicine, the field locks the person inside a social environment that strengthens the dread rather than the hope. The realities of physician daily life—exceedingly long work hours and sleeplessness that erode body, soul, and social relationships; the strong competitiveness with peers over superiors' admiration and over rising through the ranks in academic medicine; the constant and often brutal criticism from these superiors; and the repeated failure to live up to professional and moral standards—increase the dominant criticism-based affect and decrease the regulatory mechanisms aimed to reduce it. I find it remarkable that most physicians, especially young ones, are oblivious to this social dynamic. In fact, they tend to accuse themselves of its ramification, putting the persecutory internal other on a pedestal: "There is always some doctor who 'manages to do it all,' and the trophy—a superior's respect and academic rank—goes to them and not to me."

An important characteristic of the immersion pattern is this: The medical establishment absorbs immersed physicians virtually without any effort on its part. Talented young people are simply pounding on its doors, begging to be admitted.

Extraction

A different pattern pertains to extraction, whereby a specific social context actively extracts individuals from their comfort zone by luring them in, often via a subtle and/or indirect force. As noted in Chapter 4, such social contexts work hard to map the characteristics of eligible individuals and then to attract them. Individuals either do not know that they are being lured or they dismiss it as unimportant. In either case, they experience their attraction to the putative social context as their choice or, worse, as reflecting their self-actualization. In Chapter 4, I provided the example of commando units attracting potential soldiers. Two additional examples of luring social contexts are more illustrative for our present purposes: high-tech companies and cults (discussed at length at the end of this chapter).

At the time of this writing in 2023, stock markets have been plummeting globally, particularly for biomedical and technology stocks. High-tech companies are trying to recover by recruiting outstanding code writers and offering higher salaries. However, at least in Israel, salary increases have not seemed to lure droves of code writers in and recruitment appears to be slow. Why? I am not completely sure, but we can glean clues from some of my patients with depression who used to work as code writers, got burned out, and left the industry. Although they were making a lot of money, they could not stand the job. The code writers provided various reasons why, which boil down to two factors: (a) they felt they were losing control over their schedule, which was overpowered by their employer; and (b) they felt that the job, albeit lucrative and (sometimes) cognitively challenging, was inherently meaningless. The job did not enable them to make the kind of impact on the world that was commensurate with their moral or political values. So they left and have no intention of returning, regardless of the seductive salaries involved.

The Overlapping and Cyclical Nature of the Three Patterns

Several points concerning action, immersion, and extraction require elaboration. First, note that the action pattern does not exclude immersion or extraction. In fact, the action pattern (i.e., generating stress and degenerating support and positive events) forms a putative social context that either extracts the individual or serves as the vessel for their immersion in a painful social context. Put differently, through a confluence of action/immersion and action/extraction, the social context (e.g., the medical establishment) propels individuals to generate problems for themselves.

Second, and to echo the theoretical and clinical work of Paul Wachtel (1994, 2009, 2014), the process is cyclical: The reformulated depressive position propels action, immersion, and extraction, which solidify the position ad infinitum. This is what Wachtel meant by the "inner" and "outer" becoming complementary. In fact, as Wachtel (2009, 2017) argued, over an extended period of time, the inner and outer are enmeshed and they form a rigid, closed system that is incredibly resistant to outside input and hence to change.

Be advised, however, that being rigid and resistant to change does not guarantee serenity. To the contrary, with increasing iterations, rigid/resistant systems erode their ability to hold their constitutive components together. At a certain point, they spill over. This is where depression becomes complicated.

FIVE COMPLICATIONS OF DEPRESSION RESULTING FROM ECODYNAMICS

Table 5.1 describes the ecodynamic patterns that may lead to the complications of depression discussed in Chapter 1. The first column of this table pertains to the five complications of depression: chronicity, heterogeneity, comorbidity, health and legal problems, and suicidality (see Chapter 6). Note that I start with chronicity in this chapter, whereas I started with heterogeneity in Chapter 1. This is for didactic purposes, because the chronicity complication is easiest to analyze in terms of ecodynamic patterns.

The second column of Table 5.1 refers to the putative ecodynamic pattern involved in the depression complication: namely, action, immersion, and extraction. For some complications, some patterns are more central than others. The table therefore labels patterns as either primary or secondary. The third column describes how the ecodynamic pattern leads to the depression complication. The final column identifies the specific mechanisms emanating from the various ecodynamic patterns lead to their resultant depression

TABLE 5.1. Ecodynamics of Complex Depression

Complication	Ecodynamic pattern	Description	Known mechanisms
Chronicity	**Primary** Action **Secondary** Immersion and extraction	The reformulated depressive position constantly generates a negative social environment feeding back to the reformulated depressive position.	Dependent interpersonal stress Low perceived social support A dearth of positive life events Scarring
Heterogeneity	**Primary** Immersion **Secondary** Extraction	The reformulated depressive position gravitates toward exosystem and/or macrosystem social systems that allow some symptoms but disallow others.	Societal norms; possibly generation of dependent interpersonal stress
Comorbidity (Type C)	**Primary** Action, immersion, and extraction	The reformulated depressive position is not contained by the social context, leading to an additional disorder.	Unknown; possibly neurocognitive, such as persistent negative thought
Health and legal problems	**Primary** Action, immersion, and extraction	The reformulated depressive position spirals out of control, leading to other problems.	Unknown; possibly hostility and inflammation
Suicidality	**Primary** Action, immersion, and extraction	The reformulated depressive position leads to a social trap: the social context does not allow authentic living.	Perceived burdensomeness and thwarted belongingness

complications. To note, these mechanisms are speculative in most cases, owing to the highly theoretical nature of this book.

Chronicity

Considerable literature has been devoted to the interpersonal nature of chronic depression (in particular, see Joiner, 2000a; Pettit & Joiner, 2006). Action is the chief mechanism through which depression chronicity is created and maintained. Specifically, according to many distinguished theorists and investigators (Coyne, 1976a, 1976b; Depue & Monroe, 1986; Hammen, 1991; Joiner, 1994, 2000a; Zuroff, 1992; Zuroff et al., 2004a), depression maintains itself by creating a negative social environment, particularly one marred by interpersonal stress dependent on the person's behavior (in Hammen's terms, *dependent* interpersonal stress) and replete with social support and positive events. Subservient to this theory and research are the studies cited in Chapter 2, which focus on active generation of a negative social environment by depressive personality dimensions (Zuroff, 1992), the most pronounced of which is self-criticism (for a review, see Shahar, 2015a).

What is missing from theory and research on chronic depression is scarring. Per *Erosion* (Shahar, 2015a), personality (now focusing on the reformulated depressive position) generates a negative social context that produces depressive (and anxious) mood and symptoms and these feed back to the depressive position.

Heterogeneity

The first step in shedding light on heterogeneity is understanding that all symptoms, physical and psychiatric, are communicative events; namely, they confer signals and messages to members of the person's social environment (e.g., Bowen, 1978; Watzlawick et al., 1967). Within depression research, this point has been markedly illuminated in evolutionary-based studies constituting symptoms such as lethargy and hopelessness as signals of social submission (L. E. O'Connor et al., 2002). Put differently, a putative symptom represents something that is important for the sufferer to convey to others. If this is so, two conclusions follow: (a) The sufferer feels that it is socially allowable to convey this message via this symptom; as a result, (b) the sufferer feels that some messages are socially disallowable, either generally or through the specific symptoms.

The last point concerning socially disallowed symptoms is remarkably important in the context of depression heterogeneity: Some depressive symptoms and/or behaviors are notoriously frowned upon when conveyed by some people. Take, for instance, crying propelled by negative affect. There is a very popular song in Israel, performed by successful singer Avner Gadassi, titled "Men Cry at Night." Its two most important lines can be translated from Hebrew as follows:

Men cry at night, their voice is unheard
Men cry at night, an absent cry

These lines are in accordance with the research on male depression (reviewed in Chapter 1), which is usually characterized by agitation and hyperactivity (e.g., workaholism) rather than by mellow lethargy. In many cultures, men are simply forbidden to become mellow or lethargic, because this stands in sharp contrast with their traditional role as providers and performers. When men are unable to resist the inner urge to cry, they better do it unnoticed; otherwise, they will likely incur insults from others, paying with shame and humiliation for their authentic expression of depression (see Joiner, 2011). Who allows and/or disallows symptomatic expressions? In Bronfenbrenner's (1977, 1994) terms, this is the macrosystem, pertaining to cultural norms and values (see also Chapter 4, this volume). The entire fields of medical anthropology and cross-cultural psychiatry are dedicated to understanding the effect of culture on psychopathological expression, and such research has shed penetrating light on a wide range of psychiatric disorders (e.g., Lewis-Fernández & Kleinman, 1995).

Although I am not a medical anthropologist, I have studied the effect of Jewish-Israeli culture and norms on one possible risk factor for depression, anxiety, and related psychopathology: namely, heroic self-representations (Israeli et al., 2018; Itamar & Shahar, 2014; Shahar, 2013a; Shahar, Bauminger, & Itamar, 2020). I define *heroic self-representations* as individuals' perception of themselves as heroic, which is manifested via three self-views: self as conqueror, self as savior, and identification with cultural heroes (*heroic identification*; see Shahar, 2013a). Although I expect these self-views to be relevant universally, they assume a special meaning in the Jewish-Israeli culture, owing to the myth of the *tzabar* (the Hebrew word for cactus): the new Israeli Jew who is independent, courageous, and tough (i.e., thorny, albeit sweet "from inside") and is the antagonist of the vulnerable, rootless, diaspora Jew (Almog, 2000). Indeed, my colleagues and I demonstrated that during a military escalation involving missile attacks on Israeli citizens, self as savior and heroic identification interacted with stress to predict an increase in anxious mood (Israeli et al., 2018).

Individuals, however, do not passively identify with cultural values and norms. If they did, we would not witness the vast within-culture variability demonstrated in the research (Fischer & Schwartz, 2011; Sagiv & Schwartz, 2022; Twito-Weingarten & Knafo-Noam, 2022). Instead, I propose that individuals differentially identify with cultural norms and values actively (if at times unknowingly) by navigating into social arenas that epitomize them. Using the terms offered in Chapter 4, they do so through immersion and extraction. In the Jewish-Israeli culture and concerning the *tzabar*, this pertains to many late adolescents doing everything within their power to be admitted to the special forces of the Israel Defense Forces (IDF).

I believe one has to be Israeli to appreciate the appeal of serving in the IDF special forces. When I try to explain this appeal to my U.S. counterparts,

I begin by likening it to the notion of receiving academic education at the elite U.S. universities, the latter arguably comprising part of the American dream. Yet I believe that the appeal of serving in the special forces is stronger because of the central, virtually sacred, role that the IDF (still) occupies in the Jewish-Israeli culture. Because Israel is a small nation that is (still) threatened militarily by enemies across the Middle East, the state espouses mandatory army service for all of its citizens: 32 months for men and 24 months for women, usually commencing at age 18 years. Although forgoing such mandatory service is possible, most youth do enlist. Many begin training at age 15 years or younger for the special forces qualifying examinations, including for the various commando/intelligence units and Air Force fighter pilot school. Such training is grueling, both physically and mentally. This effort pales to that required after actual admission and subsequent training. After training ends, an active service full of challenges and threats begins. Individuals who complete special forces service are admired by Israeli society at large. Doors are opened to them in the worlds of academia, business, and public service, and many (if not most) step in and assume high places in Israeli society.

Yet some individuals with distinguished IDF service under their belt and highly successful jobs also suffer from depression, anxiety, PTSD, and other disorders. And they suffer in silence, as noted in the song by Avner Gadassi. A major reason for the silent nature of this suffering is that these people are demonstrated heroes. Suffering from psychiatric symptoms stands in contrast with the *tzabar*, robbing individuals of their heroic image (and, frequently, of their illustrious reserve military service, which they cherish). I know this not just because I heard or read about it: I confront this in my practice, and it was a major source of inspiration for the heroic self-representation theory (Shahar, 2013a).

One person who epitomized the tension between heroism and distress was Lieutenant Colonel Yonatan (Yoni) Netanyahu. For non-Israeli readers (and perhaps even for Israelis of the younger generation), the Netanyahu name is most strongly associated with Yoni's brother, Binyamin (Bibi) Netanyahu, the Israel prime minister as of this writing. However, of Ben-Zion and Cela Netanyahu's three sons, it was Yoni, the elder, who was destined for glory and prominence. Although all three sons served at Sayeret Matkal (the top IDF commando unit), it was Yoni who ascended in the ranks and became its chief commander. It was Yoni who led the squad that stormed the Entebbe Terminal in Uganda during Operation Thunderbolt, rescuing Israeli and Jewish passengers abducted on an Air France flight and held captive. It was Yoni who was the only soldier to lose his life in this ultimately successful military mission, one that exemplified the global fight against terrorism. And it was Yoni who (posthumously) reached international fame after his two brothers published a collection of his personal letters, revealing him as an emblem of the *tzabar*: a fierce warrior and military leader but at the same time a poetic and romantic soul.

My colleagues and I used the collection of Yoni's letters (Netanyahu & Netanyahu, 1977, 2001) with the aim to publish the first iteration of a comprehensive psychobiography of him (Shahar, Bauminger, & Itamar, 2020). We selected Yoni because we were interested in (a) the link between heroism and emotional distress and (b) the way in which culture (in this context, the Jewish-Israeli culture through the *tzabar*) affects both. Alongside undisputed documentations of Yoni's bravery and military skills, there were reports (admittedly controversial) that he was markedly, clinically depressed before his death (Zonder, 2006, p. 129). We circumvented the controversy of whether Yoni was clinically depressed by focusing on three uncontested facts. First, heroism can lead to marked emotional distress, whether "clinical" or not (Beggan, 2019; Israeli et al., 2018). This is particularly noted for military and political leaders whose courage is largely acknowledged (Ghaemi, 2011, 2012). Second, per the evidence reviewed in Chapter 1, even "subsyndromal" levels of distress might incur tremendous functional impairment. Third, alongside the zest, sparkling wit, and endearing benevolence and care for which Yoni was known throughout his life and career, his letters conveyed immense suffering, composed particularly of utterances concerning sadness, death, meaninglessness, and loneliness. Consider, for instance, a letter he wrote to his friend, Rina, on April 20, 1963, when he was only 17 years old:

> I live, but in a world that's shattered and ruined. I study, but I don't learn a thing. Why am I like this and not different? I'm sorry that I'm not like the others. . . . In that case, it would have been better not to have been born at all. (Netanyahu & Netanyahu, 1977, 2001)

Likewise, Yoni's last letter, written to his romantic partner, Bruria, shortly before his death in Entebbe (June 29, 1976), expressed overwhelming sadness:

> I keep asking myself: Why? Why now of all times? Is it that my work doesn't absorb, doesn't hold me? Wrong! On the contrary, it possesses me and I don't want it to. I do things because they have to be done, and not because I want to. And the same haunting question returns—can I let myself live like this, work like this and wear myself out? And the answer is always that I must persevere and finish what I have begun—that I have an obligation not only to the job, but to myself as well—but how do I know if I can hold out for another ten months? (Netanyahu & Netanyahu, 1977, 2001)

Moreover, Yoni's letters revealed that his distress transpired before his army service and grew steadily throughout, often while he was performing his most heroic feats. Or, more likely, his distress grew because of these deeds, as illustrated in this letter to Bruria written on February 1, 1975:

> I was sad when I talked to you. Now the sadness has faded a little, and it's remote—hovering, touching but not quite touching. I feel a special sort of sadness when I'm with you, yet not entirely with you; for instance, when we're talking on the phone.
> After a while I rang up Tutti [Yoni's ex-wife] and told her I was in the army and was sad—because I wanted to be with you. And she was very surprised, because I'd never told her that there were times when I had found it hard in the army. Perhaps I didn't have it so hard in the past, because by now I've been in the army for so many years, and lately I've begun to miss the tension and the interest that I used to feel in the earlier period. Still, I sometimes had bad stretches even then, but I never told her anything about them.
> I remember a few years ago, there was a whole month of nothing but border crossings, and on three consecutive occasions I had encounters with Arabs (very deep inside their territory), and on one of them I killed a man, for the first time at such close range—about two feet—and I emptied an entire clip of bullets into him till he stopped twitching and died. And each time, when I came home, I wouldn't tell her about it, just hold her tighter each time. It was hard then.
> To kill at such very close range isn't like aiming a gun from a hundred yards away and pulling the trigger—that's something I had already done when I was young. I've learned since how to kill at close range too—to the point of pressing the muzzle against the flesh and pulling the trigger for a single bullet to be released and kill accurately, the body muffling the sound of the shot. It adds a whole dimension of sadness to a man's being. Not a momentary, transient sadness, but something that sinks in and is forgotten, yet is there and endures . . . (Netanyahu & Netanyahu, 1977, 2001)

Could you imagine Yoni going to his superiors and sharing the sadness and fatigue he reflected in these letters? I would say, no way. As emphasized previously, people usually express what they feel is allowable, and a commando fighter is not allowed to be sad and fatigued. But who brought Yoni, and the other commando fighters, to the commando? The answer is, of course, they did. And why? Because of the immersion (primarily) and extraction (secondarily) ecodynamic patterns described in Chapter 4 and in Table 5.1.

In this respect, it is interesting to note how closely related heroism and self-criticism are. First, they are shown to correlate empirically (Shahar, 2013a). Second, in Yoni's letter, there is a formidable example of ruthless self-criticism that serves as the basis for heroism. Yoni wrote this letter to his troops in the armored battalion he commanded before he stepped into the role of chief commander of Sayeret Matkal. This battalion was essentially shattered after the 1973 war; after Yoni assumed command, it became the leading battalion in the entire brigade. This is a segment of his farewell note to the soldiers:

> I believe that there can be no compromise with results. Never accept results that are less than the best possible, and even then look for ways to improve and perfect them. I believe that the greatest danger in the life of a unit is to lapse into self-satisfaction. I would like the men of this battalion always to be a bit worried—perhaps there is something else we might have done, something we might have improved and didn't. (Netanyahu & Netanyahu, 1977, 2001)

So individuals like Yoni immerse themselves within the very social context that demands them to be sad, fatigued, and worried, without conveying these experiences.

My overarching point is this: We can make sense of the specific composition of depressive symptomatology for a specific individual by understanding how the transaction between their personality dynamics and their social context channels the expression of symptoms: namely, how it encourages some symptoms while prohibiting others. The psychotherapy case presented in Box 5.1 further illustrates this heterogeneity.[1]

Comorbidity (Type C)

Recall that in Chapter 1, I described Type C depression comorbidity as a pattern whereby depression brings about, or contributes to, another disorder. From the perspective advanced here, how does this happen? This happens similarly to the way in which depression becomes chronic over time: When the reformulated depressive position cannot be contained by the social context, it brings about additional disorders.

Consider the general, pervasive effect of the social context on psychopathology. Decades ago, stressful life events were shown to prospectively predict depression onset (e.g., G. W. Brown & Harris, 1978), and this effect has been demonstrated repeatedly. However, stressful events have also been shown to precipitate a wide array of other syndromes and disorders, including generalized anxiety disorder (Sheerin et al., 2018), obsessive–compulsive disorder (Abba-Aji et al., 2020; Murayama et al., 2020), substance use (Pascoe et al., 2020), somatization (Ran et al., 2020), PTSD (whereby stressful events other than the trauma are predictive; see Pedrini et al., 2021), and even psychosis (Ayesa-Arriola et al., 2020; Martland et al., 2020). Perceived social support is another contextual factor that appears to be prospectively

---

[1]This case has been modified to disguise the patient's identity and protect their confidentiality.

> **BOX 5.1**
> ## CASE EXAMPLE OF HETEROGENEITY IN COMPLEX DEPRESSION
>
> David, a 50-year-old man, seemed to me to be an incarnation of Yoni Netanyahu: an illustrious military leader with a history of dangerous missions under his belt and a record of excellence in academia and business. He was a family man, a dedicated and loving husband and father. He was also suffering from recurrent major depression that assumed an atypical form.
>
> David had been receiving treatment from me for more than a year. Recently, we took time to examine the psychodynamic meaning of the hypersomnia he exhibited when depressed. To me, it was most important to understand the hypersomnia for three reasons. First, when David was not depressed, he was full of zest and life and applied his bountiful energy and numerous skills to all of his various life domains; hence, his depressive hypersomnia appeared to be out of character. Second, even when he was depressed, David's mood sometimes brightened in the face of positive events, primarily via successes in his military missions and following loving, reciprocal transactions with his wife. Third, events in David's relationship with his wife appeared to be temporally correlated with his depressive hypersomnia.
>
> In the session during which we discussed David's hypersomnia, it became clear to us that underlying the excessive need to sleep when depressed was his semiconscious experience of being trapped socially. In these situations, David felt that he had disappointed either his work or army environment or his wife (or both). Because he was so disciplined and performance oriented, he had a hard time snapping or starting a quarrel. In addition, for reasons described in the earlier discussion on Yoni, David had difficulties with public expressions of his misery. Consequently, sleeping (namely, being alive but unconscious) presented itself as a plausible solution.

involved in the onset and maintenance of diverse psychopathology, either additively (Lagdon et al., 2021) or by buffering the adverse effect of trauma and/or stressful life events (McLaughlin et al., 2020). With regard to positive life events (the third contextual actor considered in this treatise), much less research exists. However, the extant research implicates these events in the prediction of depression and anxiety (Shahar & Priel, 2002), general adjustment (Hussong et al., 2022), and recovery from psychosis (L. Davidson et al., 2006).

The point here is that the reformulated depressive position either creates these contextual factors (action) or gravitates toward them (immersion, extraction), and they then lead to other psychopathologies that feed back to the reformulated depressive position, culminating in chronic depression. This, I believe, is what accounts for findings evincing Type C comorbidity.

Think about special forces soldiers who develop psychopathology throughout their dangerous service. The research is mixed with respect to whether these soldiers differ from their non–special forces counterparts in terms of the prevalence of depression, PTSD, and other syndromes and disorders. Some studies suggest no difference (Hoge et al., 2004), others indicate a lower prevalence among special forces soldiers (Hanwella & de Silva, 2012), and still others suggest a higher prevalence among them (Hing et al., 2012). Regardless of these possible differences, mental health problems among special forces soldiers are a serious challenge. In an interesting study, Osório et al. (2013) examined predictors of PTSD in a sample of elite Portuguese soldiers deployed in Afghanistan. Using multiple logistic regression, the investigators found that combat exposure was the only predictor of the presence versus absence of PTSD. But who or what brought these soldiers into highly dangerous combat? You guessed correctly: The soldiers did (i.e., the immersion pattern).

The mechanisms accounting for Type C comorbidity (i.e., connecting the reformulated depressive position to psychiatric disorders other than depression) are unknown. However, I believe they are likely related to neurocognitive rigidity, possibility reflective of impaired executive function, and may serve as such mechanisms (for research on the role of impaired executive function in comorbidity, see Crisci et al., 2021; Menghini et al., 2018). Various negative repetitive styles of thinking (e.g., rumination, anxiety sensitivity) may reflect such impaired executive function (Zetsche et al., 2018).

Health and Legal Problems

The scenario of depression-related health and legal problems is similar to that described for Type C depression comorbidity, except here depression transfers the individual not merely to another form of psychopathology but to a different domain (i.e., that of physical health and/or legal problems). I illustrate this next, focusing on a single health problem (chronic physical pain) and a single legal problem (youth violence).

Chronic Physical Pain
As noted in Chapter 1, chronic physical pain is a formidable, highly treatment-resistant medical condition that devastates individuals, families, and societies.

For decades, the governing opinion among pain experts has been that depression (and anxiety), which are highly prevalent in chronic pain, are caused by the pain and its serious functional consequences (see Banks & Kerns, 1996; Hendler, 1984; Max et al., 2006; Orhurhu et al., 2019). More recently, however, the possibility of an inverse effect has been recognized, in which depression brings about and/or exacerbates pain (Lerman et al., 2015; Magni et al., 1994; Patton et al., 2021; Sachs-Ericsson et al., 2017; Woo, 2010). We might ask: Why would depression exacerbate chronic pain? Herein, I surmise that it is not depression per se but the reformulated depressive position that propels pain. My colleagues and I conducted two studies on self-criticism in chronic pain that help illustrate this idea (Rudich et al., 2008, 2010).

Zvia Rudich, Sheera Lerman, and I sought to understand how pain physicians experience patients with pain who arrive at their first visit to a specialty pain clinic (Rudich et al., 2008). Rudich, a very astute pain physician, has contributed many ideas and insights to my pain and depression research program. Lerman, currently on the faculty of Johns Hopkins School of Medicine, was one of my first doctoral students and the first to write her dissertation on chronic pain. We surmised that the first visit to a specialty pain clinic is of great importance because patients often arrive at this visit demoralized and exhausted from an arduous journey along the paths of the medical establishment (e.g., starting with seeing an orthopedist, then a rheumatologist, a neurologist, a psychiatrist, etc.). Such demoralization may either increase or decrease as a function of that first visit, but this, in turn, is dependent on how the physician experiences the patient. Hence, we asked physicians at the specialty pain clinic of Soroka University Hospital in Beer-Sheva, Israel, to rate patients during their first visit to the clinic on the extent to which they (the physicians) predicted that patient pain and functioning would improve (both on a scale of 0–100). Before they entered the physician's office, patients sat in the waiting room and completed a battery of self-report questionnaires that assessed pain severity, depressive symptoms, social support, and self-criticism. The pain physicians were aware that patients were completing questionnaires as part of an ongoing research project but were not aware of the nature of these questionnaires or patients' responses, of course.

We observed that physicians' ratings of expected improvement in patient pain were almost identical to their expected improvement in patient functioning (namely, $r = .80$). Therefore, we averaged both projections into a single composite score. In general, this score was tilted toward a favorable projection of patient improvement (i.e., $M = 61.28$); however, variability among patients was quite high ($SD = 20.57$), rendering the mean of limited importance. We then predicted this variability in physician evaluation using the study variables, and we found that a single variable emerged as a unique predictor: self-criticism. The higher the patient's self-criticism, the less favorable their physician's projection of their future improvement ($\beta = -.40$; $p < .05$). Based on these results, we opined the following:

> The specific active ingredient in patients' self-criticism that might lead to physicians' pessimism regarding outcome is yet to be determined. Nevertheless, we speculate that patients with elevated self-criticism convey marked dissatisfaction with their treatment and disbelief in the possibility of recovery, and this, in turn, is likely to demoralize the attending physician. Our group is currently examining this possibility. (Rudich et al., 2008, p. 213)

Indeed, we have. Five months, on average, after the patients' first visit, we reassessed their pain severity and depressive symptoms. We found that physicians' evaluation of patients' improvement after the first visit predicted patients' levels of depression and the affective component of pain (i.e., the experience of pain as "attacking" or "punishing"). We then surmised the following:

> Possibly, physicians in our studies were able, even after the first encounter, to astutely identify and predict the course of clinically complex, and psychiatrically co-morbid patients, and to foresee poor prognosis based on their impression of their patients. . . . Another possibility is that physicians' pessimism influences medical decision-making, which, in turn, adversely affect prognosis. (Rudich et al., 2010, p. 450)

Of the two possibilities noted (i.e., physicians serving as super psychological assessors or playing an iatrogenic role in the treatment process and course), my vote goes squarely to the latter over the former. The reasons are straightforward: Physicians are not trained to evaluate their patients' psyche, and their prognosis was predicted based on patients' personality (i.e., self-criticism; Rudich et al., 2008). These studies suggest a vicious cycle in which patients' self-demoralization (self-criticism) demoralizes their new physicians, in turn derailing treatment and outcomes. This possibility is further corroborated by additional research conducted independently in my group and in Belgium, showing that self-criticism is a strong predictor of pain (Kempke et al., 2013; Lerman et al., 2012) and of poor response to a multidisciplinary treatment program for chronic pain (Kempke et al., 2014).

In this book, however, I treat self-criticism as a proxy of the reformulated depressive position. Accordingly, and consistent with the action pattern, it is highly likely that the reformulated depressive position generates interpersonal strife and a dearth of contextual protective factors that increase individuals' chronic pain. As in the case of major depression, this process is likely to occur both within pain-related treatment, as in the previously described findings of Rudich and colleagues, and in the natural environment of patients with chronic pain. Yet the iatrogenic effect of individuals on their pain-related treatment merits special attention, because it elucidates a potentially noxious immersion pattern. To understand this, we must acknowledge the special features of the medical system within which patients with chronic pain dwell.

Numerous quantitative and qualitative studies attest that the medical system represents a large segment of the problem for patients with chronic pain rather than the much-hoped-for solution. Consider, for instance, a qualitative study published in the leading journal *Pain*, in which narrative accounts of 20 patients with chronic back pain were analyzed using a phenomenological approach (Walker et al., 1999). The investigators identified the underlying theme emerging from these analyses: "in the system." This theme pertained to participants' experience of being trapped within the medical, social security, and legal systems, which induced anger, helplessness, and powerlessness (instead of providing assistance). Specifically, the authors offered the following:

> People with back pain found themselves, from an early stage, entrapped within various systems, the most important of which were the health care system, the benefits system and (for those involved in compensation claims) the legal system. Participants felt misunderstood and stigmatised, particularly when there was no obvious sign of pathology to validate their suffering.
>
> These experiences made it difficult to come to terms with their current situation and most could see no future for themselves. (Walker et al., 1999, p. 622)

As suggested by Walker et al. (1999), one of the most noteworthy ways in which the medical system confers such powerlessness is by making the patient with chronic pain feel insignificant. Consider the following quote from a patient named Stan:

> They treat you as if you don't understand what [they are] talking about. . . . I'd like to be spoken to on my own level; it's as if he's saying to me, well I've been to college and university and you are just a lowly person. (p. 623)

Another patient, Mike, offered the following:

> The system doesn't work. . . . It doesn't inform you, it doesn't keep you on regular observation to make sure you are doing the things that are not going to be detrimental to your future . . . it doesn't give you the back-up

you need to alleviate the pain in the future, especially in the long term . . . they're trying really to cover up the fact that they haven't got a clue what they're trying to treat because nothing will show up on the X-rays. (Walker et al., 1999, p. 623)

These accounts from Stan and Mike provide clues as to how the reformulated depressive position may render patients with chronic pain immersed in a noxious system, which then exacerbates stress and pain. While features of this system are likely to demoralize any individual, people who already harbor criticism-based affect, affect-regulatory maneuvers such as counteracting deficiency (e.g., resenting others and making them feel deficient) or compulsive purposefulness (e.g., intensely pushing for an immediate cure), and mental representations of the self as flawed and others as punitive or judgmental are likely to inadvertently aggravate health care practitioners and evoke rejection (either subtle or explicit) that in turn solidifies their sense of insignificance and deficiency. At a certain point, the lines separating pain, self, and systems become blurred, and an overarching sense of entrapment prevails (e.g., see Stensland, 2021).

Youth Violence
Youth violence is a major public health problem globally, with serious consequences for perpetrators, victims, and societies at large. Unlike the lay tendency to construe perpetrators as "bad" and victims as "affected by the bad," research points to a large segment of youth (in some studies, the largest) experiencing both, which is referred to as the *bully–victim* pattern (Goldbach et al., 2018; Kochel et al., 2015; Nansel et al., 2001). Moreover, these youth appear to suffer from mental and physical health consequences more than their bully and victim counterparts (Henrich & Shahar, 2014; Sterzing et al., 2014). In addition, although the prevalence of bullies or victims decreases throughout adolescence, the prevalence of bully-victims increases (Centers for Disease Control and Prevention, 2011). These cursory epidemiological findings strongly suggest that youths immersed in the bully–victim pattern are trapped in a system of violence that gradually amalgamates during adolescence.

Could it be that depression—or more precisely, the reformulated depressive position—is one determinant of these action and immersion patterns? I believe so. In Chapter 1, I referred to longitudinal research attesting to the predictive effect of depressive symptoms and/or a depression diagnosis on youth violence. Even after controlling for depressive symptoms, self-criticism also predicted externalizing problems among youth, including aggression and violence (Leadbeater et al., 1999; Shahar, Gallagher, et al., 2004; Zahra et al., 2021).

This effect of self-criticism may constitute a proxy for a deeper effect of the reformulated depressive position.

To illustrate, I turn to one of my favorite movies, *Good Will Hunting* (1997), starring Ben Affleck and Matt Damon (who also wrote the script) and directed by Gus Van Sant. The protagonist, Will Hunting (Matt Damon), is a closeted, self-taught math and science genius from South Boston who works as a janitor at the Massachusetts Institute of Technology. Will anonymously solves extremely difficult math puzzles posted by Professor Gerald Lambeau on the blackboard, thus stunning Lambeau and his students. In an attempt to identify the mysterious puzzle solver, Lambeau posts an even more difficult puzzle on the blackboard and almost catches Will in the act of solving it. After he flees from Lambeau, Will meets Skylar, a young British woman studying at Harvard.

The scene I find most relevant here, which attracted my attention even as a young man watching the film for the first time, happens the day after Will meets Skylar. He is in the car with his best friend, Chuckie Sullivan, and their other friends. While Chuckie is driving, Will yells for him to pull over. He points to a basketball court nearby and locates an adolescent boy who presumably bullied him in the past. "I know him from juvie," Will shouts. The "gang" pulls over, enters the court, and engages in a fight with the boy and his friends. The police arrive and they arrest Will. During his trial, the judge releases Will to Lambeau because he promises that he will take Will under his wing and teach him math. Lambeau further promises the judge that he will arrange psychotherapy for Will. A new period in Will's life begins. He eagerly learns math from Lambeau and, in the process, reveals even greater talent than the professor had imagined. After Will mocks a few therapists and derails treatment, Lambeau takes him to his college roommate, Dr. Sean Maguire (Robin Williams). Maguire is an unorthodox psychotherapist who eventually earns Will's trust and gains entry into his inner world. During a stormy therapy session, Will reveals that his father physically abused him during childhood.

Let us pause and ponder the story so far. When I first watched the film, I was amazed that Will (already dealing with numerous, quite serious, problems) actually initiates a gang fight with a past bully, the outcome of which is highly likely to end miserably. Indeed, if it were not for Lambeau, Will would likely have ended up in jail, forsaking the glorious career he develops later and continuing as a criminal. So why did he do it? The obvious reason is revenge: This was an opportunity to get back at a boy who had bullied him in juvenile detention. I believe that this reason is superficial. Yes, revenge is involved but not necessarily, or only, with the adolescent boy. It is revenge taken symbolically against an abusive father.

Why would Will seek to take symbolic revenge against his abusive father? After all, the abuse is in the past. Except that it isn't. When he works with Maguire, Will not only acknowledges having been physically abused by his father. He also describes how he stood up to his father with defiance when being brutally beaten—what I refer to as *counteracting deficiency* (Chapter 4) and Melanie Klein (1940) called a *manic defense*—only to be attacked from within (namely, construing the abuse as his fault). Individuals who study the various forms of childhood abuse or work with individuals who have been abused are familiar with this stance, which is referred to as *turning against the self* in psychoanalysis (Ferenczi, 1949; S. Freud, 1915, 1936; see also Filipas & Ullman, 2006; Lassri et al., 2018). It takes a stormy and semiviolent therapeutic exchange, during which Will provokes Maguire by insulting his deceased wife (i.e., transference defiance) and Maguire loses his temper and holds Will forcefully, for Will to acknowledge he has turned against himself and then to process this defense and release it while Maguire echoes in a somewhat hypnotic manner: "It's not your fault."

When Will sees the adolescent abuser on the basketball court, he is well "cooked" (i.e., primed to immerse himself in a bully–victim system). Such immersion often masks the deep depression experienced by violent adolescents or those diagnosed with conduct disorder (Shahar, Gallagher, et al., 2004). In *Good Will Hunting*, two powerful people (Lambeau and Maguire), through their empathy, nurturing, and tolerance of Will's aggression, eventually prevent him from becoming fully immersed in a system of violence. The change they exert in Will's life is both internal and external. Internally, Lambeau and Maguire provide a *corrective emotional experience* (Alexander & French, 1946) that activates benevolent mental representations of other people and of relationships, thereby diluting the toxic reformulated depressive position. Externally, Will is pulled away from a system of violence and toward "work and love" (a phrase attributed to S. Freud), thereby gravitating to positive social contexts. I describe this remedial process further in Chapter 8, which touches on therapy.

I offer one final note concerning the possible mechanisms connecting depression to health and legal problems. Research is far from elucidating such mechanisms but by way of hypothesis generation, I offer hostility as a unified mechanism. I presented hostility earlier as a possible mediator of the effect of depression on delinquency, violence, and crime. This refers not only to the affective component of hostility but also to the cognitive component, anger rumination (Denson, 2013) and a hostile attribution bias (Klein Tuente et al., 2019). That both components are likely to culminate in aggression and violence is straightforward. However, hostility has been shown repeatedly to serve as a risk factor for poor physical health and physical illness (T. W. Smith, 1992; Vandervoort, 2006). In addition, recent research suggests that hostility, particularly chronic, may be translated by the body as multisystemic inflammation that erodes health and brings about physical illness over time (e.g., Graham et al., 2006; Kendall-Tackett, 2007).

Absent from this chapter is the treatment of how depression spirals into suicidality. Suicidality is the most ominous complication of depression, which is why I dedicate the next chapter to suicidal depression.

6

SUICIDAL DEPRESSION

A Case Study of Complex Depression's Most Severe Consequence

Hope is a necessity for normal life and the major weapon against the suicide impulse.

—Karl A. Menninger

In a fascinating article, Ali and El-Mallakh (2022) offered an analysis of what appears to be the oldest record of a depressed individual contemplating killing himself: a 4,000-year-old Egyptian papyrus of a man "journaling" his plight. The authors were particularly intrigued by the man's sense of worthlessness: "Look, my name is reeking; Look, more than carrion's smell/ on Harvest days/when the sky is hot" (p. 4). When such worthlessness accompanies the loneliness and hopelessness voiced by this man, suicidal depression develops. The authors concluded, "The presentation of depression, the reasons for considering suicide, and the process by which an individual works through those thoughts do not appear to have varied significantly over the past 4,000 years" (p. 7).

Indeed, they have not. As noted in the Introduction and throughout this book, depression is a very serious risk factor for suicide—likely the most

https://doi.org/10.1037/0000377-007
Complex Depression: The Role of Personality Dynamics and Social Ecology, by G. Shahar
Copyright © 2024 by the American Psychological Association. All rights reserved.

serious of all (Alqueza et al., 2023; Hawton et al., 2013; Miret et al., 2013). Suicidal depression occupies a central place in my research and clinical endeavors (e.g., Shahar, Rogers, et al., 2020). In fact, as gleaned from the Introduction, I did not really choose to deal with suicidal depression: It has chosen me.

In Chapter 5, I identified suicidality as the last of several complications caused by three ecodynamic patterns: action, immersion, and extraction (Table 5.1). Because suicide is by far the most dangerous potential outcome of complex depression, I devote an entire chapter to it. This chapter explains how the reformulated depressive position translates into suicidal ideation, suicide attempts, and eventually death by suicide. This explanation builds on and extends my earlier theoretical publications on this topic (Shahar, 2018, 2021b). Central to the theoretical effort here, I attempt to align reformulated object relations theory with the most prominent theory of suicide: namely, the interpersonal–psychological theory of suicide (IPTS) established by Joiner and colleagues (Chu et al., 2017; Joiner, 2005; M. L. Rogers et al., 2021; Van Orden et al., 2010). I begin by describing the IPTS. Then I relate the IPTS to the reformulated depressive position, arguing that the integration between the two perspectives illuminates the way in which individuals trap themselves into a social context from which they may only escape by killing themselves. This entrapment, I contend, stands behind what Joiner and colleagues identified as an acute suicide crisis. I illustrate this with the case of my stepfather, Zvika.

INTERPERSONAL-PSYCHOLOGICAL THEORY OF SUICIDE

The IPTS represents lifelong, monumental scholarship and research on the determinants of suicidality. Although the theory is primarily interpersonal, it also draws on cognitive behavioral and biological evolutionary perspectives. Thus far, the IPTS has not been linked with psychodynamic thought. This is understandable, given Joiner's (2000a, 2000b) dismay with the nonscientific mentality of the psychoanalytic establishment (a dismay that I share but seek to circumvent; see Chapter 3, this volume). Hence, the following pages represent what is, to my knowledge, the first attempt to link the IPTS with a reformulated psychoanalytic stance, and I hope to convince you (and Joiner) that such a linkage is fruitful.

According to the IPTS, in order for individuals to be able to die by suicide, they must possess both *the desire* and *the ability* to do so. The desire to die by suicide emanates from two psychological states: perceived burdensomeness and thwarted belongingness. The ability to die by suicide is predicated on a person's ability to transcend evolutionary self-preservation and to gradually acquire fearlessness of death.

Perceived burdensomeness pertains to individuals' view that their existence burdens their social context, including their family, friends, and acquaintances. Consequently, the individual believes that these people would all be better off without them (de Catanzaro, 1995; Noyman-Veksler et al., 2017; Van Orden et al., 2006). *Thwarted belongingness* refers to the experience of an individual being alienated from others and not an integral part of a family, circle of friends, or another valued group. This idea is an iteration of Durkheim's (1897) famous study linking social alienation and suicide and is based on a massive body of research implicating social support in suicide prevention (e.g., Kleiman et al., 2014).

An *acquired ability to enact lethal self-injury* pertains to the repeated attempt to physically hurt oneself, representing a tenacious fight with self-preservation motives. Empirical evidence is consistent with the IPTS: past suicidal behavior habituates individuals to the pain and fear of self-injury, making future suicidality more likely (G. K. Brown et al., 2000; Nock et al., 2006; Orbach et al., 1997; Van Orden et al., 2008).

The IPTS postulates that the three risk factors just described (perceived burdensomeness, failed belongingness, and acquired capacity) work in tandem. In particular, this theory suggests that the joint occurrence of perceived burdensomeness and failed belongingness is sufficient to produce the desire to die, and this desire translates into lethal or near-lethal behavior only in the presence of the acquired capacity for lethality. The interactive nature of at least two of the three risks is demonstrated in numerous studies (Chu et al., 2017).

The Reformulated Depressive Position and the Interpersonal-Psychological Theory of Suicide

Recall that the reformulated depressive position comprises three elements embedded within a fourth, higher order one. The three elements are criticism-based affect, affect-regulatory maneuvers aimed at diffusing criticism (counteracting deficiency, downregulating authenticity, and compulsive purposefulness), and mental representations of the self as appeasing a judgmental other. These are embedded within a time axis whereby the reformulated depressive position is remembered as occurring in the past, is enacted in the present, and is projected into the future. In the case of depression progressing to suicidality, the time axis is the most important element. More specifically, the future is the most important sub-element within the time axis. Here is why.

When depressed individuals project their self-with-other representations into the future, what they most project is hope. This projection is not merely in the cognitive-reflective sense (namely, an abstract scenario where they feel good and their lives are good) but rather in the relational sense: the hope that others will accept and validate them for who they authentically are. Underlying this hope is the construal of the projected other as providing redemption, of absolving them from the constant need to diffuse criticism-based affect via the aforementioned regulatory maneuvers. At the same time, however, these individuals are haunted by their past and present over the dread that others will hurt them as they always have and always do. Tragically, while depressed individuals project both hope and dread for the future (Mitchell, 1995b), their interpersonal behavior is governed by the latter rather than by the former. Thus, in an attempt to counteract deficiency, they project criticism onto others, thereby provoking rejection and loss. The rejection and loss activate demeaning, criticism-based affect and mental representations of judgmental and punitive others; this occurs alongside the aforementioned downregulation of authenticity, which, in Winnicott's (1965) terms, diminishes the true self and bolsters the false self. Hope is still maintained via compulsive purposefulness, but the latter depletes ego resources. Ultimately, the failure to "generate" an accepting other erodes hope and introduces frustration and resultant agitation; these affects further alienate others, thereby trapping the person in interpersonal turmoil. Others thus are either abandoning, leading to thwarted belongingness, or fiercely accusing and thus begetting perceived burdensomeness: "My mere existence is an offense." The person is left alone at the mercy of their inner world, which at this point is completely merciless. Because depression "locks" the person in their inner world (depressive rumination), their encounters with the outside world become increasingly harsh. Suicidal patients with depression in my practice often describe their suicidal ruminations as stormy screams. Outer reality is no longer available as a respite from these screams: The person has already burned all bridges and/or realizes that they are likely to invoke hurt in any interpersonal turn. The only way to stop the screams is to cease being aware, and the only way to secure this is to die (Baumeister, 1990). This state of affairs pertains to what Joiner and colleagues called *acute suicidal risk* (M. L. Rogers et al., 2019). Now the sufferer has a new goal, a new sense of meaning, or a new way to salvage their self-image: They can succeed in dying. This is incumbent on two conditions. The first is stealth: If people close to the sufferer know that they are going to kill themselves, they will intervene. This is why acute suicide risk tends to be under clinicians' radar. The second is the fear of death, which requires practice to overcome and leads to what Joiner and colleagues called *acquired capacity*. When the sufferer has practiced enough, they are ready to stare death down (Joiner et al., 2016).[1]

CASE EXAMPLE OF THE ECODYNAMICS OF SUICIDAL DEPRESSION: MY STEPFATHER, ZVIKA

Herein, I use the death by suicide of my stepfather, Zvika, to illustrate the theoretical postulates described earlier concerning the ecodynamics of suicidal depression. As is likely expected, this is not easy for me. But I find it helpful for a few reasons. First, discussing it helps me work through the experience of being a suicide survivor (and doubly so, as my biological father also killed himself, but the dynamics of his suicide was, I believe, very different than that described in this treatise). It is also helpful because I am "close to the data": I knew Zvika for more than 30 years and have access to reports about him from my brother and sister, his distant family members, and my mother's (unfinished) memoir and the letters he wrote her that became available to me shortly after her recent death. This proximity to the data renders the following analysis a mixture of (a) psychological autopsy (i.e., a clinical-psychological procedure aimed at understanding the determinants of a victim of suicide using the information they have left behind) and (b) ethnography (i.e., an anthropological methodology whereby the investigator immerses themselves within a certain social context and reports on their impression reflectively) (Marcus, 1995; for application to the understanding of suicide, see also Pearson & Liu, 2002). In fact, because some of the materials I use to analyze Zvika's suicide are mine (e.g., letters he wrote to me, my own memories of him), my analysis includes strong elements of autoethnography (T. E. Adams et al., 2015). To the extent that ethnography requires a large measure of reflexivity and skepticism (Lichterman, 2017), autoethnography requires even more. Accordingly, the analysis is offered here as an illustration rather than a demonstration, and its validity is invariably "bracketed" (Roth, 2013).

---

[1] I find it an incredible testament to Joiner's perceptiveness that based on analyses of video clips of sufferers just before their death by suicide, he and his colleagues observed that completers tend to have an abnormally slow blink rate. As these authors noted, a particularly slow blink rate is characteristic of action that is frightening and daunting, which is exactly what a suicidal act is (Duffy et al., 2022; Joiner et al., 2016).

Zvika's History

Zvika married my mother when I was 1 year old. Because he was the male figure who actually raised me, my recollections of him are complex and multifaceted. There was the Zvika who was sparkling with charm, wit, and wisdom, and there was the Zvika who became so rigid that he could not be reasoned with. There was the dedicated and trustworthy Zvika who had others' needs in mind and who would go to great lengths to be there for them, and there was the Zvika who attempted to shrug all responsibilities in order to be completely free. There was the meditative, philosophical Zvika who would patiently engage in deep discussions with anyone interested, and there was the Zvika who was overtaken by rage and fear and sought to humiliate and hurt.

Zvika was born in occupied Poland during World War II. His parents were already in one of the ghettos and managed to escape to the then-Soviet Union in unknown ways. It was, as could be expected, a long and arduous escape, during which Zvika's father died. His mother, an outstandingly resilient and brilliant matriarch, managed to raise Zvika in the Soviet Union under the harshest conditions. They both "made Aliya," or immigrated to Eretz Israel (State of Israel), when Zvika was 7 or 8 years old. They resided in Jerusalem, where Zvika attended a boarding school. It was a harsh educational facility. Zvika attracted negative attention because he was an immigrant. I recall him joking about being humiliated for the way he dressed and spoke. He also alluded to various family members with whom he had adopted a bully-victim pattern.

My sister, Lilach, noted that Zvika was taken to boarding school because his mother was depressed. At that time, the numerous traumas that she had endured "caught on," and she had difficulty functioning. Yet Zvika was an only child and was his mother's entire world. Zvika and other family members were keenly aware of the tension between his mother's strengths and vulnerabilities; this contributed to the tension Zvika experienced while being both the center of his mother's attention and at the same time experiencing her depression as abandonment.

Zvika took his mandatory army service in infantry. He served as a paramedic and apparently was a very good one. During his mandatory service, war erupted in 1967 (also known as the Six-Day War). After his discharge from the military, Zvika decided to become an educator and worked as a high school teacher for years without an academic education (a not-uncommon scenario in then-emerging Israel). He oscillated between various fields of study and thus never completed a degree, which haunted him for the rest of his life.

Zvika's first marriage, which bore my stepsister, Iris, was stormy. He met my mother shortly after his divorce. They began dating slowly and later married. Owing to his extraordinary intellectual talents, Zvika got a job in the Israeli aircraft industry as an engineer despite not having the proper diploma. My sister, Lilach, was born in 1972. Life for the five of us was quite difficult. The Yom Kippur War erupted in 1973. Zvika served as a combat paramedic on reserve duty, and he experienced numerous battles and resultant horrors. After the war, we experienced long periods of economic hardship, and Zvika developed a serious cardiac illness that led to three cardiac arrests, one of which nearly killed him. There were other serious stressors with which we (as a family) had to deal that will not be described here. Rather, I conclude this brief history with a description of Zvika's immersion in a spiritual cult, which ultimately propelled his death by suicide.

Rising Tensions Between the Self and the Social Context: When Zvika's Depression Became Really Complex

One tension Zvika harbored was that between rationality and spirituality. He was a very gifted engineer with a strong background in mathematics and computer science and he was highly versed in physics, biology, and chemistry. His knowledge of the humanities was incredible. Zvika spoke approximately six languages and was highly knowledgeable in philosophy, history, and the arts. He was particularly attracted to mystical experiences and sought to understand the transcendental: deities, supernatural phenomena, and altered consciousness. This was common knowledge in our family, and my mother often complained about how Zika would repeatedly pursue communities and gurus who promised access to transcendental experiences and the afterlife. Zvika would enter such a community, make a huge impression, become highly enthusiastic, and then quickly find himself in a clash with the community leader and/or key community members. He would then become disenchanted and leave, only to resume pursuit of another community.

Around 2000, Zvika learned about the Fourth Way, a comprehensive mystical-religious (non-Jewish) philosophy developed by George Gurdjieff and his student Paul Ouspensky. Here is how my mother described the encounter in her memoir:

> Zvika and I both loved reading books. Our privet library was comprised of hundreds of books filling every [shelf] in the house. We were fond of going to bookshops together and we always found books to purchase. One day, when we were in Tel-Aviv together, we entered [the] Stimatzky book branch. I sought books on alternative medicine and Zvika looked for books on the occult.

Suddenly, Zvika came over and showed me a book with a marker inside. The book was *The Fourth Way*, and the marker had a phone number written on it. The phone number, it was written, was of a member of the Israeli society propagating the messages appearing in the book. Zvika's face lit [up] as if he found a gold treasure. "You see?" he said, "we did not come here [to the store] in [vain]. Someone above directed me into this [shelf] where this book was placed. Tomorrow I will call this phone number."

"What is this book?" I [my mother] asked.

"It is something I spent all my life searching for," Zvika replied earnestly.

Zvika looked very content. The next day, he told me that he indeed called the number, and found out that there is indeed a group of people managing a school that teaches the Fourth Way. His mood brightened, and he started to attend this school, first once weekly, and then twice weekly. At that time, I too took various courses in alternative medicine at various places in our hometown. Our children were now adults, were out of the house, and it [was] certainly the time for both of us to embark on new learning experiences for self-growth. Little did I know that this interface between my husband's character and his pursuit of the occult and the nature of the Fourth Way school will lead to an incalculable tragedy. (Lavie, 2022)

And indeed, it did. The 2 years after Zvika's encounter with the Fourth Way group and school were marred by one crisis after another. In brief, within months, Zvika was completely engrossed in cult activities. My mother learned that he had transferred almost all of their hard-earned savings to the cult. He isolated himself from virtually all of his former friends and acquaintances. He found a girlfriend and became increasingly violent at home. After he threatened to kill both my mother and himself, Zvika was forced by court order to move out of their house. After all his financial resources had been drained, Zvika quickly learned that he was no longer adored by the cult. He began having verbal altercations with some politically strong cult members and, sure enough, was kicked out. Eight months after Zvika left home, he was found dead in a motel room. He had turned on a gas stove and taken sedatives to fall asleep while inside.

As noted in the Introduction, I was at Yale School of Medicine at this time and was starting a new and exciting chapter in my life. I was completing my postdoctoral training and becoming a Yale faculty member, and my then-wife was pregnant with our daughter. I followed the slew of crises from afar, incredulous and helpless. I called Zvika several times in an attempt to reason with him, but he pushed me away with contempt ("How typical of you. You are trying heroically to sever a Gordian knot [referring to the escalation in his relationships with my mother], but you do not have a sword and you are no Alexander"). After numerous attempts, I ceased trying. I still feel guilty about ceasing, even though Zvika was right: I did not have a sword. When

I learned that Zvika threatened to kill my mother and himself, I told everyone around me that he would indeed kill himself. At the time, they thought I was being "hysterical." The rest is history.

AN ECODYNAMIC ANALYSIS OF ZVIKA'S COMPLEX DEPRESSION

My ecodynamic analysis of Zvika's suicide is based on three steps. First, I characterize his psychopathological symptoms. Second, I relate Zvika's personality to the reformulated depressive position (described in Chapter 3). Finally, I focus on the ecodynamic patterns leading from the reformulated depressive position to Zvika's suicide.

Psychopathology

It is without question that Zvika had repeated and severe bouts of depression throughout his life. This was part of the family folklore, and Zvika even joked about it. At various points, Zvika was even prescribed antidepressants (selective serotonin reuptake inhibitors), which he found quite helpful. His depressive manifestation faithfully took hold in accordance with the description of male depression (e.g., Addis & Mahalik, 2003), with agitation frequently replacing overt sadness as well as physical symptoms, escapist behavior (not so much at work but directed toward mystical interests), and periodic isolation from people close to him. Another feature of Zvika's depression was his dependence on two substances: nicotine and food (such dependence is more common in male depression). He smoked rebelliously even after his cardiologists warned of its dangers, and he consumed massive amounts of food, particularly when depressed (which also brings Zvika's depressive manifestation closer to atypical depression).

It would be tempting to surmise that Zvika's depression was actually bipolar, because he was radiant and charming at times. Agitation in general, and agitated depression in particular, is considered a marker of bipolar spectrum disorder or the "soft-bipolar" spectrum (Akiskal et al., 2003). However, I do not believe that Zvika suffered from a bipolar disorder. First, there was no genetic history of bipolar disorder in his family. Second and speaking from personal experience, Zvika had many apparently contradictory sides, but I never saw these sides appear or disappear as a function of mood. Rather, I saw them come and go as a function of self: These were self-states (Bromberg, 2009), largely dissociated, that would alternate based on stressful events and relational vicissitudes, and the alteration encompassed much more than mood. While the comorbidity between dissociation and bipolar disorder cannot be ruled out (Kefeli et al., 2018), a previous meta-analysis showed that of myriad psychiatric disorders investigated, dissociative experiences are lowest in bipolar disorder (Lyssenko et al., 2018).

The hypothesized centrality of dissociation is further corroborated in the overwhelming trauma Zvika experienced throughout his life: from escaping the horrors of the Holocaust as an infant-turned-child to experiencing a very difficult immigration to Israel at a young age, school bullying in adolescence, and the horrors of war in young and older adulthood. He once told my sister, Lilach: "The wars I have witnessed finished me." The following description is from my mother's memoir:

> He also provided detailed accounts of his regiment's participation in the fighting [of the Six-Days War in 1967], and at that evening he focused on a tough event he experienced in one of the battles.
>
> While his regiment was storming forward, he and his fellow paramedics run into several Egyptian wounded soldiers. He saw a wounded Egyptian soldier with a broken leg screaming in pain and rushed to him to provide medical aid. He sat with his face turned toward the wounded soldier and began treating the broken leg, when suddenly he heard an awful yell by a fellow paramedic: "Zvika, watch out!" Instinctively, he turned around and laid on his right side.
>
> Turned out that while he was treating the wounded's leg with his back exposed, the wounded lifted a big dagger and tried to stab him in the back. The fellow paramedic's yell saved his life, because it made him stepped aside and the wounded actually stabbed himself at the stomach and eventually died. (Lavie, 2022)

Reformulated Depressive Position

As noted in Chapter 3, the reformulated depressive position consists of strong ties between four components: (a) criticism-based affect, but also a fragile modicum of hope; (b) three affect-regulatory maneuvers aimed at alleviating criticism (namely, counteracting deficiency, downregulating authenticity, and compulsive purposefulness); (c) mental representations of a deficient but appeasing self in relation to a punitive but seductive (hope-invoking) other; and (d) the time axis, whereby the triangle consisting of affect, its regulation, and mental representations is remembered in the past, enacted in the present, and projected into the future.

In Zvika's case, all were strongly manifested. Even in his suicide letter, the centrality of guilt—both as a felt emotion and as an emotion sought to be invoked in the other (i.e., me)—is clear (see the Introduction, this volume). In addition, anger and insult appear in the letter through their denial. The letter also includes other emotions not directly related to the reformulated depressive position (e.g., confusion and love). This makes sense. People are much more than their single position. Indeed, Zvika was a person capable of loving, as demonstrated in my mother's memoir and the letters he wrote to her. This makes his death all the more tragic.

Additional criticism-based affects were apparent in Zvika's behavior throughout his life, the two most dominant of which are shame and contempt. Shame and shaming are paradigmatic in the development of personality and psychopathology in general and depression in particular (Farr et al., 2021; P. Gilbert, 2000; Scheff, 2001). Contempt is a more complex emotion that is usually directed at depressed individuals (Joiner et al., 1992) but is likely to propel interpersonal stress, arguably leading to depression (Roseman, 2018). At the same time, Zvika expressed hope (a noncriticism-based emotion that nevertheless belongs to the reformulated depressive position) throughout his life, usually with respect to a perceived impending redemption by others, communities, or pursuits. When Zvika's hope died, he went along with it.

All three affect-regulatory maneuvers described in the reformulated depressive position are characteristic of the way Zvika regulated his distress. Specifically, contempt toward others ("turning against the other") is the epitome of counteracting deficiency (Roseman, 2018). Zvika also counteracted deficiency every time he developed an uplifting spiritual project that he thought would redeem him, this time for good. Such spiritual projects were also tied to compulsive purposefulness: Upon developing the project, Zvika was completely immersed, investing all of his time, energy, and (particularly toward the end of his life) money. Downregulating authenticity was revealed in the peculiar way in which Zvika treated his job: He did not like it and it did not entice him, but he felt that a job was something people did so they would have the means to engage in pursuits they really liked. This meant that Zvika, a formidable intellectual and operational force, was largely estranged from the social context in which he spent most of his day.

As for mental representations of the self and others, I believe that parental representations played a major role in Zvika's dynamics. I am referring specifically (a) to Zvika's representation of maternal figures as nurturing and admiring on the one hand and judgmental and punitive on the other, primarily tacitly; and (b) to a blurry, almost absent, representation of paternal figures. Earlier, I alluded to Zvika's mother being a strong matriarch. I knew her very well and she, too, made a huge impression on me. As a grandmother, she was perfect: caring, inspiring, nurturing, and accepting. As a mother to Zvika, however, she was not only nurturing but also highly critical. Throughout their lives, Zvika attempted to obtain her approval, which she gave only partially—with an elusive promise to provide full approval sometime in the future, contingent on his performance, which always fell short of her standards. As for the paternal representation, Zvika never really knew his father. Growing up without a father is a difficult predicament, one that incurs grave implications for personality development among children, including a likelihood of developing malignant self-criticism (Reuven-Krispin et al., 2021; see also Culpin et al., 2013). Father absence frequently leads to "father hunger" (Herzog, 1982). Juxtaposed against blurry representations of parental figures, the type of fathers "adopted" throughout the person's life are likely to be seen as omnipotent and omniscient. In Zvika's case, these were the gurus he sought throughout his life.

This brings us to the fourth component of the reformulated depressive position: the time axis. I have highlighted the centrality of the future, fueled by the power of *hope:* to be accepted by the other for what one authentically is. In Zvika's life, such hope was constantly directed toward gurus and their followers. One by one, Zvika selected these gurus (i.e., *exciting objects*, in Fairbairn's, 1944, terms), only to be renounced once he became disenchanted. Lamentably, the last guru and followers renounced him after draining his resources.

Ecodynamics

The scene described in my mother's memoir, in which Zvika finds a note in an obscure book on a bookstore shelf, appears to be taken right out of a movie. But this is exactly what cults do: They spread seductive marks aimed at extracting individuals from their natural social context. Here is my mother's recount of the financial disaster that ensued from Zvika's relationship with the cult:

> And then I began fathoming the financial aspect of this problem: The financial tragedy. I started to look at our bank accounts and the financial reports and this made me shudder. All our money from 30-years of savings was gone. . . . I asked my husband (about this . . .) . . . "I do not allow you to ask me where the money is!" he yelled . . .
> "But you promised," I told him in one of our conversations, "Right there, in your mother's house in Haifa, on the Carmel Heights, you promised that we will be together forever, that you worship me, that I am your redemption angel . . . and now you are going to ruin both of lives because of this cult? Now? That we are both old and sick? What is going on with you? Let us start our life anew. Can't you see what this cult is doing to you? To us? To our family?". . . He stood aloft, condescending, and impervious, and said, "The cult is the most important thing in the world to me. The cult is now my family." He then walked out of the house, slamming the door behind him. (Lavie, 2022).

Zvika was extracted from his social context and immersed into the cult. As long as he had the resources to buy his redemption, he felt fine. Unfortunately, when he was drained of his resources, he was seen by his "new family" as a burden and hence was abandoned. His hope for future redemption was tarnished. When my sister, brother, and I offered a helping hand, he actively pushed us away (action). Such was the power of the humiliation and self-loathing he felt. He was left with nothing. Perceived burdensomeness and thwarted belongingness then came full circle: Dying by suicide was the only successful thing he thought he could accomplish.

7
PRACTICAL IMPLICATIONS FOR ASSESSMENT
Evaluating Complex Depression Through the Reformulated Depressive Position and Ecodynamics

So what exactly is depression? The answer to that question is complex: There are some things we know about depression, and some things we do not know, and both sets of things inform evidence-based assessment of depression.
—Joiner et al., 2005, p. 267

My general philosophy of assessment was outlined previously (Shahar, 2015a, 2019). In brief, I view assessment as the point of convergence between two seemingly opposite (both mandatory) aspects of our creed: schematics and poetics. *Schematics* pertains to the scientific basis of clinical psychology (evidence-based practice). *Poetics* refers to the importance of understanding the unique (idiographic) context of the suffering individual—one that extends beyond the general (nomothetic) laws of empirical science, expressed via the person's language and deciphered through methods drawn from the humanities (Shahar, 2010; Teo, 2017). When the two converge, a detailed, rich, and pragmatic picture of the individual is attained.

This chapter demonstrates how such assessment can be conducted with respect to complex depression. Specifically, I discuss assessment of the complex manifestation of symptoms, the reformulated depressive position, and ecodynamics. For each component, I first outline the type of information needed and the suitable instruments. I then present ways in which this information is integrated for use in case formulation and treatment planning. This integration is based on measures I recently developed—the Depression Complexity Scale (DCS), the Reformulated Depressive Position Inventory (ReDPI), and the Ecodynamics Questionnaire (EDQ)—which are described later. Psychometric validation studies of these measures are underway, and you are invited to contact me both to receive updates on the most current findings and to collaborate on further validation.

I wish to emphasize that I deliberated extensively about whether to present the DCS, the ReDPI, and the EDQ in this book. I developed these measures only recently. I have circulated them among clinicians treating complex depression (psychotherapists and psychopharmacologists alike) and received very encouraging feedback. I am about to begin collecting data that will test their psychometric properties. The natural course of scale development would be to develop the scale, collect psychometric data, and then publish psychometric findings in a journal. That process will take a good number of years. I am eager to learn whether these measures are psychometrically sound and, if so, to enter them into practical use. Therefore, I decided to publish the present versions in this book and to call on the international research community to join me in testing the psychometrics of these scales and improving them if need be. This call is made in the same spirit that inspired the amazing international collaboration among laboratories across the world in an attempt to understand the makeup of COVID-19. Because I argue that complex depression constitutes a pandemic that is more alarming than COVID-19, it is incumbent on me to facilitate a similar international research collaboration.

ASSESSING THE SYMPTOMS AND COMPLEXITY OF DEPRESSION

To determine the symptomatic picture of depression and how complex it is (and in what way), the clinician must use various *symptom measures.* Within depression research and treatment (but also in other fields), the distinction between self-report measures and semistructured interviews is paramount. Virtually every clinician is familiar with the Beck Depression Inventory–II (BDI-II; A. T. Beck et al., 1996) and the Center for Epidemiologic Studies Depression Scale (CES-D; Radloff, 1977). Semistructured interviews aimed at assessing psychopathology are less well known and thus are used less often in clinical practice despite their superior psychometric properties. The most extensively studied semistructured interviews are the Structured Clinical Interview for the *DSM* (SCID; First et al., 1995), the Diagnostic Interview Schedule (Robins et al., 1981), the Schedule for Affective Disorders and Schizophrenia (SADS; Endicott & Spitzer, 1978), the Mini International Neuropsychiatric Interview (MINI; Sheehan et al., 1998), the Longitudinal Interval Follow-Up Evaluation (LIFE; Keller et al., 1987), and the Diagnostic Interview for *DSM-5* Anxiety, Mood, and Obsessive-Compulsive and Related Disorders (DIAMOND; Tolin et al., 2018). Somewhere in between is the Hamilton Rating Scale for Depression (HRSD; Hamilton, 1967), which is a clinician rating scale.

Existing Tools to Assess Depression

How does one select the right measure from a plethora of alternatives and synthesize information arriving from self-report measures (e.g., BDI-II), clinician ratings (e.g., HRSD), and research-grade semistructured interviews (e.g., SCID)? Even though almost 20 years have passed since its publication, I believe that the most useful article addressing this question was offered by Joiner et al. (2005). In a special issue dedicated to empirically based assessment of psychopathology and published in the prestigious journal *Psychological Assessment*, Joiner and colleagues reviewed the current state of depression science, identified gaps in extant knowledge, and disentangled the factors clinicians must consider when assessing depression. Specifically, Joiner et al. (2005) noted that currently it is not known whether depression is a binary (yes or no) category (taxon) or a continuous variable. They also described available self-report, clinician-based, and semistructured interviews and evaluated their psychometric properties and incremental validity (i.e., the extent to which a measure adds information over other measures). The authors highlighted the wide spectrum of depressive symptoms, particularly that it extends beyond negative affect, and discussed various subtypes of depression. In addition, they underscored the importance of chronicity, comorbidity, and bipolarity, with the latter pertaining to the presence of hypomanic features within unipolar depression. Joiner et al. (2005) also addressed the impact of demographics and culture on depression and its assessment. Finally, they emphasized the importance of assessing suicidality in the context of depression assessment and diagnosis. Based on their findings, Joiner et al. (2005) offered the following recommendations:

> On the basis of available knowledge, our recommendation for the optimal evidence-based depression assessment in clinical settings includes (a) the SCID

to establish formal mood disorder diagnoses; (b) the MINI module on melancholic features to supplement the SCID; (c) the Seasonal Pattern Assessment Questionnaire (Rosenthal et al., 1987) to assess for the possibility of a seasonal component to any diagnosed mood disorder; (d) the BDI-II to assess severity of depressive symptoms and short-term change in depressive symptoms; and (e) the LIFE to formally assess remission of disorder once BDI-II scores are stably low for many weeks. For mass screening situations, the CES-D and BDI-II seem to be wise choices. (p. 275)

I basically agree with the authors' algorithm, although I suggest the following relatively minor modifications. First, with respect to self-report measures, we must invariably include the Beck Anxiety Inventory (BAI; A. T. Beck et al., 1988) alongside the BDI-II because it is extremely important to observe the extent to which patients present with anxiety alongside their depression (see Chapter 1, this volume) and how this presentation changes over time. The BAI and BDI-II constitute a successful pair because Beck and colleagues developed the BAI so that it overlaps minimally with symptoms of depression.

Second, in terms of other self-report measures, I recommend invariably including the Brief Symptom Inventory (BSI; Derogatis, 1982). The BSI is a 53-item measure tapping nine symptomatic constellations (depression, anxiety, somatization, obsessive-compulsive disorder, hostility, interpersonal sensitivity, phobic anxiety, paranoia, and psychoticism) and three global indices of distress. The BSI has several unique advantages: It (a) relies on a vast body of research evidence (most of which is freely available in the public domain), (b) includes norms from diverse international populations, (c) obtains information on a large symptomatic spectrum, (d) includes symptoms that may underlie atypical and/or complex depressive manifestations (e.g., hostility, anxiety, and depression, which may indicate agitated depression), (e) includes a suicidal ideation item, and (f) is sensitive to therapeutic change.

Third, with respect to semistructured interviews, I believe that the DIAMOND is on its way to replacing the SCID, SADS, MINI, LIFE, and other alternatives as the first choice in this category because it includes a very useful screener, is easier to administer, and is very sensitive to change and recovery. I use the DIAMOND in my practice; whether my prediction is correct remains to be seen, however.

Finally, any robust indication of bipolarity should essentially terminate the clinical assessment of unipolar depression. Consistent with Akiskal et al. (2003), I am of the opinion that even minor indications of hypomania render construal of the patient as suffering from bipolar spectrum disorder, in turn pushing the inquiry beyond the scope of this book. I define a robust indication of bipolarity as bipolarity that appears in at least two sources of information (e.g., a self-report measure and a clinical interview).

Per Chapter 1, it is crucial that the clinician also assess clients' physical health and illness and any legal problems (in addition to depression), as these are often comorbid with complex depression.

The Depression Complexity Scale

Even if we assume that all of the information is in place, it is still unclear how the clinician should synthesize it such that the results will enable evaluation of the complexity of depression and, by extension, aid treatment planning. This is the time to introduce the DCS, an ultra-brief, clinician-based measure of depression complexity, which is presented in Exhibit 7.1.

With a format the follows the BDI-II and BAI, the DCS targets five domains of complexity: symptom typicality, chronicity, comorbidity, health and legal problems, and suicidality. Within each domain, the highest scores tap not only the extent to which depression is complex but also the extent to which it burdens treatment—both psychotherapeutic and pharmacological. Scores range from 0 to 15, with higher scores representing greater complexity.

EXHIBIT 7.1. The Depression Complexity Scale (DCS)

This form is to be completed by the clinician or by a trained evaluator.

Instructions

Please think of a patient you are treating for depression and rate the patient's condition on the following five domains: manifestation, chronicity, comorbidity, health and/or legal problems, and suicidality.

1. **Manifestation**
    - (0) _____ Stereotypic manifestation, with no atypicality and no hints for bipolarity.
    - (1) _____ Stereotypic manifestations, with some hints for bipolarity not confirmed by other data sources.
    - (2) _____ Atypical manifestation, with atypical presentation or agitated depression.
    - (3) _____ Bizarre manifestation, with psychotic or dissociative features.

2. **Chronicity**
    - (0) _____ First or second onset.
    - (1) _____ Relapse (more than two episodes) with distinct periods of remission.
    - (2) _____ Chronic low-key manifestation (e.g., dysthymia).
    - (3) _____ Double depression: acute episodes superimposed on a chronic low-key manifestation.

(continues)

EXHIBIT 7.1. The Depression Complexity Scale (DCS) (*Continued*)

3. Comorbidity

(0) _____ No comorbidity: a standalone unipolar depressive picture.

(1) _____ Straightforward comorbidity: depression secondary to anxiety, stress-related, or personality disorder (Type B comorbidity).

(2) _____ Depression propels other conditions: indications that depression brings about other mental disorders such as conduct or substance use disorder (Type C comorbidity).

(3) _____ Comorbidity with more than two disorders without clarity as to causal relationships.

4. Health and/or Legal Problems

(0) _____ No health or legal problems.

(1) _____ Some problems (health, legal, or both), but depression can be treated without addressing them.

(2) _____ A serious health or legal problem, and depression cannot be treated without addressing it.

(3) _____ Serious health and legal problems, and depression cannot be treated without addressing both.

5. Suicidality

(0) _____ No suicidality: no past attempts or nonsuicidal self-injury (NSSI), no current ideations, and no current plans.

(1) _____ Little suicidality: no past attempts or NSSI, but passive suicidal ideations (i.e., without plans or preparation).

(2) _____ Significant suicidality: more than two past attempts or current plans and preparation, or a history of chronic NSSI and current suicide ideation of any form.

(3) _____ Very serious suicidality: more than two past attempts and imminent plans and/or preparation.

ASSESSING THE REFORMULATED DEPRESSIVE POSITION

What does it take to assess the reformulated depressive position? Recall that this position comprises four components: (a) criticism-based affect, (b) regulatory processes that reinforce this affect, (c) schemas and scripts of the self and others that are consistent with self-criticism, and (d) a time axis that considers past and present influences as well as projections of the self in the future. Fortunately, all of these exist (in abundance even, in some cases). For the purposes of this work, let us examine criticism-based affect, regulatory affect mechanisms pertaining to counteracting deficiency, downregulation of authenticity, compulsive purposefulness, and mental representations of self with others.

The ancient, albeit still useful, notion of *affective tone* developed by Rapaport et al. (1946) is particularly conducive here. It pertains to the overarching emotional tone of the respondent. To the extent that criticism-based emotions dominate this tone, the reformulated depressive position could be said to exist.

Existing Tools to Assess the Reformulated Depressive Position

Self-report checklists of felt emotions are used extensively in research. The Positive Affect Negative Affect Scale (PANAS; Watson et al., 1988) is likely the most commonly used self-report. Existing norms of the expanded form (PANAS-X; Watson & Clark, 1994) enable use of the PANAS in the clinic. Scales are also available for clinicians interested in rating their patients' emotions (e.g., Kramer et al., 2021). Clinicians who use projective tests such as the Thematic Apperception Test (TAT; Murray, 1943) can apply validated coding systems in order to extract measures of emotions from the narrative provided by respondents to pictures containing social interactions (e.g., McAdams et al., 2001, 2004). Alternatively, various machine-learning procedures exist that allow the interested clinician to compare patients' narratives—derived from either projective tests or transcribed sessions—against norms extracted from social media, thus assessing the prevalence of emotions expressed in language (e.g., Guo, 2022). Regardless of the measure used, the aim here is to establish the extent to which critical, demeaning affect (e.g., contempt, disgust, hate, and dislike) alongside hope is prevalent in a patient's inner world.

To assess how patients regulate criticism-based affect, I recommend that clinicians use excellent self-report and projective measures of coping styles and defense mechanisms. Although I cannot review these here, I recommend consulting Young (2022). Herein, I provide specific recommendations as to the coping, defense, and regulatory maneuvers that should be assessed using the measures just described.

To evaluate how patients counteract deficiency, the clinician should look for manic defenses such as denial (e.g., ignoring external reality indicating self-flaws), undoing (e.g., trying to rewrite reality that indicates flaws, or working even harder after failure), projection of critical-based affect ("It is you who is humiliating me, not me humiliating you"), avoidant coping style (e.g., avoiding efforts to rectify failures), turning against the other (e.g., criticizing others on a regular basis), and reaction formation (namely, reacting with self-enhancement to feelings of inadequacy). I also encourage clinicians to watch for future developments with respect to already promising cognitive tasks that distinguish between explicit and implicit expression of mellow affect such as sadness. For instance, Granger et al. (2021) found that euthymic individuals appear to express negative content more prevalently in implicit cognitive tasks compared with explicit tasks, a discrepancy they labeled *depression avoidance*. Future studies may apply these cognitive tasks to criticism-based emotions and gather norms that may make these tasks useful as clinical assessment tools.

To evaluate patient downregulation of authenticity, I suggest that clinicians use measures designed to test the *autonomous motivation* component in self-determination theory—that is, patients doing things because they want to do them. Low levels of autonomous motivation are certainly a strong indicator of downregulated authenticity. In addition, I recommend that the clinical watch for *isolation* as a defense mechanism (e.g., describing painful events without the expected mental pain). Because zest and vitality require the ability to experience and express emotion, the dominance of isolation in a patient's inner world is highly suggestive of the absence of these qualities, which emanate for inner obstacles posed in the way of authenticity.

Compulsive purposefulness is easy to recognize from respondents' behavior and from an open-ended clinical interview. Nevertheless, I urge the clinician to also look for indications of rationalization as a defense mechanism. *Rationalization* pertains to the tendency to supply seemingly logical reasons for one's behavior, except these reasons are not genuine (e.g., "I work long hours because I have to, not because I am escaping being alone with my thoughts or being intimate with my spouse").

What about mental representations of self with others? They are easy to assess. Strongly validated self-report, projective, or semiprojective measures of mental representations of self and others are available, and research using many of these was summarized earlier. In my clinical practice, I use two such measures with almost every patient: the Object Relations Inventory (ORI) by Sidney Blatt and colleagues (Blatt et al., 1988; Huprich et al., 2016) and the Social Cognition and Object Relations Scale (SCORS) by Drew Westen and colleagues (Westen et al., 1985; for a more recent version, see Stein et al., 2015). The ORI uses a procedure that elicits free descriptions of the self and others (e.g., parents, friends, therapists), which are scored using a manual developed by Blatt and colleagues. The ORI was informed by Blatt's integration of Jean Piaget's cognitive development theory and psychoanalytic object relations theory. The SCORS is yet another procedure for scoring texts (primarily TAT narratives) using a manual that integrates psychoanalytic object relations theory and social-cognitive theory. Both the ORI and SCORS provide scoring for content and structural dimensions.

The Reformulated Depressive Position Inventory

So what should a clinician do when they have obtained all of the pertinent information on the various components of the reformulated depressive position? Exhibit 7.2 presents the ReDPI.

Like the DCS, the ReDPI is a clinician-based measure. Completion of the ReDPI is predicated on the clinician's relatively good acquaintance with not only the patient's personality but also object relations theory and the reformulated depressive position presented in Chapter 3. Like the DCS, the ReDPI is also brief and pragmatic. It includes three sections: The first is for clinician assessment of patient criticism-based affect. Four affects are assessed, including two self-directed (shame and guilt) and two other directed (contempt and hostility). The second section enables clinician assessment of patient affect-regulatory maneuvers, including counteracting deficiency, downregulating authenticity, and compulsive purposefulness (with two items for each). The third section taps patients' mental representations of the self as deficient and the other as judgmental (two items each). The ReDPI concludes with two items that characterize the patient's attempt to find acceptance in relationships. Like the DCS, higher scores represent greater dominance of the reformulated depressive position.

ASSESSING THE ECODYNAMICS OF COMPLEX DEPRESSION

Ecodynamics is likely the most challenging domain to assess because it has not been addressed in previous assessment literature, and this book is the first, to my knowledge, to describe ecodynamics in complex depression. However, any assessment of ecodynamics is predicated on comprehensive assessment of the patient's social context and their transactions with this context, which is seldom done in the clinic (see Chapter 4 for a discussion of the mentalistic fallacy). This is regrettable, given that there are many self-report measures for assessing contextual variables such as stressful events, perceived and received social support, and positive life events. In my practice, which includes many adolescent and young adult patients, I use the Brief Adolescent Life Event Scale (BALES; Shahar, Henrich, Reiner, & Little, 2003). The BALES is an abbreviated measure of negative and positive life events that are likely to be dependent on the respondent's action. This measure is used in research

146 • *Complex Depression*

EXHIBIT 7.2. The Reformulated Depressive Position Inventory (ReDPI)

This form is to be completed by the clinician or by a trained evaluator.

Instructions

Think of your patient and rate them in terms of the stable characteristics described, using the following scale:

0	1	2	3	4
Strongly Disagree	Somewhat Disagree	Don't Know	Somewhat Agree	Strongly Agree

Affect

Your patient tends to feel:
- (a) Shame _____
- (b) Guilt _____
- (c) Contempt _____
- (d) Hostility _____

Affect Regulation

When your patient feels one or more of the above emotions, they:
- (e) "Rev themselves up" by attending to their own strengths, often in an exaggerated manner. _____
- (f) Attempt to put their own needs aside and "do what is right." _____
- (g) Immerse themselves in work. _____
- (h) Belittle others to protect their self-image. _____
- (i) Try to figure out how "others wish them to be." _____
- (j) Focus on short- and long-term goals. _____

Mental Representations

Self-Representations

Your patient:
- (k) Experiences themselves as fundamentally deficient. _____
- (l) Tends to berate themselves. _____

Other Representations

Your patient:
- (m) Experiences other people as judgmental. _____
- (n) Experiences other people as unforgiving of mistakes and flaws. _____

Representations of Relationships

Your patient:
- (o) Attempts (either consciously or unconsciously) to assuage a punitive other. _____
- (p) Harbors a chronically frustrated yearn to be accepted by others for who they truly are. _____

internationally. Unfortunately, there are no established norms to date, so my use of the BALES is impressionistic. There is also a young adult version of the BALES scale (Shulman et al., 2009). Of course, other good life event scales are in use in both research and practice, including the Social Climate Scales by Rudolf Moos (1994/2003) and the Comprehensive Scale of Stress Assessment (Sheridan & Smith, 1987). Both are excellent psychometrically, but I suspect that their length would deter clinicians. These assessments capture numerous life events specific to time periods (e.g., daily, weekly) and populations and many good measures of perceived and received social support.

Existing Tools to Assess the Ecodynamics of Complex Depression

Semistructured interviews of life stress and social support are superior to self-report measures (Monroe, 2008). However, they take a great deal of time to administer. Thus, I believe that in their current state, semistructured interviews are prohibitive for use in clinical practice—with a single exception. I am currently working to adopt Connie Hammen's (1980) UCLA Life Stress Interview (see Chapter 1) to clinical practice, although at this point I cannot anticipate when it will be ready.

Let us assume, however, that the clinician has all of the pertinent information about transactions between the patient and their social contexts, including those with higher order systems such as the mesosystem (e.g., interactions involving immediate microsystems "over the patient's head"), exosystem (e.g., child school, adult workplace), macrosystem (e.g., societal norms and values), and chronosystem (e.g., passage of time both within and across generations). What can a clinician do with this information? How can they translate it the various patient-context patterns described in Chapters 4 and 5?

The Ecodynamics Questionnaire

Enter the EDQ, which is presented in Exhibit 7.3. As with the DCS and the ReDPI, the EDQ was developed recently, has received very encouraging feedback from clinicians, and will soon be tested psychometrically.

Like the DCS and the ReDPI, the EDQ is a clinician-based measure. Unlike the former measures, however, the clinician cannot complete the EDQ without an explanation of the theory espoused in this book. This explanation must be clear and succinct in order for the clinician to both absorb and apply it to a single patient: I attempted to do exactly this in developing the EDQ. The questionnaire opens with a brief description of three types of person–context exchanges relevant to complex depression: action, immersion,

EXHIBIT 7.3. The Ecodynamics Questionnaire (EDQ)

To be completed by the clinician or by a trained evaluator.

Instructions

The aim of this questionnaire is to help you assess the way your patient interacts with their social environment. Generally speaking, a person's social environment is complex, in that it is composed of various systems. However, for the purpose of this questionnaire, focus on the following systems:

- Family of origin (FoO)
- Romantic relations (RR)
- Occupation or education (OE; namely, work and/or school)
- Friendships (Fr)
- Hobbies and leisure activities (HLe)

For each of these five systems, note whether your patient interacts with the system in a way that is consistent with the following patterns:

1. **Action (A):** The patient actively generates stress in the context of their interpersonal relationship with system members (A1). Moreover, the patient actively refrains from engaging with system members around enjoyable/fulfilling activities (A2), and also actively derails mobilization of social support from these members (A3).

    Anchoring examples: Individuals behave provocatively, thereby eliciting rejection. They decline invitations for recreational activities and refrain from seeking help when they are in distress.

2. **Immersion (Im):** The patient actively selects themselves into a system, even if they do not have to. The patient actively identifies with the system's culture, norms, and values and attempts to actualize them in their own behavior. Such actualization often comes at the expense of the patient's authentic voice, thus causing them suffering.

    Anchoring examples: Perfectionistic individuals self-select to highly competitive and achievement-based social contexts (e.g., top colleges).

3. **Infatuation (Inf):** The patient's personality dynamics is highly compatible with characteristics of the social setting, a scenario described in occupational psychology as person–environment fit. Moreover, both the person and the system are attracted to each other.

    Anchoring examples: Neighborhoods and communities seek specific types of inhabitants who also seek them (e.g., rural neighborhoods seeking individuals preferring to live in the periphery).

4. **Extraction (Ex):** The social system actively extracts the patient out of their comfort zone by luring them in, often via a subtle and/or indirect force. More specifically, the social context maps those characteristics of the individual that are likely to attract them to the context and then plants cues that activate these individual characteristics. Individuals are largely unaware that they are lured in. Rather, they experience their attraction to the social context as their own selection, based on choice.

    Anchoring examples: Shopping malls are physically designed to attract potential shoppers. Military intelligence agencies, such as the U.S. Central Intelligence Agency or the Israeli Mossad, collect information on potential human assets and then lure them in based on that information. Proanorexia websites seek adolescents with body image problems.

	Instructions
Please use the following table to insert the relevant patterns (A1, A2, A3, Im, Inf, and/or Ex), if they fit, in the pertinent columns. Importantly, more than one pattern may fit each system.

	FoO	RR	OE	Fr	HLe
Patient Patterns					

and extraction. I also include the infatuation pattern because it provides a strong contrast with immersion and extraction, thereby sharpening their meaning. Next, the clinician is asked to consider the patients' transactions with five microsystems: family of origin, romantic relationships, occupation or education, friendships, and hobbies and leisure activities. For each system, the clinician should note which of the four patterns exist. A simple count of three of the four patterns that are involved in complex depression comprises the score yielded by the EDQ.

CASE FORMULATION WITH THE DEPRESSION COMPLEXITY SCALE, THE REFORMULATED DEPRESSIVE POSITION INVENTORY, AND THE ECODYNAMICS QUESTIONNAIRE

I am a staunch believer in case formulation and treatment planning, including setting specific treatment goals and envisioning, with the patient, the time frame within which these goals are likely to be attained (Shahar & Ziv-Beiman, 2020). It should be emphasized that case formulation and treatment planning are invariably tentative.

My aim in developing the DCS, the ReDPI, and the EDQ was to facilitate case formulation. It is hoped that with these instruments, the clinician will gain appreciation of (a) how complex the patient's depression is and (b) how transactions between the patient's personality and social context contribute to this complexity. The more complex the depression, the lengthier the treatment (Schramm et al., 2020; Seligman, 1995) and the greater number of professionals likely to be involved in therapy, either directly or indirectly (e.g., prescribing psychiatrists, counselors, advisors, physicians, and law enforcement experts). Chapter 8 provides a case example that illustrates how the three measures described in this chapter can be used to inform treatment with a client who has complex depression and suicidal ideation.

8

PRACTICAL IMPLICATIONS FOR PSYCHOTHERAPY

Specific Interventions for Treating Complex Depression

Patients often have within themselves adaptive structures which they have sought all of their lives to attain but which have been unexpressed because they've been caught up in pathology. We free those adaptive elements.
—Sidney Blatt (Dimitrovsky 2007, pp. 315-316)

In this chapter, I address the implications of the reformulated object relations theory, the reformulated depressive position, and ecodynamics theory in psychotherapy with complex depression. To note, I neither present a comprehensive treatment package nor do I believe there should be one. Good treatment modules exist, but they need added perspective: namely, how to think about the various obstacles that therapists confront in the treatment of complex depression, what to anticipate, how to prioritize intervention, and how to synthesize the various processes taking place. These are the issues I target in this chapter.

The points I offer are tied to my definition of integrative psychotherapy (e.g., Shahar, 2013b, 2021a, 2021b). In my clinical work, I strive to consider every intervention and every exchange with the patient from three orientations: psychodynamic, existential, and cognitive (Shahar, 2021a). I make it a point to enter into and remain in a dialogue that represents each. I use psychodynamic, existential, and cognitive techniques both in my work and to guide development of my own techniques. This integration is demonstrated next, and discussion of the various points is accompanied by a therapy vignette.

TREATING A SUICIDAL PATIENT WITH COMPLEX DEPRESSION: A CASE EXAMPLE

Meet Lori.[1] She just turned 22 and is a professional athlete. Lori's sister, Natasha, is 30 years old and a lawyer at a leading law firm. Lori and Natasha were born in Israel to Russian immigrants. Their parents are both educated but, like many Russian immigrants, had a tough time acclimating to Israel. When Lori was 10, her father had a major depressive episode in which he caused a terrible car accident and was seriously injured. He then lost his job. Lori did not learn of her father's depression and mental health problems until she was 13. She began to develop depression at that age and ultimately dropped out of school. The depression worsened, and she was exempted from mandatory service in the Israel Defense Forces (IDF). Although this exemption was certainly justifiable, Lori was isolated further socially when the few friends she had left to serve in the IDF and severed their ties with her.

Things with Lori's family then went from bad to worse. Her father's brother developed depression and eventually died by suicide, which led to major family turmoil. Shortly thereafter, Lori made her first suicide attempt at age 19. She was referred to a prescribing psychiatrist. A wide range of psychotropic medications were attempted, but Lori did not respond to any of them. She was therefore deemed to be suffering from treatment-resistant depression. Three very serious suicide attempts then ensued, the last leading to day hospitalization at a psychiatric facility. After discharge, the psychiatrist overseeing the day hospitalization program referred Lori to me for therapy.

I have been treating Lori for the past 2 years, which have been quite eventful. During this time, she again became very suicidal and was referred for a special ketamine treatment known for efficacy in promptly reducing suicidality (e.g., Abbar et al., 2022). The treatment delivered in that Lori's suicidal urges subsided, but she reported still being depressed—albeit without

---

[1]This case has been modified to disguise the patient's identity and protect their confidentiality.

the gnawing emotional pain that drove her to attempt suicide in the past. Lori's father had also demonstrated increasingly severe cognitive decline, which of course adversely affects her mood.

Four central issues have surfaced during therapy. First, it became clear in the first month of treatment that Lori is suffering from social anxiety disorder (SAD). This disorder is characterized by considerable discomfort or distress in social situations and by a behavioral pattern of shyness. SAD is highly comorbid with unipolar depression (Adams et al., 2016) and seriously interferes with an individual's relationships, daily routine, and school and work. These adverse effects of SAD are also evident in Lori's life: Although she is interested in developing a romantic relationship, she has had problems with dating. Her work as a fitness instructor at a local gym is also impeded by her shyness and difficulty meeting and conversing with gym clients. In general, comorbid double depression and SAD render Lori markedly isolated socially. Her only ongoing connections are with Natasha and with me (over the last couple of years). Natasha has moved away and her visits are infrequent, and Lori engages in therapy with me once a week; thus, she is lonely most of the time.

Second, athletics is Lori's primary outlet. She is very good at sports, and practicing and competing provide her with a modicum of content unparalleled by other activities. Nevertheless, over the last couple of years, she has experimented with illegal performance enhancers that complicate her physical health and put her at risk for legal trouble.

Third, although Lori contributes constructively to the therapeutic alliance and has made significant strides in her work with me, one pattern remains an obstacle: Lori is reluctant to connect the repeated surfacing of depression with events occurring in her social context, primarily with her family and dating life. I find this very puzzling because (to me) the link is obvious. At the beginning of therapy, Lori simply dismissed my attempts to turn her attention to this link. Later, she acknowledged "seeing" it intellectually but rarely "feeling" it.

Fourth and highly related to the third pattern are the bouts of hopelessness that Lori experiences. These bout are, of course, perfectly correlated with the surfacing of her depression; yet during those times, hopelessness stands out in terms of its viciousness and resistant to counter facts. In fact, we used to call Lori's hopelessness *The Story*, referring to the story she tells herself about her life. The major aim of therapy has been to help her consider The Story as a creation of her own mind rather than the objective truth and to begin building an alternative story (see Spence, 1982). That Lori collaborates with me in doing so is a testimony to her fortitude.

I rated Lori with the three instruments described in Chapter 7: the Depression Complexity Scale (DCS), the Reformulated Depressive Position Inventory (ReDPI), and the Ecodynamics Questionnaire (EDQ). Her score on the DCS was 13 of 15: She demonstrated atypical manifestations or agitated depression (2), double depression (3), Type C comorbidity (with substance use and SAD [2]), serious health and legal problems (concerning the performance enhancers [3]), and very severe suicidality (3). Her score on the ReDPI was 55 of 64, with clear indications of criticism-based emotions, mental representations of self as deficient and appeasing and of others as judgmental, and a strong yearn to be accepted. Defensive processes centered primarily around downregulating authenticity ("doing what is right," "what others wish me to do"), but there were also some indications of counteracting deficiency ("putting others down") and compulsive purposefulness ("focusing on short- and long-term goals"). Finally, on the EDQ, Lori exhibited a strong action pattern in old contextual domains, primarily espousing passive-aggressive maneuvers that isolated her from other people. In the family domain, an immersion pattern was also evident in which Lori had tremendous difficulty separating herself from her family. For instance, she still lived with her parents and was absorbed in her father's difficulties even when it was clear that this was bad for her.

FOUR INTERVENTIONS FOR TREATING COMPLEX DEPRESSION

Next, I discuss four interventions for treating complex depression: providing psychoeducation, instilling remoralization, using ecodynamic practice to diffuse toxic patient–context exchanges, and altering the reformulated depressive position. I will demonstrate their implementation in Lori's therapy.

Intervention 1: Providing Psychoeducation

For readers coming from psychodynamic and/or humanistic–existential psychotherapeutic perspectives, the prospect of educating patients about psychological processes at the beginning of therapy may sound strange if not "disenfranchising" (e.g., Bohart et al., 1998). However, this is not the case. In fact, I argue that gently and flexibly educating patients about the unfolding of insight-oriented therapy may actually advance psychodynamic and humanistic–existential growth (Shahar & Govrin, 2017). By providing a cognitive-affective frame of the patient's suffering and how it will be addressed in treatment, the therapist not only supplies pertinent information but also delivers strong messages of commitment and hope. For patients with complex depression, the therapist's commitment and hopeful vision are sorely needed.

The psychoeducation that I recommend therapists provide to patients with complex depression is straightforward and threefold:

1. Explain to patients that their depression manifests in complex ways (e.g., explain how depression is connected to agitation), may beget further depression (e.g., explain chronicity), is likely to propel other disorders (e.g., explain Type C comorbidity), contributes to their health and/or legal problems, and, of course, leads to suicidality.

2. Convey to patients that their depression is not synonymous with their entire self and identity; rather, it largely (not exclusively) emanates from how they experience the world and situate themselves within it. Specifically, use nontechnical terms to explain the meaning of a position, how it colors all cognitive processes, and how it modulates emotions and shapes behavior. Emphasize the theme of malignant criticism. Differentiate between the type of criticism that is constructive and may assist in self-improvement and the type that is toxic and accounts for their demoralization. Show how criticism colors not only how patients experience themselves but also how they experience others. Prime them to investigate (with you) how the theme of malignant criticism explains what happens in their relationship with you (i.e., transference and countertransference).

3. Illuminate for patients how their behavior interacts with their social context, and use nontechnical terms to explain the action, immersion, and extraction patterns discussed earlier. Specifically, show patients how they may generate stress and degenerate social support and positive events (action), and how they may lock themselves within a social system that erodes their well-being (immersion and extraction).

With respect to psychoeducation in complex depression, timing is everything. First, the three elements just described are best introduced successively. There is no point in talking to patients about person–context exchanges before you present the theme of malignant criticism and how it shapes their inner world. Similarly, if patients' inner world is addressed first and too early in therapy, it may be experienced as far-fetched and intrusive. Patients come to therapy with acute suffering of complex depressive symptoms, which should be addressed first in terms of psychoeducation. Thus, I usually provide psychoeducation about complex depression as part of the initial assessment and treatment planning period (unfolding over the first two to four sessions). I then wait for a *spontaneous gesture* (Winnicott, 1971) from the patient, such as a description of an event in their life, a free association, or a dream, before I present the theme of malignant criticism. I reiterate this theme over several sessions while formulating (in my head) the various ecodynamic patterns. I then wait for another opportunity in which patients describe an interpersonal exchange that reflects action, immersion, and extraction, and I discuss malignant criticism with them. This discussion is relatively succinct in that I point out the patterns and invite patients to investigate them further with me.

Let us use Lori's therapy to illustrate. Helping Lori see how living with her parents markedly aggravates her complex depression is a major challenge. Because treatment has been complicated, I waited about 8 months into our sessions before I began hammering this point home. I had already provided some psychoeducation for complex depression and the reformulated depressive position, although I had not fully implemented this intervention. Finally, when Lori alluded to worsening of her depressive symptoms in one session, I asked what had happened with the family that week. Here is our exchange:

LORI: Nothing, really. All the same.

GOLAN: I find it hard to believe that absolutely nothing has happened.

LORI: Well, you know, I snapped at my dad again. I can't stand him and I can't stand myself for doing this.

GOLAN: What happened that made you snap at him?

LORI: Well, as I have told you many times, he enters into my room unannounced, and starts sharing his problems with me. I f---ing don't know how to solve his problems! I just don't know and he doesn't get it, so I snapped at him.

GOLAN: You are assuming that it is your job to solve his problems, and this assumption is all but new.

LORI: [Snappishly] Well, what would you do if your dad entered your room, asking you to solve his problems?

GOLAN: Probably what you did. But you don't need me now as "you." I think you need me as "me" working with you to understand what happened to you then, both inside and outside in your reaction to your dad, and how that is related to the fact that you feel extra bad this week.

LORI: [Sarcastically] Go ahead. Make my day.

GOLAN: [Trying to lighten the atmosphere] Let me try to make both our days. Time and time again, you have told me about how you feel guilty over your dad's condition.

LORI: [Increasingly curious but acting bored] Yeah . . .

GOLAN: We don't feel guilt over people we don't care about.

LORI: You don't need to be Professor Shahar to know that I love my dad.

GOLAN: Correct. And you don't need to be any type of professor to know that, in your family, you all love each other. Greatly. And are committed to each other. Perhaps overly.

LORI: What do you mean?

GOLAN: I mean that you are trapped. You can't live in your parents' house without feeling guilty and without snapping at your dad, because your dad will continue to seek your help. That's the way it is in your family. And as long as you are there, you will continue to feel that it is your job to help him—except that you can't, so you will continue to be mad about both him and yourself.

LORI: What you are saying is that I need to leave the house.

GOLAN: One doesn't need to be a professor to realize this. But since you are raising professorial issues, let me tell you what we know from research and clinical experience: There are social situations that entrap us. They do so because they ignite our personality tendencies. For instance, some individuals are prone to guilt. Social situations in which close others in the guilt-prone person's milieu deflect responsibility their way, this is bound to induce guilt. It is almost mathematical. No matter how many meds you are taking, it is going to happen and you will become more depressed. There are only two ways out of this: Change the social dynamics if you can; and if not, extract yourself from the situation. Yes, sometimes this means leaving home.

I repeated the terms *trapped* and *extract yourself from the situation* delicately but consistently through many sessions. After a prolonged period of time, Lori told me that she is beginning to prepare to find a place to rent. She experienced this as her own idea, which was the best possible scenario. At this time, she is living outside of her parents' home.

Intervention 2: Instilling Remoralization

In Chapter 1, I highlighted the fact that demoralization is different from depression, derails treatment outcomes, and is likely to ensue from chronic depression. To push the envelope further, I argue that demoralization is likely to stem from forms of complex depression such as heterogeneous manifestation, chronicity, comorbidity, health and legal problems, and suicidality because all of these are likely to devastate sufferers' lives and to lead to unsuccessful treatments.

Consider Lori. She has received nearly every pharmacological treatment in every psychiatric protocol. Before she came to therapy with me, she had received two forms of psychotherapy: one cognitive behavior therapy and another psychoanalytic. When Lori tells me that she is "fundamentally ill and untreatable," she is unknowingly echoing many of her counterparts. There is a very good question that patients with complex depression ask their therapist, either explicitly or implicitly: "Why should you be the one who will succeed in helping me?" This question may have many answers, none of which are good. There is no evidential basis for these patients to suppose that we will succeed after all of these calamitous failures; even if there were, it is not a cognitive issue. They feel untreatable.

Patients with complex depression, consciously or not (usually a bit of both), seek to convince the therapist that they are untreatable. They do so in numerous ways, which can be grouped into two clusters: (a) creating havoc in their social relationships and (b) impeding therapy (Shahar, Blatt, Zuroff, Krupnick, & Sotsky, 2004). There are more than 50 ways in which patients attempt to demoralize the therapist, akin to what Kleinian psychoanalysts call *projective identification*. So what is a therapist to do?

Over the years, I have developed the following heuristics that help me combat patient demoralization and instill even small measures of remoralization.

Take Care of Your Demoralization First

Elsewhere, I alluded to the gnawing need to (almost) constantly be in therapy ourselves and to surround ourselves with psychotherapy supervisors and peers with whom we can consult (e.g., Shahar, 2004, 2015a). No matter how important and senior we think we are, these dictums hold. Next, I further explain why this is so.

Realize That Demoralization Is Not Static

As Larry Davidson and I have argued (Davidson & Shahar, 2007a, 2007b), people are locomotive. They are always "on the move" or, as Heidegger would say, they are "ahead of themselves" (Cooper, 1999; Shahar, 2010). Thus, when you begin therapy with someone suffering from complex depression (or any other form of complex psychopathology, for that matter), please assume that the worst is yet to come and perhaps rapidly. Doing so enables you to be "on your toes" and observe the ways in which patients unwittingly engage in vicious interpersonal cycles both within and outside therapy.

Engage With Patients' Adaptive Schemas
No matter how much they suffer and how deeply they engage in vicious interpersonal cycles, patients also have adaptive internal presences. In psychoanalysis, we call these *good objects* (my mentor Blatt referred to them as *adaptive structures*; Dimitrovsky, 2007). Following the language we use in this book, these would be *adaptive interpersonal schemas and scripts* or, more generally, *adaptive positions* (Shahar & Mayes, 2017, in press). In fact, in a rare instance in which Blatt drew from Kleinian object relations theory, he, John Auerbach, and colleagues referred to Betty Joseph's (1983) relatively nascent notion of healthy projective identification and upgraded it to *adaptive projective identification*: patients, even seriously disturbed ones, evoke in their therapist a sense of warmth and compassion that can then be internalized by the patients, in turn building their resilience (Auerbach & Blatt, 2001; Blatt et al., 1996).

I advise you not to wait for patients to identify their adaptive structures, however. In a manner akin to Alexander and French's (1946) notion of corrective emotional experience, I advocate actively infiltrating patients' (very toxic) inner world as a good object. Examples of ways to achieve this include increasing the frequency of therapeutic sessions, being available to patients online, and utilizing self-disclosure (see elaboration in Shahar, 2015a). The therapist can even use Milton-Eriksonian suggestive and persuasive techniques such as pacing and leading, in which they adjust their speech, language pattern, and behavior to match the patient. This approach helps establish a sense of safety, and the therapist then can lead the patient to realms conducive to treatment as they deem suitable (Erickson, 1980).

Lest you deem me clinically naïve, I quickly point out that I do not expect this process to be easy, quick, or even successful in the short to moderate term regardless of the means used to infiltrate patients' inner world as a good object. On the contrary, I expect the most complex patients (those who occupy a particularly toxic and tenacious criticism-based inner world) to strongly dismiss the very notion that anyone, let alone the therapist, is "good." Nevertheless, the more that patients observe therapists attempting to establish themselves as a good object, the more they come to respect therapists' stamina in the face of patient tests and provocations and through therapeutic rupture. In turn, the likelihood of patients' adaptive structures paving their way to the therapy office is greater, in turn setting in motion positive, resilience-related interpersonal cycles.

Utilize Active, In-the-World Interventions
Elsewhere, I described my penchant for active techniques that inherently involve patients in daily activities "outside their mind" (Shahar, 2013b, 2015a, 2021a; Shahar & Davidson, 2009; Shahar & Govrin, 2017). The ostensive rationale here is existential, drawn from philosophical ideas such as Kierkegaard's action over reflection, Heidegger's being in the world, and Sartre's fundamental project, among others (see Cooper, 1999). The underlying idea is to help patients stay away from their toxic depressive position for long hours throughout the day while we process this position psychodynamically in therapy sessions. Active, in-the-world interventions are also likely to increase patients' self-efficacy, because the reward emanating from enjoyable activities is likely to be immediate and noticeable. My favorite active, in-the-world intervention is behavioral activation (Dimaggio & Shahar, 2017), whereby patients are encouraged to systematically schedule enjoyable and/or meaningful activities in their daily routine and then execute these activities even if they "don't feel like it." Behavioral activation not only yields powerful antidepressant (primarily antianhedonic) effects but, in the context of integrative psychotherapy, may also lead to what Yalom (1980) called *heightened existential awareness* (i.e., increased awareness of one's responsibility, free choice, and ability to create meaning in a chaotic world; see Shahar & Govrin, 2017). Other well-regarded, active in-the-world interventions are Viktor Frankl's (1975) dereflection, which involves directing attention to outward interests and away from the inner world (e.g., by volunteering), and detailed inquiry into interpersonal exchanges, often espoused by interpersonal psychoanalysts (Sullivan, 1954). The latter is likely to heighten awareness of the action and immersion ecodynamic patterns.

Work With the Future
Moran Schiller and I described previously how deliberate and systematic work with future representations may take a central place in psychodynamic-integrative therapy with depressed patients (Shahar & Schiller, 2016b). Patients with complex depression often manifest demoralization as an assault on their own future: either they cannot conceive such a future or they envision it in the most dreadful of terms. Moran and I proposed to combat patients' assault on their future in three ways: fighting for the future, explicating the future, and playing with the future.

Fighting for the future involves embracing a methodically optimistic (more accurately, nonpessimistic) stance toward patients' future. Specifically, fighting for the future consists of explicitly, but not belligerently, resisting patients' grim depiction of their future. At times, patients may express dismay at this therapeutic stance and may label it as unempathic and even condescending. However, I am discovering that some patients actually yearn for the therapist's resistance to pessimistic future scenarios. Such yearning, coupled with gratitude for the therapist's resistance, is often expressed later in therapy.

Explicating the future consists of the therapist providing gentle, sometimes subtle, encouragement to patients to imagine their own future, even when they declare that their future is actually unimaginable. Numerous auxiliary therapeutic techniques may be summoned in this quest, including guided imagery, semihypnotic or hypnotic suggestions, and cognitive restructuring, particularly the trial-based version in which patients alternate between the role of a prosecutor ("You have no future") and a defense attorney ("Yes, I do, and this may be it"; see de Oliveira et al., 2012).

Playing with the future entails engaging with patients to show symbolically what their future may look like. In Shahar and Schiller (2016b), we described the case of Luck, a 24-year-old law student suffering from crippling depression. Luck's mandatory army service and past occupational and academic history were illustrious, but he struggled to get out of bed when he was depressed. Luck began playing PlayStation and orchestrated wars between his team (a bunch of players he assembled from all over the world) and other teams, which helped him get out of bed when depressed. Although Luck's parents were horrified that all he did was play PlayStation, we later learned that this was how Luck prepared for his recovery: The occupational pursuits that propelled this recovery were highly similar to the role he occupied in his PlayStation wars.

Of the various points comprising remoralization work, I believe that working with the future is the most important. Recall that the time axis is one of the chief components of the reformulated depressive position: the future has a special place in the time axis as experienced by individuals. I emphasize the link between Blatt's notion of patients' adaptive structures and adaptive projective identification, and I also note the importance of working with patients on their future. In treating a patient with complex depression, a therapist may sometimes feel that nothing works, that the patient is stuck and is pushing away any attempts to "hold" their future (Winnicottianly speaking), and that indeed there is no future for the patient. However, I repeatedly observe that if we persevere, an adaptive structure within the patient may suddenly awaken and voice an interest in having a future in ways we could never anticipate.

I recently learned that after a very bad period in which she could absolutely form no mental representation of her own future, Lori decided to enroll in a bachelor of computer science program at a nearby community college. She certainly has the skills to succeed. Up to this point, she had insisted that she would not be able to complete high school matriculation exams. When I asked why she set this ambitious (but in my opinion, realistic) goal to return to school when she previously ridiculed her likelihood of accomplishing even more basic goals, all she could say was, "I am fed up living this way." In the past, being fed up used to propel Lori toward a suicide attempt. Now, Lori is experiencing a different kind of fed up: This one has self-compassion, playfulness, and even humor. I am eager to see how Lori's pursuit of this goal pans out, and I am determined to play an active part in helping her realize it.

Intervention 3: Using Ecodynamic Practice to Diffuse Toxic Patient-Context Exchanges

I strongly recommend that psychotherapists engage directly with patients' social ecology. I advocate reaching out to patients' family members, friends, and romantic partners and to school personnel, workplace officials, and other pertinent people in their social network when needed (e.g., physicians in pain clinics where patients are treated). Of course, this is contingent on patient consent but I have discovered that with adequate psychoeducation, the majority of patients consent.

The purpose here is twofold: (a) to gather information on the aforementioned action, immersion, and extraction patterns and then (b) to intervene directly to minimize these patterns while simultaneously working with patients to help them identify and prevent them.

The theoretical umbrella guiding me in intervening with patients' social ecology is diverse. In addition to the aforementioned ecodevelopment theory put forth by Bronfenbrenner, I draw from interpersonal psychoanalysis, the Tavistock model of organizational psychodynamics, and psychodynamic social work theory (e.g., Caputo & Tomai, 2020; Fraher, 2004; Mishna et al., 2013). Their common denominator is the realization that individuals' unconscious material is activated but also shapes features of social context. For instance, Borg (2003) introduced the notion of *community character*, which pertains to the unconscious representation of implicit rules, stereotypes, rituals, and laws governing and limiting interactive patterns within a community and thus describes group-level, self-protective mechanisms. Similarly, the Tavistock model of organizational psychodynamics, which is heavily influenced by

Kleinian and neo-Kleinian psychoanalysis (primarily Bion, 1961), posits that organizations are constantly threatened by uncertainty, which summons anxiety. Thus, organizations espouse similar defenses against anxiety that individuals use to manage anxiety in the psyche. For instance, projective identification pertains to the tendency of a social group or organization to project its own unwanted experiences onto another group or organization. By espousing these defenses, organizations regulate their members' experience, providing them with relief from anxiety on the one hand but restricting their freedom on the other (Fraher, 2004; Menzies, 1960). In addition to these theoretical sources, I draw from two leading family-systems theories: Minuchin's structural family therapy (e.g., Colapinto, 2019; Minuchin & Nichols, 1998) and Bowen's (1978) family theory. The former emphasizes how family structures (e.g., coalitions) reflect power relationships within the family. The latter is highly compatible with the former and highlights the extent to which family members are self-differentiated versus undifferentiated from other members and how family interactions bolster versus hinder self-differentiation.

While I consider the practice of ecodynamics important, I also emphasize its use to augment individual psychotherapy. The primary goal of individual psychotherapy (in my opinion) is to help patients change their maladaptive mental structures—those that render them vulnerable to psychopathology (see Intervention 4). Individual psychotherapy is not aimed at changing the social ecology, although it may do so indirectly.

Working With Action

The specific tactical goals of ecodynamic practice are derived from the putative pattern that is considered detrimental to the patient. When this pattern is action, the goal is to first contain the reverberations of patients' maladaptive action (primarily stress generation and degeneration of social support). Next, ecodynamic practice facilitates working through the psychodynamic processes propelling this maladaptive action (namely, working through the reformulated depressive position). Finally, the ecodynamic practice aims to help patients prevent maladaptive action. Realistically, however, this aim can only be realized when the former two aims are at least partly realized.

Here are some examples of ecodynamics use to manage action:

- Meet with family members with whom the patient has volatile relationships. Help these family members understand the patient's inner dynamics and how to react to the patient's gestures (provocations) in a way that prevents strife-generating clashes with the patient.

- Meet with school personnel to improve their relationship with an adolescent patient.

- Establish frequent contact with friends and family members of suicidal patients to develop safety plans, promptly gather information on increased suicide risk, and short-circuit patients' tendency for seclusion and help negation.

Working With Immersion

When the pattern is immersion, the goal of ecodynamic practice is to facilitate patients' self-differentiation (Bowen, 1978). Doing so requires reaching out to key members of the patient's social environment to help them work with the patient individually. This work enables the patient to view themselves as psychologically separate (or at least separable) from these key members (e.g., parents, bosses) and enables the patient to secure a psychological distance between themselves and the values, norms, and culture of the social environment. This dilutes the centrality of the patient's reformulated depressive position in their psyche. Examples of ecodynamic practice with immersion include the following:

- Work with parents and young patients, separately and jointly, to realize similarities and differences between their and their parents' character ("You are violent just like your father" or "Depressed again, just like your mother").

- Help school personnel realize that adolescent patients are under peer pressure that may account for their problem behaviors (e.g., commission of violence or substance use, leading to depression).

- Work with members of any social system to help the patient out of a social trap, which I label the *axis of criticism* (ACRIM), related to the previous two items (Shahar, 2015b; Shahar & Henrich, 2013). ACRIM is a scenario whereby patients' self-criticism and criticism from significant others—also known as *critical expressed emotion* (Fahrer et al., 2022)—feed each other, particularly under stress. Awareness on the part of patients and significant others of the language of criticism paves the way toward containing ACRIM and increases the likelihood of successfully severing the reformulated depressive position (see Intervention 4).

- Work with medical team members to help them understand how they inadvertently strengthen the patient's sick role (e.g., pity), thereby derailing their resilience.

Working With Extraction

When the putative pattern is extraction, ecodynamic practice is extremely hard. The reason is straightforward: The relevant social context is keenly interested in maintaining control of the patient, and the therapist reaching out poses an inherent threat to this interest. My clinical experience has taught me that when extraction is operative, three possibilities exist for an effective ecodynamic practice. First, reaching out to key members of the relevant social context may help the therapist gain better understanding, even if the members representing the social context still resist the prospect of releasing their hold over the patient. Second and far less likely, ecodynamic practice may convince at least one key member of the relevant social context to begin loosening the ties of extraction. If this happens, then other key members may follow suit and the patient may have a potential ally in their quest for self-differentiation. Finally and possibly most likely, a failed attempt to reach out to relevant key members may be discussed in individual therapy, in turn energizing the patient to break free on their own.

Strategies for Interacting With Patients' Social Contexts

What maneuvers are executed by the therapist interested in the practice of ecodynamics? I believe that the therapist needs to do four things: (a) identify key members and reach out to them; (b) empathize with these individuals' viewpoints when meeting with them; (c) advocate for the patient during the course of such a meeting; and (d) if the meeting goes well, mediate between the patient and key members. Allow me to explain.

Not all members of the putative social context are adequate candidates for reaching out. Adequate candidates (a) have a sufficient standing (political power) within the social context, (b) are likely to be favorable toward the patient, or (c) may have an interest in changing the maladaptive ecodynamic pattern in point. These parameters are not always easy to map; they are invariably pondered about with the patient, and mistakes may happen. When the social context in point is the family, parents are almost always potential candidates, even when the patient is no longer a minor. However, the therapist may realize that one or both parents are not amenable for joint work, challenging the therapist to seek an alternative within or outside the family.

Once a key member is selected, the therapist should reach out politely and ask to meet to understand what is happening with this patient in this particular context. During the meeting, it is extremely important for the therapist to try to understand the key member's point of view and empathize with it, even if the therapist comes to the meeting completely aligned with the patient's perspective (as we, individual psychotherapists, often do). Citing the late, well-known relational psychoanalyst Phillip Bromberg (1996), the therapist must be able to "stand in the spaces" and hold both the patient and key member's points of view, at least within themselves. If the therapist feels that they managed to convey an empathic sentiment to the key member during this meeting, the therapist may cautiously attempt to advocate for their patient by presenting the patient's point of view. The therapist must be prepared to be dismissed in this attempt, which is likely to be a dismissal of the patient's subjectivity; if and when this happens, the therapist is advised to refrain from responding argumentatively. Instead, positive reframing of the key member's reaction is in order (e.g., "This helps me better understand your point of view"), followed by a request for another meeting. Often times, advocacy is released slowly and in small doses.

If some advocacy has been carried out successfully, then the therapist may consider mediating between the patient and the key member. I use the term *consider* because this is not always the best option. At times, a small dose of advocacy is enough and the patient and key member can take it from there. Other times, mediation is required. I make it a point to offer mediation to both the patient and the key member in nondemanding terms, suggesting it as a possibility or an idea that may or may not be good. If accepted, mediation is done via a joint meeting or two. The purpose of this entire process is to open avenues in the patients' social context and let them walk those themselves.

Intervention 4: Altering the Reformulated Depressive Position

The central goal of psychotherapy with people suffering from complex depression is to ameliorate the reformulated depressive position. I take this a step further by arguing that any therapeutic modality that is proven effective for noncomplex depression (for a review, see Guideline Development Panel for the Treatment of Depressive Disorders, 2022) but that does not produce a change in the reformulated depressive position is destined to be ineffective in ameliorating complex depression. The rationale for this seemingly bold statement is covered thoroughly in the previous chapters and can be summarized here with a single sentence: to the extent that the reformulated depressive position lies dormant in patients' inner world following therapy, it will then activate the ecodynamic patterns that will lead to a relapse and likely a more complex one.

To illustrate, take two empirically supported therapeutic packages that have been compellingly shown to alleviate depressive symptoms and disorders, including chronic depression: interpersonal psychotherapy (IPT; Klerman &

Weissman, 1994) and cognitive behavioral analysis system of psychotherapy (CBASP; McCullough, 2000, 2006). Both treatments appear to have comparable efficacy vis-à-vis reducing depression (Schramm et al., 2011).

IPT was developed in the context of treatment for acute, major depressive disorder but was quickly adapted to chronic and suicidal forms of depression (Markowitz, 1998; Tang et al., 2009). This brief (16 weekly sessions) manualized therapy modality draws heavily from the interpersonal psychoanalytic schools of thought represented primarily by Harry Stack Sullivan and Karen Horney, primarily from their focus on interpersonal causes of psychopathology. Unlike interpersonal psychoanalysis, IPT does not attempt to directly change patients' inner life; it aims to change patients' social environment by training them to improve their interpersonal conduct. Although no homework is provided, active interpersonal and emotion-based techniques are utilized in each session; examples include assigning patients the "sick role" and educating them about the interpersonal context of depression, detailed interpersonal inquiry, decision, analysis, role playing, and others. One or more of the following four interpersonal areas are targeted for change: complicated grief, role transition, role dispute, and impaired interpersonal skills. IPT therapists explicitly refrain from working on transference–countertransference exchanges, although they may be aware of them. Unlike psychodynamic psychotherapy, IPT does not utilize free associations and/or dreams as vehicles for understanding unconscious conflict, arguably because the latter two are not construed as a major causal agent in the onset and maintenance of depression.

IPT certainly helps in alleviating depressive symptoms, even in chronic and suicidal depression. However, both research and clinical practice suggest that this effect is not long lasting. Indeed, if IPT were effective in managing the complex manifestation of depression described here, we would all be using it and the problem of complex depression would be solved. Clearly, this is not the case: I believe that the reason is IPT does not alter patients' criticism-based affect, criticism-related affect-regulatory maneuvers, and toxic mental representations of self with other. When these exist below the radar of symptomatic improvement, they are likely to give rise to depressive ecodynamics. This is unfortunate because IPT techniques can be easily integrated with psychodynamic work that is likely to be effective in ameliorating the reformulated depressive position. In fact, two therapeutic packages appear to integrate dynamic and interpersonal work: dynamic interpersonal therapy and the core conflictual relationship theme method. Dynamic interpersonal therapy (Lemma et al., 2011) was developed in London, England. The core conflictual relationship theme method is a version of supportive expressive psychotherapy developed originally by Lester Luborsky (1984) at the University of Pennsylvania in Philadelphia, and further upgraded by Jacques Barber (currently at Adelphi University in New York) and colleagues (Wiseman & Barber, 2004).

CBASP is an integrative therapeutic modality developed specifically for chronic depression. Similar to IPT, CBASP focuses on patients' interpersonal context, predicated on the assumption that their interpersonal behavior is problematic and in turn leads to social disconnection. Unlike IPT, however, the therapist intensely uses the therapeutic relationship in CBASP to provide feedback to patients on the type of behavior that is directed to the therapist and may also lead to their isolation. This is akin to transference work in psychodynamic psychotherapy, with the exception that unconscious material (affect and defense, conflict, mental representation) is not illuminated. In addition to this focal intervention, CBASP also includes a host of behavioral, cognitive, and problem-solving interventions, all applied to interpersonal material. James P. McCullough, the originator of CBASP, also strongly recommended that this therapy be augmented with antidepressant medications (McCullough, 2000). While CBASP traditionally lasts for 12 weeks, there have been recent calls to extend the length of treatment (Schramm et al., 2020).

As with IPT, I believe that CBASP is fundamentally an excellent therapeutic modality, but it falls short of providing a comprehensive solution to complex depression because it does not go far enough in addressing the deep-seated components of the positions. This gap is even more poignant for CBASP than IPT for three reasons: First, CBASP is already defined as an integrative therapy, and its reliance on transference work is inherently included in the CBASP protocol. Thus, unlike IPT therapists who refrain from addressing the therapeutic relationship, including therapeutic ruptures, in CBASP the road from working on these ruptures to working on affect, defense, and mental representation is very short. Second, psychodynamic work is already shown to be effective in reducing not only noncomplex depression but also treatment-resistant depression compatible with the various manifestations of complex depression described here. Specifically, in the Tavistock Adult Depression Study (TADS; D. Taylor, 2015), Fonagy et al. (2015) showed that a manual-based, long-term psychodynamic psychotherapy lasting for approximately 18 months (sessions held once weekly) decreased treatment-resistant depressive symptoms more than nonpsychodynamic treatment as usual. The TADS manual is based on a prototypical psychodynamic therapy inspired predominantly by classical psychoanalysis and British object relations theory. The treatment consists of a profound investigation of affect, conflict, defense, object relations, and transference exchanges, conducted in a receptive and empathic atmosphere that attunes not only to the past but also to the here and now. Further analyses of the TADS data revealed that patients who were particularly self-critical did not benefit from this type of treatment (Rost et al., 2019), suggesting that even this excellent treatment is limited in terms of diffusing the reformulated depressive position. I wonder whether an integration of CBASP with the psychodynamic TADS modality would actually yield effects for self-critical patients. As an integrative psychotherapist applying interventions included in both modalities, I am inclined to answer this question in the affirmative.

This treatise is certainly not intended to teach the psychodynamics-oriented reader how to conduct psychodynamic psychotherapy. Instead, I offer two points of emphasis that I find helpful for neutralizing the reformulated depressive position via psychodynamic work: (a) dilute the reformulated depressive position's impact and (b) circumvent the reformulated depressive position.

Diluting the Impact of the Reformulated Depressive Position
First and foremost, psychodynamic work should aim to dilute the impact of the reformulated depressive position. My clinical experience is teaching me that the best way to do this is to process (with the patient) the links between the three components of the reformulated depressive position: affect, regulatory maneuvers, and mental presentations. Namely, whenever patients bring up one of these components (e.g., affect), I wait for them to connect it to another component (e.g., affect-regulatory maneuver) and then I immediately comment on this link in a way that questions the extent to which it is mandatory: "Just because you feel shame doesn't necessarily mean that you need to immerse yourself in work." When a comment like this is iterated and reiterated (Rogerian therapists may call it a *reflection*, whereas psychoanalytic ego psychology therapists would label it an *interpretation of defense*), this likely opens patients up to the possibility that the way they regulate their affect is iatrogenic and they should experiment with other regulatory material. The same tactic should be applied to the link between affect and mental representations of self and others ("Your experience of shame is not necessarily a smoking gun proving that you are deficient") and affect-regulatory maneuvers and mental presentations ("It may sound tragic, but just because you will now immerse yourself in work doesn't necessarily mean that your boss will turn out to be an accepting person").

My underlying assumption, developed in the course of clinical work, is that the weaker the links between the three components of the reformulated depressive position, the less central the place it occupies in the psyche. In Lori's case, extensive work has been done to weaken the three links—especially that between affect and mental representations of self and others.

LORI: [Opening the session] So I am in the pits. Nothing changes, nothing works.

GOLAN: In what way does nothing change?

LORI: Same old stuff. I am buried at home, doing nothing. Feels like wanting to do nothing. But that is because I am nothing.

GOLAN: Wow, that was a smart move!

LORI: What do you mean?

GOLAN: I mean smart from the point of view of The Story that this bullying part of you is advancing, the one we have been discussing all along. See how this part just made the move from feeling bummed out, feeling that you want to do nothing, to describing yourself as "a no thing."

LORI: [Dismayed] Golan, you are just playing with words. You know exactly what I mean.

GOLAN: No, I am not playing with words, at least not this time. And yes, I know what this bullying part of you means: This part means to convince you that you are what you feel. Time and again, we are seeing this: You decide what you are based on what you feel. Provided, of course, that the feeling is negative. When you feel somewhat good, like that time you won that tournament, this did not make you think good things about yourself.

LORI: Because it was transient. A glitch in time.

GOLAN: Everything is transient, and the bully's story really doesn't hold, logically speaking: If you feel bad, you are bad. If you feel good, this is transient and has no bearing on you. Doesn't make sense. But I am not trying here to argue with the bully's logic. I am trying to show you how the bully narrates his story.

LORI: [Sarcastically] So please go ahead and indulge me. Tell me how.

GOLAN: Well, it was just here in the room: jumping from feeling to self-description. When you declare that you are nothing, what else could be said? There is really nothing else to add. End of story. But this is what we are trying to do: Instead of ending the story, we are trying to reread it.

LORI: You are trying. I have given up.

GOLAN: No, you haven't, or you wouldn't be here. But it is tough to reread a story that is so compelling. Plus, this is the one story you feel and think you have. If I "take" this story away from you, you will be story-less. A good reason to be sarcastic.

LORI: [Smiles in admission]

Circumventing the Reformulated Depressive Position
The second key point in neutralizing the depressive position is that psychodynamic work should aim to circumvent the reformulated depressive position by focusing on adaptive, resilience-related components. Such components pertain to positive affect, adaptive affect-regulatory maneuvers, and positive mental representations of an obvious emotion such as joy.

However, I am more interested in identifying instances in which patients experience two other types of positive affect: enthusiasm and curiosity. Enthusiasm is rarely distinguished from other forms of positive affect (Frenzel et al., 2009; for a focus on displayed enthusiasm, see Moè, 2016), while curiosity has recently been examined as a distinct emotional quality that serves as a robust dimension of resilience (Denneson et al., 2017). Together, I submit that they comprise the affective basis of authenticity or, in Winnicott's (1965) terms, the *true self*. Even the most disturbed patients use affect-regulatory maneuvers, although I admit that this is often difficult to see. My particular favorite is humor, which is considered a salient protective factor. I strive to identify and emphasize even the slightest expressions of patient humor, and I try my own humor on them on a trial-and-error basis. Finally, with respect to positive mental representations of the self and others, my experience teaches me that even in the most depressed life story, encounters with nurturing and supportive others can be identified. In fact, owing to an apparently inherent bias toward negative autobiographical memories in depressed patients, these individuals are more likely to bring up positive descriptions of other people compared with positive self-descriptions. When this happens, I encourage patients to elaborate and then link them to position affect (primarily enthusiasm and curiosity) and adaptive affect-regulatory mechanisms (e.g., humor). In this way, resilience-related positions are forms, and focusing on them activates the very adaptive structures emphasized by Sidney Blatt. And with the mention of Blatt, I come full circle in this treatise. This seems like an adequate place to conclude it—for now.

EPILOGUE
Afterthoughts and Looking to the Future

For numerous reasons, epilogues are my favorite part to write. The most important reason is likely also the most straightforward: When I write the epilogue, this means that I have completed the journey. Good, bad, or ugly, the deed is done. Now it is time to sit back and reflect (not relax). Epilogues are offered as a collection of afterthoughts on the journey and of half-baked plans for building on it for the purpose of envisioning the future. Accordingly, as I thank you, dear reader, for accompanying me in this expedition, allow me to unravel this collection and present my afterthoughts and related plans for the future.

AFTERTHOUGHTS ON COMPLEX DEPRESSION

In this segment, I explicate on several afterthoughts and reflections on the materials presented in this treatise.

---

https://doi.org/10.1037/0000377-010
Complex Depression: The Role of Personality Dynamics and Social Ecology, by G. Shahar
Copyright © 2024 by the American Psychological Association. All rights reserved.

Afterthought 1: The Extension of Self-Criticism Into Ecodynamics

I concluded *Erosion* with the following words: "So it looks like self-criticism and I are stuck with each other. It is rather ironic that this has become clear as I turn the final page on such a prolonged (2-decade) segment of my life's work" (Shahar, 2015a, p. 161). Almost a decade later and reflecting on this treatise, I can say that I am still stuck with self-criticism but the two of us are not alone: We are joined by additional personality processes—namely, those that comprise the reformulated depressive position. Moreover, through this treatise, these personality processes and I have managed to extend ourselves beyond the inner world and toward the social context, thus developing the ecodynamics theory. Although the seeds of this extension were present in *Erosion*, I am gratified that they have matured in this book. The more comprehensive our depiction of the person nested in their various contexts, the closer we will get to understanding their suffering.

Afterthought 2: We Still Have a Long Way to Go

Despite the progress in theory and research on unipolar depression outlined in this treatise and elsewhere, I find it amazing that we (the scientific and clinical community) are far from understanding it to the point of minimizing its toll, if not eradicating it altogether. To wit, this highly unsatisfactory state of the field is not unique to unipolar depression: it is easily applicable to virtually all other mental disorders. My amazement, however, stems both from the fact that depression is one of the first mental disorders recognized and documented in writing and from the enormous efforts of scientists to understand it and of clinicians to control it (and of scientists-clinicians such as myself to do both).

In trying to fathom the reasons for the limited success in understanding and treating unipolar depression, I identify two: one refers to the condition and the other to the nature of our scientific understanding. With respect to the nature of depression, it is important to highlight the dynamic nature of this clinical condition. Depression mutates not only within and between individuals but also within social contexts and across time. Thus, it is easy to forget that it was not long ago that we did not have internet and thus could not develop depression and suicidality online (Morrison & Gore, 2010; but see Odgers & Jensen, 2020; the magnitude of the effect of the internet on depression is far from being settled). With respect to our scientific understanding, the inverse is true: scientific understanding is constrained by the methodology and technology that enables it, and both the methodology and technology are developing relatively slowly. Later, I refer to recent developments in methodology and technology and how these correspond to the theory advanced in this treatise.

Afterthought 3: Unexpected Advances

Although scientific inquiry evolves slowly, it often does so in unexpected ways. We are currently witnessing such an unexpected turn: one that materializes past calls for the synthesis of the quantitative sciences and technology on the one hand and the hermeneutic disciplines (the humanities, social theory, and anthropology) on the other (Snow, 1959; see also the Introduction, this volume). Manifestations for such synthesis are numerous, including the emerging fields of historiometry (quantitative study of outstanding figures; Simonton, 1998), digital humanities (application of computing/digital technologies to various disciplines within the humanities, such as literary texts; Eve, 2022), genetic epidemiology (study of the interplay between genetic and environmental factors in population health and disease; Seyerle & Avery, 2013), developmental origins of health and disease (Heindel & Vandenberg, 2015), network science (Börner et al., 2007), and others. The more these interdisciplinary fields thrive and the more central their influence on the training of the next generation of scientists, practitioners, and scientist-practitioners, the better situated we will be in terms of understanding and solving major problems, including unipolar depression. I hope that this book, which is written from an interdisciplinary perspective, constitutes a step in this direction. Let us now consider future plans for research and practice.

FUTURE DIRECTIONS IN RESEARCH

The following are three central future directions for empirical research that emanate from the present treatise.

Gradations of Depression Complexity

Throughout the book and particularly in Chapter 1, I have implied that depression complexity is a categorical variable presumably composed of three levels: noncomplex depression, moderately complex depression, and highly complex depression. Although such classification is reasonable, it is far from being supported by research for the simple reason that research into the distribution of depression complexity does not exist. This is so because currently there is no consensus definition of depression complexity. In fact, the few existing definitions of depression complexity are a posteriori (i.e., derived from exploratory data analysis) and quite narrow (i.e., they focus only on chronicity or only on suicidality). This gap in the present state of the science is exactly why I wrote this book. Indeed, the Depression Complexity Scale (DCS; presented in Chapter 7) is, to my knowledge, the only theory-based measure of depression. Accordingly, utilization of this measure in research should provide information about the distribution and gradation of depression complexity. Such information is crucial for clinical assessment and treatment planning. Statistical techniques such as taxometrics (Schmidt et al., 2004) should target the possibility that depression complexity is continuous rather than binary or categorical (i.e., exhibiting a taxon).

Network Analysis of the Reformulated Object Relations Theory

The network approach to psychopathology in general (Borsboom & Cramer, 2013; Fried et al., 2017) and to depression in particular (e.g., Fried et al., 2016) has drawn substantial attention in the clinical literature. Central to this approach is the idea that depression (or any other type of psychopathology) is best understood as a dynamic system in which a web of symptoms interact which each other in specific constellations, resulting in vicious circles that are often hard to escape. Accordingly, more severe psychopathology is characterized by a denser network in which the system is more resistant to change (Pe et al., 2015).

The network approach is particularly relevant to testing the reformulated object relations theory advanced here. Specifically, I theorized in Chapter 3 that the reformulated depressive position is characterized by strong links (i.e., a *denser network* in network theory) between demeaning affect, its regulation, and criticism-based mental representations of the self and others. Thus, it could be hypothesized that the denser the network comprising these elements, the more complex the manifestation of the depression. State-of-the-science methods for estimating networks using Gaussian graphical modeling (Epskamp & Fried, 2018) with the *qgraph* package in R statistical software (Epskamp et al., 2012) can be implemented to test this hypothesis. Implementation of such a study is very high on my to-do list.

In the context of empirical research efforts aimed at testing the reformulated object relations theory, special attention should be given to tracking the developmental trajectories of the reformulated depressive position. Original theoretical writings of Klein and her followers, as well as of other theoreticians working from the framework of object relations theory, have posited that the depressive position develops very early (i.e., roughly after 6 months of life; see J. R. Greenberg & Mitchell, 1983). This would be very difficult, albeit not insurmountable, to examine empirically. An alternate hypothesis is that the reformulated depressive position develops during the first 5 years of life, which could shed some light on the phenomenon of preschool depression (Luby, 2010). My hunch, however, is that the reformulated depressive position develops slowly over the first decade of life and then peaks during early adolescence, when abstract thinking matures in a way that leads to the formation of clearly delineated mental representations of self-in relations, including the ability (or, in the case of depression, the failure) to develop a sense of agency (McAdams, 2013). To the extent that such a hypothesis is confirmed, this could shed light on the surge in depression-spectrum psychopathology in early adolescence (Hammen, 2009).

Systematic and Rigorous Assessment of the Social Context

The ecodynamics theory advanced in this book pertains to eight patterns of person–context exchanges (see Chapter 4). Three patterns are particularly pertinent to the understanding of complex depression: action, immersion, and extraction. The Ecodynamics Questionnaire (EDQ) presented in Chapter 7 appears adequate for assessing tumultuousness. The EDQ can be augmented by self-report and interview-based measures of life stress, perceived social support, and positive life events. In turn, these measures can provide a good picture of how much the person generates stress and suffers from a dearth of perceived social support and positive life events.

Immersion and extraction pertain to the extent to which a person embeds themselves in a putative social environment (which exacerbates their depression). What measures may augment the EDQ in assessing this embeddedness? Herein, I turn your attention to social network analysis (SNA), a quantitative interdisciplinary procedure for investigating the properties of the social context using networks (similar to that noted in the previous item) and graph theory (e.g., Kadushin, 2011; Scott & Carrington, 2014). Several SNA indices may highlight the extent to which the putative social context "closes in" on the person, including *density* (the proportion of direct ties in a network relative to the total number possible), *cohesion* (the degree to which actors are connected directly to each other by cohesive bonds), and *homophily* (the extent to which actors form ties with similar versus dissimilar others; similarity can be defined by demographic, temperamental, and personality characteristics). While some research exists regarding the relevance of these indicators to the understanding of depressive symptoms (Morita et al., 2022), I am not aware of similar research focusing on SNA and depressive vulnerability.

Neurobiology

Last, but far from least, is the importance of directing future research efforts to understand neurobiological processes implicated in the reformulated depressive position. Earlier, I (Shahar, 2016) invoked the hypothesis that genetic polymorphisms suspected in the onset of depression (e.g., the serotonin-transporter-linked promoter region [5-HTTLPR] and brain-derived neurotrophic factor [BDNF] polymorphisms; see Caspi et al., 2003; Fratelli et al., 2020) are actually *self-focus genes*, propelling us to look inside regardless of mood for the purpose of knowing ourselves. Consistent with this view is research tying 5-HTTLPR and BDNF to attention in general (Chiao & Blizinsky, 2010) and to depressive rumination in particular (Hilt et al., 2007). The link between these polymorphisms and self-focused attention and/or self-criticism on the one hand and self-knowledge on the other is likely mediated by activity of lateral cortical structures (Longe et al., 2010), particularly the dorsal lateral prefrontal cortex (Hooley et al., 2005, 2009; Longe et al., 2010; Northoff, 2007). Furthermore, connectivity involving the right superior anterior temporal lobe and the subgenual cingulate cortex and adjacent septal region during self (versus other) blaming was shown to predict depressive relapse (Lythe et al., 2015). The next steps in this neuroscientific endeavor include examining (a) the links between activation of these brain structures in the context of self-critical tasks, (b) activities of brain structures involved in the perception of punitive others (for efforts leading the way, see Halamová et al., 2022 and Kanovský et al., 2022), (c) brain activity underlying self-critical demeaning affect such as guilt and shame (Miyauchi et al., 2022), and (d) brain activity implicated in defense mechanisms and coping strategies, particularly those geared toward regulating self-critical, demeaning affect (e.g., Cieri & Esposito, 2019).

FUTURE DIRECTIONS FOR PRACTICE

In this section, I describe numerous future directions for psychological practice.

Assessment

The three questionnaires that I have developed and described in Chapter 7—the DCS, the Reformulated Depressive Position Inventory, and the EDQ—should not be assumed to be sufficient for the assessment of complex depression, the reformulated depressive position, and ecodynamics. In the previous section dedicated to future directions in research, I noted several ways in which ecodynamics could be further assessed (e.g., SNA). Herein, I note briefly that several existing assessment procedures could be adopted for assessment of the reformulated depressive position in clinical practice. I refer first to the Shedler–Westen Assessment Procedure (SWAP-200; Shedler, 2022; Westen et al., 2012). This psychodynamically informed, clinician-based psychological test aims to assess deep layers of an individual's personality with an emphasis on the personality–psychopathology link. The SWAP-200 asks clinicians (or people highly knowledgeable with the target person, when used in other contexts) to rate the target person on a set of 200 personality-descriptive items. Respondents use a 1- to 7-point Likert scale to classify a limited number of items into each level. This procedure, also known as the Q-sort (S. J. Beck, 1962; Block, 1961), forces the rater to choose between the characteristics that are most representative and less (or least) representative of the target person. The Q-sort procedure requires considerable effort from the rater, but this effort pays off because the end result is a profile of personality traits, processes, and disorders that predict highly relevant behaviors and shed light on an extant clinical picture. My clinical experience with the SWAP-200 is not only fruitful in its own right but its 200 items include all of the descriptors needed to cover the basic elements of the reformulated depressive position: self-critical demeaning affect, affect regulation, and mental representations of self and others. I therefore plan to reach out to the SWAP originators in an attempt to collaborate for the purpose of deriving a SWAP-based measure of the reformulated depressive position.

Psychotherapy

Although I alluded to the following issue in Chapter 8, I reemphasize here that the most challenging part of treating people with complex depression (and more generally, treating people with complex and treatment-resistant psychopathology) is therapist demoralization. To reiterate from previous chapters, such demoralization is practically inevitable because patients (a) drill their own demoralization into the therapist's psyche (projective identification) and also (b) create the type of social environment that (owing to its tumultuous and even hostile nature) depletes the therapist's energy, often rendering them helpless and hopeless (e.g., Shahar, 2004).

Accordingly, here is an opportunity to reemphasize what was noted earlier: Don't go at it alone. I have highlighted the need to constantly receive supervision and (more often than not) to supervise yourself while working with complex cases. Here I add the wonderful potential of *peer supervision*, which pertains to a formal, ongoing, and stable framework within which a therapist both consults and provides consultation to another therapist (one that preferably works with a similar type of clientele). The structure of this exchange is complementary and reciprocal rather than hierarchical and is likely to bolster openness and a sense of comradery (Amanvermez et al., 2020; Golia & McGovern, 2015). Such openness and comradery are powerful remedies of demoralization that ensues from working with complex cases. We discover that (a) we are not alone in the demoralization, (b) there are numerous ways to address it, and (c) there is profound meaning in surviving it. Moreover, almost invariably, peer supervision is not purchased, making in particularly cost-effective. For all of these advantages, I increasingly gravitate toward this approach, often as an add on to the more traditional form of supervision. My experience thus far is highly positive.

Another major challenge for psychotherapy with complex depression, which was noted in Chapter 8 but could and should be developed further, is the tenacity with which patients experience their work through their reformulated depressive position. As I posited in *Erosion* (Shahar, 2015a), malignant self-criticism may be particularly appealing (i.e., addictive) because it is compelling: It provides a powerful explanatory framework for how the self and world are built. As a consequence and in a manner reminiscent of Sigmund Freud's (1914) early recognition of the tenacity of neurosis, it is very difficult (and often insufficient) to change this position solely by using insight-oriented psychotherapeutic techniques such as psychodynamic interpretation. As strongly argued by Freud (1914), patients may gain insight into the presence and determinants of the reformulated depressive position, only to be strongly influenced by this position immediately afterward. Even "warmer" psychodynamic work—such as relieving the position in the therapeutic relationship, in the transference, and then reflecting on such relieving—would often not be enough to nullify the formidable power of the position. As you already know, I am strongly in favor of using active/directive techniques, alongside exploratory ones, in psychotherapy with complex depression (see Chapter 8). Nevertheless, despite the potential of these active/directive (primarily cognitive behavior techniques) to augment exploratory, psychodynamic, and existential work (see Shahar & Govrin, 2017), they are likely not enough to undermine the toxic position, at least not in the short term. Because I am cognizant of the devastating effects of viewing the self and world from the perspective of the reformulated depressive position, I am constantly looking for new ways to short-circuit them. My hunch is that a potentially useful avenue for undermining the reformulated position is already waiting on the other side of the door.

More specifically, I am interested in interventions such as psychedelic-assisted psychotherapy (Reiff et al., 2020), digitally induced psychedelic experiences (Carhart-Harris et al., 2022), virtual reality techniques (Falconer et al., 2014), and hypnotherapy (Harris, 2021). Their common denominator is that they allow the therapist to work with the patient for the purpose of inducing visual-perceptual experiences (e.g., visions of colors, sights, and sounds, or attention to avatars). In my opinion, these visual-perceptual alterations enable the patient to feel that they are entering a new experiential world, one not governed by previous perceptions and convictions. I believe that this is a first step in which the patient summons from within thoughts and feelings that are inconsistent with those cognitions and emotions that propel their psychopathology. From here, patients (already under the influence of the special techniques) can begin to experience the self and others in a different, more benign way. Consistent with this supposition, initial research has demonstrated that compassion-based virtual reality reduces self-criticism (Falconer et al., 2014), as does consumption of the natural psychedelic ayahuasca (Domínguez-Clavé et al., 2022). I believe that in the future, we will see these types of interventions as a conducive, perhaps essential, element of treating complex depression.

References

Abba-Aji, A., Li, D., Hrabok, M., Shalaby, R., Gusnowski, A., Vuong, W., Surood, S., Nkire, N., Li, X. M., Greenshaw, A. J., & Agyapong, V. I. O. (2020). COVID-19 pandemic and mental health: Prevalence and correlates of new-onset obsessive-compulsive symptoms in a Canadian province. *International Journal of Environmental Research and Public Health, 17*(19), 6986. https://doi.org/10.3390/ijerph17196986

Abbar, M., Demattei, C., El-Hage, W., Llorca, P. M., Samalin, L., Demaricourt, P., Gaillard, R., Courtet, P., Vaiva, G., Gorwood, P., Fabbro, P., & Jollant, F. (2022). Ketamine for the acute treatment of severe suicidal ideation: Double blind, randomised placebo controlled trial. *BMJ, 376*, e067194. https://doi.org/10.1136/bmj-2021-067194

Abela, J. R., Webb, C. A., Wagner, C., Ho, M. H. R., & Adams, P. (2006). The role of self-criticism, dependency, and hassles in the course of depressive illness: A multiwave longitudinal study. *Personality and Social Psychology Bulletin, 32*(3), 328–338. https://doi.org/10.1177/0146167205280911

Abramson, L. Y., Metalsky, G. I., & Alloy, L. B. (1989). Hopelessness depression: A theory-based subtype of depression. *Psychological Review, 96*(2), 358–372. https://doi.org/10.1037/0033-295X.96.2.358

Adams, G. C., Balbuena, L., Meng, X., & Asmundson, G. J. (2016). When social anxiety and depression go together: A population study of comorbidity and associated consequences. *Journal of Affective Disorders, 206*, 48–54. https://doi.org/10.1016/j.jad.2016.07.031

Adams, T. E., Holman Jones, S., & Ellis, C. (2015). *Autoethnography*. Oxford University Press.

Addis, M. E. (2008). Gender and depression in men. *Clinical Psychology: Science and Practice, 15*(3), 153–168. https://doi.org/10.1111/j.1468-2850.2008.00125.x

Addis, M. E., & Mahalik, J. R. (2003). Men, masculinity, and the contexts of help seeking. *American Psychologist, 58*(1), 5–14. https://doi.org/10.1037/0003-066X.58.1.5

Aderka, I. M., Gillihan, S. J., McLean, C. P., & Foa, E. B. (2013). The relationship between posttraumatic and depressive symptoms during prolonged exposure with and without cognitive restructuring for the treatment of posttraumatic stress disorder. *Journal of Consulting and Clinical Psychology, 81*(3), 375–382. https://doi.org/10.1037/a0031523

Adorno, T. W., Frenkel-Brunswik, E., Levinson, D. J., & Sanford, R. N. (1950). *The authoritarian personality*. Harper and Row.

Ainsworth, M. D. S., & Bell, S. M. (1970). Attachment, exploration, and separation: Illustrated by the behavior of one-year-olds in a strange situation. *Child Development, 41*(1), 49–67. https://doi.org/10.2307/1127388

Akiskal, H. S., Hantouche, E. G., & Allilaire, J. F. (2003). Bipolar II with and without cyclothymic temperament: "Dark" and "sunny" expressions of soft bipolarity. *Journal of Affective Disorders, 73*(1–2), 49–57. https://doi.org/10.1016/S0165-0327(02)00320-8

Alexander, F., & French, T. M. (1946). *Psychoanalytic therapy: Principles and application*. Ronald Press.

Ali, Z., & El-Mallakh, R. S. (2022). Suicidal depression in Ancient Egypt. *Archives of Suicide Research, 26*(3), 1607–1623. https://doi.org/10.1080/13811118.2021.1878079

Almog, O. (2000). *The Sabra: The creation of the New Jew*. University of California Press.

Alqueza, K. L., Pagliaccio, D., Durham, K., Srinivasan, A., Stewart, J. G., & Auerbach, R. P. (2023). Suicidal thoughts and behaviors among adolescent psychiatric inpatients. *Archives of Suicide Research, 27*(2), 353–366. https://doi.org/10.1080/13811118.2021.1999874

Amanvermez, Y., Zeren, Ş. G., Erus, S. M., & Genç, A. B. (2020). Supervision and peer supervision in online setting: Experiences of psychological counselors. *Eurasian Journal of Educational Research, 20*(86), 249–268. https://ejer.com.tr/wp-content/uploads/2021/01/ejer.2020.86.12.pdf

Amati, D., & Shallice, T. (2007). On the emergence of modern humans. *Cognition, 103*(3), 358–385. https://doi.org/10.1016/j.cognition.2006.04.002

American Psychiatric Association. (2000). *Diagnostic and statistical manual of mental disorders* (4th ed., text rev.). https://doi.org/10.1176/appi.books.9780890420249.dsm-iv-tr

American Psychiatric Association. (2022). *Diagnostic and statistical manual of mental disorders* (5th ed., text rev.). https://doi.org/10.1176/appi.books.9780890425787

Amitay, O., Mongrain, M., & Fazaa, N. (2008). Love and control: Self-criticism in parents and daughters and perceptions of romantic partners. *Personality and Individual Differences, 44*(1), 75–85. https://doi.org/10.1016/j.paid.2007.07.020

Andersen, S. M., & Chen, S. (2002). The relational self: An interpersonal social-cognitive theory. *Psychological Review, 109*(4), 619–645. https://doi.org/10.1037/0033-295X.109.4.619

Anderson, D. M., Cesur, R., & Tekin, E. (2015). Youth depression and future criminal behavior. *Economic Inquiry, 53*(1), 294–317. https://doi.org/10.1111/ecin.12145

Angst, J., Gamma, A., Rössler, W., Ajdacic, V., & Klein, D. N. (2009). Long-term depression versus episodic major depression: Results from the prospective Zurich study of a community sample. *Journal of Affective Disorders, 115*(1–2), 112–121. https://doi.org/10.1016/j.jad.2008.09.023

Arnold, K. (2014). Intellectualization and its lookalikes. *Psychoanalytic Review, 101*(5), 615–632. https://doi.org/10.1521/prev.2014.101.5.615

Auerbach, J. S., & Blatt, S. J. (2001). Self-reflexivity, intersubjectivity, and therapeutic change. *Psychoanalytic Psychology, 18*(3), 427–450. https://doi.org/10.1037/0736-9735.18.3.427

Austin, J. T., & Vancouver, J. B. (1996). Goal constructs in psychology: Structure, process, and content. *Psychological Bulletin, 120*(3), 338–375. https://doi.org/10.1037/0033-2909.120.3.338

Ayesa-Arriola, R., Setién-Suero, E., Marques-Feixa, L., Neergaard, K., Butjosa, A., Vázquez-Bourgon, J., Fañanás, L., & Crespo-Facorro, B. (2020). The synergetic effect of childhood trauma and recent stressful events in psychosis: Associated neurocognitive dysfunction. *Acta Psychiatrica Scandinavica, 141*(1), 43–51. https://doi.org/10.1111/acps.13114

Ayuso-Mateos, J. L., Morillo, D., Haro, J. M., Olaya, B., Lara, E., & Miret, M. (2021). Changes in depression and suicidal ideation under severe lockdown restrictions during the first wave of the COVID-19 pandemic in Spain: A longitudinal study in the general population. *Epidemiology and Psychiatric Sciences, 30*, E49. https://doi.org/10.1017/S2045796021000408

Bagby, R. M., Psych, C., Quilty, L. C., & Ryder, A. C. (2008). Personality and depression. *Canadian Journal of Psychiatry, 53*(1), 14–25. https://doi.org/10.1177/070674370805300104

Baldwin, M. W. (1992). Relational schemas and the processing of social information. *Psychological Bulletin, 112*(3), 461–484. https://doi.org/10.1037/0033-2909.112.3.461

Ballard, E. D., Yarrington, J. S., Farmer, C. A., Lener, M. S., Kadriu, B., Lally, N., Williams, D., Machado-Vieira, R., Niciu, M. J., Park, L., & Zarate, C. A., Jr. (2018). Parsing the heterogeneity of depression: An exploratory factor analysis across commonly used depression rating scales. *Journal of Affective Disorders, 231*, 51–57. https://doi.org/10.1016/j.jad.2018.01.027

Bandura, A. (1977). Self-efficacy: Toward a unifying theory of behavioral change. *Psychological Review, 84*(2), 191–215. https://doi.org/10.1037/0033-295X.84.2.191

Bandura, A. (1978). The self system in reciprocal determinism. *American Psychologist, 33*(4), 344–358. https://doi.org/10.1037/0003-066X.33.4.344

Bandura, A. (1997). *Self-efficacy: The exercise of control*. W. H. Freeman/Times Books/Henry Holt.

Banks, S. M., & Kerns, R. D. (1996). Explaining high rates of depression in chronic pain: A diathesis-stress framework. *Psychological Bulletin, 119*, 95–110. https://doi.org/10.1037/0033-2909.119.1.95

Bar-Kalifa, E., & Atzil-Slonim, D. (2020). Intrapersonal and interpersonal emotional networks and their associations with treatment outcome. *Journal of Counseling Psychology, 67*(5), 580–594. https://doi.org/10.1037/cou0000415

Bar-Shachar, Y., & Bar-Kalifa, E. (2021). Responsiveness processes and daily experiences of shared reality among romantic couples. *Journal of Social and Personal Relationships, 38*(11), 3156–3176. https://doi.org/10.1177/02654075211017675

Bareket-Bojmel, L., & Shahar, G. (2011). Personality discloses: Emotional and interpersonal effects of self-criticism, openness to experiences, and experiential avoidance on self-disclosure online. *Journal of Social and Clinical Psychology, 30*(7), 732–759. https://doi.org/10.1521/jscp.2011.30.7.732

Bareket-Bojmel, L., Shahar, G., Abu-Kaf, S., & Margalit, M. (2021). Perceived social support, loneliness, and hope during the COVID-19 outbreak: Testing a mediating model in the UK, USA, and Israel. *British Journal of Clinical Psychology, 60*(2), 133–148. https://doi.org/10.1111/bjc.12285

Bareket-Bojmel, L., Shahar, G., & Margalit, M. (2021). COVID-19-related economic anxiety is as high as health anxiety: Findings from the USA, the UK, and Israel. *International Journal of Cognitive Therapy, 14*(3), 566–574. https://doi.org/10.1007/s41811-020-00078-3

Barrera, M., Jr. (1986). Distinctions between social support concepts, measures, and models. *American Journal of Community Psychology, 14*(4), 413–445. https://doi.org/10.1007/BF00922627

Barrett, T. F. (2008). Manic defenses against loneliness in adolescence. *The Psychoanalytic Study of the Child, 63*(1), 111–136. https://doi.org/10.1080/00797308.2008.11800801

Bartholomew, K., & Horowitz, L. M. (1991). Attachment styles among young adults: A test of a four-category model. *Journal of Personality and Social Psychology, 61*(2), 226–244. https://doi.org/10.1037/0022-3514.61.2.226

Baumeister, R. F. (1990). Suicide as escape from self. *Psychological Review, 97*(1), 90–113. https://doi.org/10.1037/0033-295X.97.1.90

Beck, A. T. (1983). Cognitive therapy of depression: New perspectives. In P. J. Clayton & J. E. Barrett (Eds.), *Treatment of depression: Old controversies and new approaches* (pp. 265–290). Raven.

Beck, A. T. (1996). Beyond belief: A theory of modes, personality, and psychopathology. In P. M. Salkovskis (Ed.), *Frontiers of cognitive therapy* (pp. 1–25). Guilford Press.

Beck, A. T., Epstein, N., Brown, G., & Steer, R. (1988). *Beck Anxiety Inventory* [Database record]. APA PsycTests.

Beck, A. T., Steer, R. A., & Brown, G. K. (1996). *Manual for the Beck Depression Inventory–II*. The Psychological Corporation.

Beck, S. J. (1962). The Q-sort method in personality assessment and psychiatric research. *Archives of General Psychiatry, 7*(3), 230–231. https://doi.org/10.1001/archpsyc.1962.01720030076023

Beggan, J. K. (2019). On the downside of heroism: Grey zone limitations on the value of social and physical risk heroism. *Heroism Science, 4*(2), 1–35. https://doi.org/10.26736/hs.2019.02.05

Bergfeld, I. O., Mantione, M., Figee, M., Schuurman, P. R., Lok, A., & Denys, D. (2018). Treatment-resistant depression and suicidality. *Journal of Affective Disorders, 235*, 362–367. https://doi.org/10.1016/j.jad.2018.04.016

Besser, A. (2004). Self- and best friend assessments of personality vulnerability and defenses in the prediction of depression. *Social Behavior and Personality, 32*(6), 559–594. https://doi.org/10.2224/sbp.2004.32.6.559

Beutler, L. E., Williams, R. E., Wakefield, P. J., & Entwistle, S. R. (1995). Bridging scientist and practitioner perspectives in clinical psychology. *American Psychologist, 50*(12), 984–994. https://doi.org/10.1037/0003-066X.50.12.984

Billig, M. (1999). *Freudian repression: Conversation creating the unconscious*. Cambridge University Press. https://doi.org/10.1017/CBO9780511490088

Bion, W. R. (1959). Attacks on linking. *The International Journal of Psycho-Analysis, 40*, 308–315.

Bion, W. R. (1961). *Experiences in groups*. Routledge.

Bjerkeset, O., Romundstad, P., & Gunnell, D. (2008). Gender differences in the association of mixed anxiety and depression with suicide. *The British Journal of Psychiatry, 192*(6), 474–475. https://doi.org/10.1192/bjp.bp.107.045203

Blass, R. B. (2010). Affirming 'That's not psycho-analysis!' On the value of the politically incorrect act of attempting to define the limits of our field. *The International Journal of Psycho-Analysis, 91*(1), 81–89. https://doi.org/10.1111/j.1745-8315.2009.00211.x

Blass, R. B., & Blatt, S. J. (1992). Attachment and separateness. A theoretical context for the integration of object relations theory with self psychology. *The Psychoanalytic Study of the Child, 47*(1), 189–203. https://doi.org/10.1080/00797308.1992.11822671

Blatt, S. J. (1974). Levels of object representation in anaclitic and introjective depression. *The Psychoanalytic Study of the Child, 29*(1), 107–157. https://doi.org/10.1080/00797308.1974.11822616

Blatt, S. J. (1995). The destructiveness of perfectionism. Implications for the treatment of depression. *American Psychologist, 50*(12), 1003–1020. https://doi.org/10.1037/0003-066X.50.12.1003

Blatt, S. J. (2004). *Experiences of depression: Theoretical, clinical, and research perspectives*. American Psychological Association. https://doi.org/10.1037/10749-000

Blatt, S. J. (2008). *Polarities of experience: Relatedness and self-definition in personality development, psychopathology, and the therapeutic process*. American Psychological Association. https://doi.org/10.1037/11749-000

Blatt, S. J., Auerbach, J. S., & Levy, K. N. (1997). Mental representations in personality development, psychopathology, and the therapeutic process. *Review of General Psychology, 1*(4), 351–374. https://doi.org/10.1037/1089-2680. 1.4.351

Blatt, S. J., Chevron, E. S., Quinlan, D. M., Schaffer, C. E., & Wein, S. (1988). *The assessment of qualitative and structural dimensions of object representations* (Rev. ed.). Yale University.

Blatt, S. J., D'Afflitti, J. P., & Quinlan, D. M. (1976). Experiences of depression in normal young adults. *Journal of Abnormal Psychology, 85*(4), 383–389. https://doi.org/10.1037/0021-843X.85.4.383

Blatt, S. J., Shahar, G., & Zuroff, D. C. (2001). Anaclitic (sociotropic) and introjective (autonomous) dimensions. *Psychotherapy: Theory, Research, & Practice, 38*(4), 449–454. https://doi.org/10.1037/0033-3204.38.4.449

Blatt, S. J., Stayner, D. A., Auerbach, J. S., & Behrends, R. S. (1996). Change in object and self-representations in long-term, intensive, inpatient treatment of seriously disturbed adolescents and young adults. *Psychiatry, 59*(1), 82–107. https://doi.org/10.1080/00332747.1996.11024752

Blatt, S. J., & Zuroff, D. C. (1992). Interpersonal relatedness and self-definition: Two prototypes for depression. *Clinical Psychology Review, 12*(5), 527–562. https://doi.org/10.1016/0272-7358(92)90070-O

Blazer, D. G., Kessler, R. C., McGonagle, K. A., & Swartz, M. S. (1994). The prevalence and distribution of major depression in a national community sample: The National Comorbidity Survey. *The American Journal of Psychiatry, 151*(7), 979–986. https://doi.org/10.1176/ajp.151.7.979

Block, J. (1961). *The Q-sort method in personality assessment and psychiatric research*. Charles C Thomas. https://doi.org/10.1037/13141-000

Block, J. (1995). A contrarian view of the five-factor approach to personality description. *Psychological Bulletin, 117*(2), 187–215. https://doi.org/10.1037/0033-2909.117.2.187

Block, J. (2001). Millennial contrarianism: The five-factor approach to personality description 5 years later. *Journal of Research in Personality, 35*(1), 98–107. https://doi.org/10.1006/jrpe.2000.2293

Block, J. (2002). *Personality as an affect-processing system: Toward an integrative theory*. Psychology Press. https://doi.org/10.4324/9781410602466

Bohart, A. C., O'Hara, M., & Leitner, L. M. (1998). Empirically violated treatments: Disenfranchisement of humanistic and other psychotherapies. *Psychotherapy Research, 8*(2), 141–157. https://doi.org/10.1080/10503309812331332277

Bonanno, G. A. (2004). Loss, trauma, and human resilience: Have we underestimated the human capacity to thrive after extremely aversive events? *American Psychologist, 59*(1), 20–28. https://doi.org/10.1037/0003-066X.59.1.20

Borg, M. B. (2003). Community group analysis: A post-crisis synthesis. *Group Analysis, 36*(2), 228–241. https://doi.org/10.1177/0533316403036002008

Börner, K., Sanyal, S., & Vespignani, A. (2007). Network science. *Annual Review of Information Science & Technology, 41*(1), 537–607. https://doi.org/10.1002/aris.2007.1440410119

Bornstein, R. F. (1998). Depathologizing dependency. *Journal of Nervous and Mental Disease*, *186*(2), 67–73. https://doi.org/10.1097/00005053-199802000-00001

Borsboom, D., & Cramer, A. O. (2013). Network analysis: An integrative approach to the structure of psychopathology. *Annual Review of Clinical Psychology*, *9*, 91–121. https://doi.org/10.1146/annurev-clinpsy-050212-185608

Bowen, M. (1978). *Family therapy in clinical practice*. Aronson.

Bowlby, J. (1969). *Attachment and loss* (Vol. 1). Basic Books.

Boyle, G. J. (2008). Critique of the five-factor model of personality. In G. J. Boyle, G. Matthews, & D. H. Saklofske (Eds.), *The SAGE handbook of personality theory and assessment* (Vol. 1, pp. 295–312). Sage. https://doi.org/10.4135/9781849200462.n14

Bradley, L., Noble, N., & Hendricks, B. (2023). DSM-5-TR: Salient changes. *The Family Journal*, *31*(1), 5–10. https://doi.org/10.1177/10664807221123558

Bromberg, P. M. (1996). Standing in the spaces: The multiplicity of the self and the psychoanalytic situation. *Contemporary Psychoanalysis*, *32*(4), 509–535. https://doi.org/10.1080/00107530.1996.10746334

Bromberg, P. M. (2009). Multiple self-states, the relational mind, and dissociation: A psychoanalytic perspective. In P. F. Dell & J. A. O'Neil (Eds.), *Dissociation and the dissociative disorders: DSM-V and beyond* (pp. 637–652). Routledge/Taylor & Francis Group.

Bronfenbrenner, U. (1977). Toward an experimental ecology of human development. *American Psychologist*, *32*(7), 513–531. https://doi.org/10.1037/0003-066X.32.7.513

Bronfenbrenner, U. (1979). *The ecology of human development: Experiments by nature and design*. Harvard University Press.

Bronfenbrenner, U. (1994). Ecological models of human development. In *International encyclopedia of education*. Oxford: Elsevier. Reprinted in M. Gauvin & M. Cole (Eds.), *Readings on the development of children* (pp. 37–43). Freeman.

Brothers, L. (1990). The social brain: A project for integrating primate behavior and neurophysiology in a new domain. *Concepts in Neuroscience*, *1*, 27–51.

Brown, G. K., Beck, A. T., Steer, R. A., & Grisham, J. R. (2000). Risk factors for suicide in psychiatric outpatients: A 20-year prospective study. *Journal of Consulting and Clinical Psychology*, *68*(3), 371–377. https://doi.org/10.1037/0022-006X.68.3.371

Brown, G. W. (1985). The discovery of expressed emotion: Induction or deduction? In J. Leff & C. Vaughn (Eds.), *Expressed emotion in families* (pp. 7–25). Guilford Press.

Brown, G. W., & Harris, T. H. (1978). *The social origins of depression: A study of psychiatric disorder in women*. Tavistock.

Brown, J. D., & Silberschatz, G. (1989). Dependency, self-criticism, and depressive attributional style. *Journal of Abnormal Psychology*, *98*(2), 187–188. https://doi.org/10.1037/0021-843X.98.2.187

Brunet, J., Sabiston, C. M., O'Loughlin, E., Chaiton, M., Low, N. C., & O'Loughlin, J. L. (2014). Symptoms of depression are longitudinally associated with sedentary behaviors among young men but not among young women. *Preventive Medicine, 60*, 16–20. https://doi.org/10.1016/j.ypmed.2013.12.003

Buckman, J. E. J., Underwood, A., Clarke, K., Saunders, R., Hollon, S. D., Fearon, P., & Pilling, S. (2018). Risk factors for relapse and recurrence of depression in adults and how they operate: A four-phase systematic review and meta-synthesis. *Clinical Psychology Review, 64*, 13–38. https://doi.org/10.1016/j.cpr.2018.07.005

Burton, E., Stice, E., & Seeley, J. R. (2004). A prospective test of the stress-buffering model of depression in adolescent girls: No support once again. *Journal of Consulting and Clinical Psychology, 72*(4), 689–697. https://doi.org/10.1037/0022-006X.72.4.689

Buss, D. M. (1987). Selection, evocation, and manipulation. *Journal of Personality and Social Psychology, 53*(6), 1214–1221. https://doi.org/10.1037/0022-3514.53.6.1214

Bylsma, L. M., Taylor-Clift, A., & Rottenberg, J. (2011). Emotional reactivity to daily events in major and minor depression. *Journal of Abnormal Psychology, 120*(1), 155–167. https://doi.org/10.1037/a0021662

Caputo, A., & Tomai, M. (2020). A systematic review of psychodynamic theories in community psychology: Discovering the unconscious in community work. *Journal of Community Psychology, 48*(6), 2069–2085. https://doi.org/10.1002/jcop.22407

Carhart-Harris, R. L., Wagner, A. C., Agrawal, M., Kettner, H., Rosenbaum, J. F., Gazzaley, A., Nutt, D. J., & Erritzoe, D. (2022). Can pragmatic research, real-world data and digital technologies aid the development of psychedelic medicine? *Journal of Psychopharmacology, 36*(1), 6–11. https://doi.org/10.1177/02698811211008567

Carver, C. S., & White, T. L. (1994). Behavioral inhibition, behavioral activation, and affective responses to impending reward and punishment: The BIS/BAS scales. *Journal of Personality and Social Psychology, 67*(2), 319–333. https://doi.org/10.1037/0022-3514.67.2.319

Casey, P., & Bailey, S. (2011). Adjustment disorders: The state of the art. *World Psychiatry, 10*(1), 11–18. https://doi.org/10.1002/j.2051-5545.2011.tb00003.x

Caspi, A., Sugden, K., Moffit, T. E., Taylor, A., Craig, I. W., Harrington, H., McClay, J., Mill, J., Martin, J., Braithwaite, A., & Poulton, R. (2003). Influence of life stress on depression: Moderation by a polymorphism in the 5-HTT gene. *Science, 301*(5631), 386–389. https://doi.org/10.1126/science.1083968

Celani, D. P. (1999). Applying Fairbairn's object relations theory to the dynamics of the battered woman. *American Journal of Psychotherapy, 53*(1), 60–73.

Centers for Disease Control and Prevention. (2011). Bullying among middle school and high school students—Massachusetts, 2009. *MMWR Morbidity and Mortality Weekly Report, 60*(15), 465–471.

Cerdá, M., Tracy, M., Sánchez, B. N., & Galea, S. (2011). Comorbidity among depression, conduct disorder, and drug use from adolescence to young adulthood: Examining the role of violence exposures. *Journal of Traumatic Stress, 24*(6), 651–659. https://doi.org/10.1002/jts.20696

Cervone, D., Shadel, W. G., & Jencius, S. (2001). Social-cognitive theory of personality assessment. *Personality & Social Psychology Review, 5*, 35–51. https://doi.org/10.1207/S15327957PSPR0501_3

Chadi, N., Ryan, N. C., & Geoffroy, M. C. (2022). COVID-19 and the impacts on youth mental health: Emerging evidence from longitudinal studies. *Canadian Journal of Public Health, 113*(1), 44–52. https://doi.org/10.17269/s41997-021-00567-8

Chandola, T., Marmot, M., & Siegrist, J. (2007). Failed reciprocity in close social relationships and health: Findings from the Whitehall II study. *Journal of Psychosomatic Research, 63*(4), 403–411. https://doi.org/10.1016/j.jpsychores.2007.07.012

Chang, W. C., Ng, C. M., Chan, K. N., Lee, H. C., Chan, S. I., Chiu, S. S., Lee, H. M., Chan, K. W., Wong, M. C., Chan, K. L., Yeung, W. S., Chan, C. W. H., Choy, L. W., Chong, S. Y., Siu, M. W., Lo, T. L., Yan, W. C., Ng, M. K., Poon, L. T., . . . Chen, E. Y. H. (2021). Psychiatric comorbidity in individuals at-risk for psychosis: Relationships with symptoms, cognition and psychosocial functioning. *Early Intervention in Psychiatry, 15*(3), 616–623. https://doi.org/10.1111/eip.12992

Chiao, J. Y., & Blizinsky, K. D. (2010). Culture–gene coevolution of individualism–collectivism and the serotonin transporter gene. *Proceedings of the Royal Society B: Biological Sciences, 277*(1681), 529–537. https://doi.org/10.1098/rspb.2009.1650

Chu, C., Buchman-Schmitt, J. M., Stanley, I. H., Hom, M. A., Tucker, R. P., Hagan, C. R., Rogers, M. L., Podlogar, M. C., Chiurliza, B., Ringer, F. B., Michaels, M. S., Patros, C. H. G., & Joiner, T. E., Jr. (2017). The interpersonal theory of suicide: A systematic review and meta-analysis of a decade of cross-national research. *Psychological Bulletin, 143*(12), 1313–1345. https://doi.org/10.1037/bul0000123

Cieri, F., & Esposito, R. (2019). Psychoanalysis and neuroscience: The bridge between mind and brain. *Frontiers in Psychology, 10*, 1790. https://doi.org/10.3389/fpsyg.2019.01983

Claridge, G., & Davis, C. (2001). What's the use of neuroticism? *Personality and Individual Differences, 31*(3), 383–400. https://doi.org/10.1016/S0191-8869(00)00144-6

Clarke, D. M., & Kissane, D. W. (2002). Demoralization: Its phenomenology and importance. *The Australian and New Zealand Journal of Psychiatry, 36*(6), 733–742. https://doi.org/10.1046/j.1440-1614.2002.01086.x

Clayton, P. J., & Lewis, C. E. (1981). The significance of secondary depression. *Journal of Affective Disorders, 3*(1), 25–35. https://doi.org/10.1016/0165-0327(81)90016-1

Clegg, K A., Levine, S., Zuroff, D. C., Holding, A. C., Shahar, G., & Koestner, R. (2023). A multilevel perspective on self-determination theory: Predictors and correlates of autonomous and controlled motivation. *Motivation and Emotion, 47*(2), 229–245. https://doi.org/10.1007/s11031-022-09995-6

Cloninger, C. R., & Svrakic, D. M. (1997). Integrative psychobiological approach to psychiatric assessment and treatment. *Psychiatry, 60*(2), 120–141. https://doi.org/10.1080/00332747.1997.11024793

Cloninger, C. R., Svrakic, D. M., & Przybeck, T. R. (1993). A psychobiological model of temperament and character. *Archives of General Psychiatry, 50*(12), 975–990. https://doi.org/10.1001/archpsyc.1993.01820240059008

Cocksedge, K. A., Simon, C., & Shankar, R. (2014). A difficult combination: Chronic physical illness, depression, and pain. *The British Journal of General Practice, 64*(626), 440–441. https://doi.org/10.3399/bjgp14X681241

Cohen, K., Ramseyer, F. T., Tal, S., & Zilcha-Mano, S. (2021). Nonverbal synchrony and the alliance in psychotherapy for major depression: Disentangling state-like and trait-like effects. *Clinical Psychological Science, 9*(4), 634–648. https://doi.org/10.1177/2167702620985294

Cohen, L. H., McGowan, J., Fooskas, S., & Rose, S. (1984). Positive life events and social support and the relationship between life stress and psychological disorder. *American Journal of Community Psychology, 12*(5), 567–587. https://doi.org/10.1007/BF00897213

Cohen, S. (2004). Social relationships and health. *American Psychologist, 59*(8), 676–684. https://doi.org/10.1037/0003-066X.59.8.676

Cohen, S., & Hoberman, H. (1983). Positive events and social support as buffers of life change stress. *Journal of Applied Social Psychology, 13*(2), 99–125. https://doi.org/10.1111/j.1559-1816.1983.tb02325.x

Cohen, S., & Wills, T. A. (1985). Stress, social support, and the buffering hypothesis. *Psychological Bulletin, 98*(2), 310–357. https://doi.org/10.1037/0033-2909.98.2.310

Colapinto, J. (2019). Structural family therapy. In B. H. Fiese, M. Celano, K. Deater-Deckard, E. N. Jouriles, & M. A. Whisman (Eds.), *APA handbook of contemporary family psychology: Family therapy and training* (pp. 107–121). American Psychological Association.

Compton, W. M., & Han, B. (2022). Substance use disorders are deadly. *The American Journal of Psychiatry, 179*(1), 11–13. https://doi.org/10.1176/appi.ajp.2021.21101069

Cooper, D. E. (1999). *Existentialism: A reconstruction* (2nd ed.). Wiley.

Coplan, R. J., Hipson, W. E., Archbell, K. A., Ooi, L. L., Baldwin, D., & Bowker, J. C. (2019). Seeking more solitude: Conceptualization, assessment, and implications of aloneliness. *Personality and Individual Differences, 148*(1), 17–26. https://doi.org/10.1016/j.paid.2019.05.020

Costa, P. T., & McCrae, R. R. (1998). Trait theories of personality. In D. F. Barone, M. Hersen, & V. B. Van Hasselt (Eds.), *Advanced personality* (pp. 103–121). Springer. https://doi.org/10.1007/978-1-4419-8580-4_5

Costanza, A., Vasileios, C., Ambrosetti, J., Shah, S., Amerio, A., Aguglia, A., Serafini, G., Piguet, V., Luthy, C., Cedraschi, C., Bondolfi, G., & Berardelli, I. (2022). Demoralization in suicide: A systematic review. *Journal of Psychosomatic Research, 157*, 110788. https://doi.org/10.1016/j.jpsychores.2022.110788

Costello, C. G., & Scott, C. B. (1991). Primary and secondary depression: A review. *Canadian Journal of Psychiatry, 36*(3), 210–217. https://doi.org/10.1177/070674379103600310

Cox, W. T., Abramson, L. Y., Devine, P. G., & Hollon, S. D. (2012). Stereotypes, prejudice, and depression: The integrated perspective. *Perspectives on Psychological Science*, 7(5), 427–449. https://doi.org/10.1177/1745691612455204

Coyne, J. C. (1976a). Depression and the response of others. *Journal of Abnormal Psychology*, 85(2), 186–193. https://doi.org/10.1037/0021-843X.85.2.186

Coyne, J. C. (1976b). Toward an interactional description of depression. *Psychiatry*, 39(1), 28–40. https://doi.org/10.1080/00332747.1976.11023874

Coyne, J. C. (1986). Ambiguity and controversy: An introduction. In J. C. Coyne (Ed.), *Essential papers on depression* (pp. 1–22). New York University Press.

Coyne, J. C. (1992). Cognition in depression: A paradigm in crisis. *Psychological Inquiry*, 3(3), 232–235. https://doi.org/10.1207/s15327965pli0303_5

Coyne, J. C. (1994a). Possible contributions of "cognitive science" to the integration of psychotherapy. *Journal of Psychotherapy Integration*, 4(4), 401–416. https://doi.org/10.1037/h0101161

Coyne, J. C. (1994b). Self-reported distress: Analog or Ersatz depression? *Psychological Bulletin*, 116(1), 29–45. https://doi.org/10.1037/0033-2909.116.1.29

Coyne, J. C., & DeLongis, A. (1986). Going beyond social support: The role of social relationships in adaptation. *Journal of Consulting and Clinical Psychology*, 54(4), 454–460. https://doi.org/10.1037/0022-006X.54.4.454

Coyne, J. C., & Downey, G. (1991). Social factors and psychopathology: Stress, social support, and coping processes. *Annual Review of Psychology*, 42(1), 401–425. https://doi.org/10.1146/annurev.ps.42.020191.002153

Coyne, J. C., Gallo, S. M., Klinkman, M. S., & Calarco, M. M. (1998, February). Effects of recent and past major depression and distress on self-concept and coping. *Journal of Abnormal Psychology*, 107(1), 86–96. https://doi.org/10.1037/0021-843X.107.1.86

Coyne, J. C., & Gotlib, I. H. (1983). The role of cognition in depression: A critical appraisal. *Psychological Bulletin*, 94(3), 472–505. https://doi.org/10.1037/0033-2909.94.3.472

Coyne, J. C., Kessler, R. C., Tal, M., Turnbull, J., Wortman, C. B., & Greden, J. F. (1987). Living with a depressed person. *Journal of Consulting and Clinical Psychology*, 55(3), 347–352. https://doi.org/10.1037/0022-006X.55.3.347

Coyne, J. C., & Racioppo, M. W. (2000). Never the Twain shall meet? Closing the gap between coping research and clinical intervention research. *American Psychologist*, 55(6), 655–664. https://doi.org/10.1037/0003-066X.55.6.655

Coyne, J. C., Rohrbaugh, M. J., Shoham, V., Sonnega, J. S., Nicklas, J. M., & Cranford, J. A. (2001). Prognostic importance of marital quality for survival of congestive heart failure. *The American Journal of Cardiology*, 88(5), 526–529. https://doi.org/10.1016/S0002-9149(01)01731-3

Coyne, J. C., & Smith, D. A. (1991). Couples coping with a myocardial infarction: A contextual perspective on wives' distress. *Journal of Personality and Social Psychology*, 61(3), 404–412. https://doi.org/10.1037/0022-3514.61.3.404

Coyne, J. C., Thompson, R., & Whiffen, V. (2004). Is the promissory note of personality as vulnerability to depression in default? Reply to Zuroff, Mongrain, and Santor (2004). *Psychological Bulletin, 130*(3), 512–517. https://doi.org/10.1037/0033-2909.130.3.512

Coyne, J. C., & Whiffen, V. E. (1995). Issues in personality as diathesis for depression: The case of sociotropy-dependency and autonomy-self-criticism. *Psychological Bulletin, 118*(3), 358–378. https://doi.org/10.1037/0033-2909.118.3.358

Cramer, P. (2006). *Protecting the self: Defense mechanisms in action*. Guilford Press.

Crisci, G., Caviola, S., Cardillo, R., & Mammarella, I. C. (2021). Executive functions in neurodevelopmental disorders: Comorbidity overlaps between attention deficit and hyperactivity disorder and specific learning disorders. *Frontiers in Human Neuroscience, 15*, 594234. https://doi.org/10.3389/fnhum.2021.594234

Culpin, I., Heron, J., Araya, R., Melotti, R., & Joinson, C. (2013). Father absence and depressive symptoms in adolescence: Findings from a UK cohort. *Psychological Medicine, 43*(12), 2615–2626. https://doi.org/10.1017/S0033291713000603

Cuthbert, B. N., & Insel, T. R. (2013). Toward the future of psychiatric diagnosis: The seven pillars of RDoC. *BMC Medicine, 11*(1), 126. https://doi.org/10.1186/1741-7015-11-126

Daniali, H., Martinussen, M., & Flaten, M. A. (2023). A global meta-analysis of depression, anxiety, and stress before and during COVID-19. *Health Psychology, 42*(2), 124–138. https://doi.org/10.1037/hea0001259

Davidson, K. W. (2012). Depression and coronary heart disease. *ISRN Cardiology, 2012*, 743813. https://doi.org/10.5402/2012/743813

Davidson, L., & Shahar, G. (2007a). From deficit to desire: A philosophical reconsideration of action models of psychopathology. *Philosophy, Psychiatry, & Psychology, 14*(3), 215–232. https://doi.org/10.1353/ppp.0.0127

Davidson, L., & Shahar, G. (2007b). Introducing a "Deleuze Effect" into psychiatry. *Philosophy, Psychiatry, & Psychology, 14*(3), 243–247. https://doi.org/10.1353/ppp.0.0120

Davidson, L., Shahar, G., Lawless, M. S., Sells, D., & Tondora, J. (2006). Play, pleasure, and other positive life events: "Non-specific" factors in recovery from mental illness? *Psychiatry, 69*(2), 151–163. https://doi.org/10.1521/psyc.2006.69.2.151

de Catanzaro, D. (1995). Reproductive status, family interactions, and suicidal ideation: Surveys of the general public and high-risk groups. *Ethology and Sociobiology, 16*(5), 385–394. https://doi.org/10.1016/0162-3095(95)00055-0

de Figueiredo, J. M. (1993). Depression and demoralization: Phenomenologic differences and research perspectives. *Comprehensive Psychiatry, 34*(5), 308–311. https://doi.org/10.1016/0010-440X(93)90016-W

De Fruyt, F. D., Wiele, L. V. D., & Heeringen, C. V. (2000). Cloninger's psychobiological model of temperament and character and the five factor model of personality. *Personality and Individual Differences, 29*(3), 441–452. https://doi.org/10.1016/S0191-8869(99)00204-4

de Oliveira, I. R., Hemmany, C., Powell, V. B., Bonfim, T. D., Duran, E. P., Novais, N., Velasquez, M., Di Sarno, E., Alves, G. L., Cesnik, J. A., & the Brazilian TBTR Study Group. (2012). Trial-based psychotherapy and the efficacy of trial-based thought record in changing unhelpful core beliefs and reducing self-criticism. *CNS Spectrums*, *17*(1), 16–23. https://doi.org/10.1017/S1092852912000399

Denneson, L. M., Smolenski, D. J., Bush, N. E., & Dobscha, S. K. (2017). Curiosity improves coping efficacy and reduces suicidal ideation severity among military veterans at risk for suicide. *Psychiatry Research*, *249*, 125–131. https://doi.org/10.1016/j.psychres.2017.01.018

Denson, T. F. (2013). The multiple systems model of angry rumination. *Personality and Social Psychology Review*, *17*(2), 103–123. https://doi.org/10.1177/1088868312467086

Depue, R. A., & Monroe, S. M. (1986). Conceptualization and measurement of human disorder in life stress research: The problem of chronic disturbance. *Psychological Bulletin*, *99*(1), 36–51. https://doi.org/10.1037/0033-2909.99.1.36

Derogatis, L. R. (1982). *Brief Symptom Inventory (BSI)* [Database record]. APA PsycTests.

Devanand, D. P. (2014). Dysthymic disorder in the elderly population. *International Psychogeriatrics*, *26*(1), 39–48.

Dew, M. A., & Bromet, E. J. (1991). Effects of depression on social support in a community sample of women. In J. Eckenrode (Ed.), *The social context of coping* (pp. 189–211). Springer. https://doi.org/10.1007/978-1-4899-3740-7_9

Dewsbury, D. A. (2009). Is psychology losing its foundations? *Review of General Psychology*, *13*(4), 281–289. https://doi.org/10.1037/a0017760

Dhar, A. K., & Barton, D. A. (2016). Depression and the link with cardiovascular disease. *Frontiers in Psychiatry*, *7*, 33. https://doi.org/10.3389/fpsyt.2016.00033

Dimaggio, G., & Shahar, G. (2017). Behavioral activation as a common mechanism of change across different orientations and disorders. *Psychotherapy*, *54*(3), 221–224. https://doi.org/10.1037/pst0000117

Dimitrovsky, L. (2007). Interview with Prof. Sidney Blatt. *The Israel Journal of Psychiatry and Related Sciences*, *44*(4), 309–320.

Dohrenwend, B. S., Krasnoff, L., Askenasy, A. R., & Dohrenwend, B. P. (1978). Exemplification of a method for scaling life events: The Peri Life Events Scale. *Journal of Health and Social Behavior*, *19*(2), 205–229. https://doi.org/10.2307/2136536

Domínguez-Clavé, E., Soler, J., Elices, M., Franquesa, A., Álvarez, E., & Pascual, J. C. (2022). Ayahuasca may help to improve self-compassion and self-criticism capacities. *Human Psychopharmacology*, *37*(1), e2807. https://doi.org/10.1002/hup.2807

Döpfner, M., Plueck, J., Lehmkuhl, G., Huss, M., Lenz, K., Lehmkuhl, U., Poustka, F., Schmeck, K., Fegert, J. M., & the German CBCL Study Group.

(2009). Covariation, co-occurrence and epiphenomenal correlation of empirically based syndromes in children and adolescents. *Psychopathology, 42*(3), 177–184. https://doi.org/10.1159/000207460

Dubovsky, S. L., Ghosh, B. M., Serotte, J. C., & Cranwell, V. (2021). Psychotic depression: Diagnosis, differential diagnosis, and treatment. *Psychotherapy and Psychosomatics, 90*(3), 160–177. https://doi.org/10.1159/000511348

Duffy, M. E., Buchman-Schmitt, J. M., McNulty, J. K., & Joiner, T. E. (2022). Eyes fixed on heaven's gate: An empirical examination of blink rate and suicide. *Archives of Suicide Research*, 1–9. Advance online publication. https://doi.org/10.1080/13811118.2022.2083536

Dunbar, R. (1998). The social brain hypothesis. *Evolutionary Anthropology, 6*(5), 178–190. https://doi.org/10.1002/(SICI)1520-6505(1998)6:5<178::AID-EVAN5>3.0.CO;2-8

Dunkley, D. M., & Blankstein, K. R. (2000). Self-critical perfectionism, coping, hassles, and current distress: A structural equation modeling approach. *Cognitive Therapy and Research, 24*(6), 713–730. https://doi.org/10.1023/A:1005543529245

Dunkley, D. M., Lewkowski, M., Lee, I. A., Preacher, K. J., Zuroff, D. C., Berg, J. L., Foley, J. E., Myhr, G., & Westreich, R. (2017). Daily stress, coping, and negative and positive affect in depression: Complex trigger and maintenance patterns. *Behavior Therapy, 48*(3), 349–365. https://doi.org/10.1016/j.beth.2016.06.001

Dunkley, D. M., Sanislow, C. A., Grilo, C. M., & McGlashan, T. H. (2006). Perfectionism and depressive symptoms 3 years later: Negative social interactions, avoidant coping, and perceived social support as mediators. *Comprehensive Psychiatry, 47*(2), 106–115. https://doi.org/10.1016/j.comppsych.2005.06.003

Dunkley, D. M., Sanislow, C. A., Grilo, C. M., & McGlashan, T. H. (2009). Self-criticism versus neuroticism in predicting depression and psychosocial impairment for 4 years in a clinical sample. *Comprehensive Psychiatry, 50*(4), 335–346. https://doi.org/10.1016/j.comppsych.2008.09.004

Dunkley, D. M., Zuroff, D. C., & Blankstein, K. R. (2003). Self-critical perfectionism and daily affect: Dispositional and situational influences on stress and coping. *Journal of Personality and Social Psychology, 84*(1), 234–252. https://doi.org/10.1037/0022-3514.84.1.234

Durkheim, E. (1897/1951). *Suicide: A study in sociology* (J. A. Spaulding & G. Simpson, Trans.). Routledge.

Dweck, C. S., & Leggett, E. L. (1988). A social-cognitive approach to motivation and personality. *Psychological Review, 95*(2), 256–273. https://doi.org/10.1037/0033-295X.95.2.256

Eagle, M. N. (2011). *From classical to contemporary psychoanalysis: A critique and integration*. Routledge. https://doi.org/10.4324/9780203868553

Ehrensaft, M. K., Moffitt, T. E., & Caspi, A. (2006). Is domestic violence followed by an increased risk of psychiatric disorders among women but not among men? A longitudinal cohort study. *The American Journal of Psychiatry, 163*(5), 885–892. https://doi.org/10.1176/ajp.2006.163.5.885

Ehring, T., & Watkins, E. R. (2008). Repetitive negative thinking as a transdiagnostic process. *International Journal of Cognitive Therapy, 1*(3), 192–205. https://doi.org/10.1521/ijct.2008.1.3.192

Endicott, J., & Spitzer, R. L. (1978, July). A diagnostic interview: The schedule for affective disorders and schizophrenia. *Archives of General Psychiatry, 35*(7), 837–844. https://doi.org/10.1001/archpsyc.1978.01770310043002

Enestrom, M. C., & Lydon, J. E. (2021). Relationship satisfaction in the time of COVID-19: The role of shared reality in perceiving partner support for frontline health-care workers. *Journal of Social & Personal Relationships, 38*(8), 2330–2349. https://doi.org/10.1177/02654075211020127

Engel, G. L. (1977). The need for a new medical model: A challenge for biomedicine. *Science, 196*(4286), 129–136. https://doi.org/10.1126/science.847460

Enns, M. W., & Cox, B. J. (1997). Personality dimensions and depression: Review and commentary. *Canadian Journal of Psychiatry, 42*(3), 274–284. https://doi.org/10.1177/070674379704200305

Epskamp, S., Cramer, A. O., Waldorp, L. J., Schmittmann, V. D., & Borsboom, D. (2012). qgraph: Network Visualizations of Relationships in Psychometric Data. *Journal of Statistical Software, 48*(4), 1–18. https://doi.org/10.18637/jss.v048.i04

Epskamp, S., & Fried, E. I. (2018). A tutorial on regularized partial correlation networks. *Psychological Methods, 23*(4), 617–634. https://doi.org/10.1037/met0000167

Erdelyi, M. H. (2006). The unified theory of repression. *Behavioral and Brain Sciences, 29*(5), 499–511. https://doi.org/10.1017/S0140525X06009113

Erickson, M. H. (1980). The nature of hypnosis and suggestion. In E. L. Rossi (Ed.), *The collected papers of Milton H. Erickson on hypnosis* (Vol. I). Irvington Publishers.

Erikson, E. H. (1968). *Identity: Youth and crisis*. Norton.

Ettman, C. K., Abdalla, S. M., Cohen, G. H., Sampson, L., Vivier, P. M., & Galea, S. (2020). Prevalence of depression symptoms in US adults before and during the COVID-19 pandemic. *JAMA Network Open, 3*(9), e2019686. https://doi.org/10.1001/jamanetworkopen.2020.19686

Eve, M. P. (2022). *The digital humanities and literary studies*. Oxford University Press. https://doi.org/10.1093/oso/9780198850489.001.0001

Fahrer, J., Brill, N., Dobener, L. M., Asbrand, J., & Christiansen, H. (2022). Expressed emotion in the family: A meta-analytic review of expressed emotion as a mechanism of the transgenerational transmission of mental disorders. *Frontiers in Psychiatry, 12*, 721796. https://doi.org/10.3389/fpsyt.2021.721796

Fairbairn, W. R. D. (1944). Endopsychic structure considered in terms of object-relationships. In *Psychoanalytic studies of the personality* (pp. 82–132). Routledge & Kegan Paul.

Falconer, C. J., Slater, M., Rovira, A., King, J. A., Gilbert, P., Antley, A., & Brewin, C. R. (2014). Embodying compassion: A virtual reality paradigm for overcoming excessive self-criticism. *PLOS ONE, 9*(11), e111933. https://doi.org/10.1371/journal.pone.0111933

Farr, J., Ononaiye, M., & Irons, C. (2021). Early shaming experiences and psychological distress: The role of experiential avoidance and self-compassion. *Psychology and Psychotherapy, 94*(4), 952–972. https://doi.org/10.1111/papt.12353

Fazel, S., Wolf, A., Chang, Z., Larsson, H., Goodwin, G. M., & Lichtenstein, P. (2015). Depression and violence: A Swedish population study. *The Lancet Psychiatry, 2*(3), 224–232. https://doi.org/10.1016/S2215-0366(14)00128-X

Feeney, B. C., & Collins, N. L. (2015). A new look at social support: A theoretical perspective on thriving through relationships. *Personality and Social Psychology Review, 19*(2), 113–147. https://doi.org/10.1177/1088868314544222

Ferenczi, S. (1933/1955). Confusion of tongues between adults and the child. In *Final contributions* (pp. 156–167). Hogarth.

Ferenczi, S. (1949). Confusion of tongues between the adult and the child. *The International Journal of Psychoanalysis, 30*, 225–230.

Filipas, H. H., & Ullman, S. E. (2006). Child sexual abuse, coping responses, self-blame, posttraumatic stress disorder, and adult sexual revictimization. *Journal of Interpersonal Violence, 21*(5), 652–672. https://doi.org/10.1177/0886260506286879

Fink, B. (2009). *A Clinical introduction to Lacanian psychoanalysis: Theory and technique.* Harvard University Press.

First, M. B., Spitzer, R. L., Gibbon, M., & Williams, J. B. (1995). The structured clinical interview for *DSM-III-R* personality disorders (SCID-II). Part I: Description. *Journal of Personality Disorders, 9*(2), 83–91.

Fischer, R., & Schwartz, S. H. (2011). Whence differences in value priorities? Individual, cultural, or artifactual sources. *Journal of Cross-Cultural Psychology, 42*(7), 1127–1144. https://doi.org/10.1177/0022022110381429

Fonagy, P. (1993). Psychoanalytic and empirical approaches to developmental psychopathology: An object-relations perspective. *Journal of the American Psychoanalytic Association, 41*, 245–260.

Fonagy, P., & Luyten, P. (2018). Attachment, mentalizing, and the self. In W. J. Livesley & R. Larstone (Eds.), *Handbook of personality disorders: Theory, research, and treatment* (pp. 123–140). Guilford Press.

Fonagy, P., Rost, F., Carlyle, J. A., McPherson, S., Thomas, R., Pasco Fearon, R. M., Goldberg, D., & Taylor, D. (2015). Pragmatic randomized controlled trial of long-term psychoanalytic psychotherapy for treatment-resistant depression: The Tavistock Adult Depression Study (TADS). *World Psychiatry, 14*(3), 312–321. https://doi.org/10.1002/wps.20267

Fontaine, N. M., Brendgen, M., Vitaro, F., Boivin, M., Tremblay, R. E., & Côté, S. M. (2019). Longitudinal associations between delinquency, depression and anxiety symptoms in adolescence: Testing the moderating effect of sex and family socioeconomic status. *Journal of Criminal Justice, 62,* 58–65. https://doi.org/10.1016/j.jcrimjus.2018.09.007

Fraher, A. L. (2004). Systems psychodynamics: The formative years of an interdisciplinary field at the Tavistock Institute. *History of Psychology, 7*(1), 65–84. https://doi.org/10.1037/1093-4510.7.1.65

Frank, E. (2005). *Treating bipolar disorder: A clinician's guide to interpersonal and social rhythm therapy.* Guilford Press.

Frank, J. D. (1974). Psychotherapy: The restoration of morale. *The American Journal of Psychiatry, 131*(3), 271–274. https://doi.org/10.1176/ajp.131.3.271

Frankl, V. E. (1975). Paradoxical intention and dereflection. *Psychotherapy: Theory, Research, & Practice, 12*(3), 226–237. https://doi.org/10.1037/h0086434

Fratelli, C., Siqueira, J., Silva, C., Ferreira, E., & Silva, I. (2020). 5HTTLPR genetic variant and major depressive disorder: A review. *Genes, 11*(11), 1260. https://doi.org/10.3390/genes11111260

Frenzel, A. C., Goetz, T., Lüdtke, O., Pekrun, R., & Sutton, R. E. (2009). Emotional transmission in the classroom: Exploring the relationship between teacher and student enjoyment. *Journal of Educational Psychology, 101*(3), 705–716. https://doi.org/10.1037/a0014695

Freud, A. (1936). The ego and the mechanisms of defense. In *The writings of Anna Freud* (Vol. 2, pp. 3–191). International Universities Press.

Freud, A. (1946). *The ego and the mechanisms of defence.* International Universities Press.

Freud, S. (1914). Remembering, repeating and working-through (further recommendations on the technique of psycho-analysis II). In *The standard edition of the complete psychological works of Sigmund Freud* (Vol. 12, pp. 145–156). Hogarth.

Freud, S. (1915). Instincts and their vicissitudes. *SE, 14,* 109–140.

Freud, S. (1926). Inhibitions, symptoms and anxiety. In J. Strachey, Ed. & Trans., *The standard edition of the complete psychological works of Sigmund Freud* (Vol. 20, pp. 75–176). Hogarth.

Freud, S. (1930). *Civilization and its discontents.* Hogarth.

Fried, E. I., Epskamp, S., Nesse, R. M., Tuerlinckx, F., & Borsboom, D. (2016). What are 'good' depression symptoms? Comparing the centrality of *DSM* and non-*DSM* symptoms of depression in a network analysis. *Journal of Affective Disorders, 189,* 314–320. https://doi.org/10.1016/j.jad.2015.09.005

Fried, E. I., van Borkulo, C. D., Cramer, A. O., Boschloo, L., Schoevers, R. A., & Borsboom, D. (2017). Mental disorders as networks of problems: A review of recent insights. *Social Psychiatry and Psychiatric Epidemiology, 52*(1), 1–10. https://doi.org/10.1007/s00127-016-1319-z

Frijda, N. H. (2001). The self and emotions. In H. A. Bosma & S. E. Kunnen (Eds.), *Identity and emotion: Development through self-organization* (pp. 39–57). Cambridge University Press. https://doi.org/10.1017/CBO9780511598425.005

Fu, Z., Brouwer, M., Kennis, M., Williams, A., Cuijpers, P., & Bockting, C. (2021). Psychological factors for the onset of depression: A meta-analysis of prospective studies. *BMJ Open, 11*(7), e050129. https://doi.org/10.1136/bmjopen-2021-050129

Ghaemi, N. (2011, July 30). Depression in command. *The Wall Street Journal.* https://www.wsj.com/articles/SB10001424053111904800304576474451102761640

Ghaemi, N. (2012). *A first-rate madness: Uncovering the links between leadership and mental illness.* Penguin.

Ghent, E. (1989). Credo: The dialectics of one-person and two-person psychologies. *Contemporary Psychoanalysis, 25*(2), 169–211. https://doi.org/10.1080/00107530.1989.10746289

Ghobadzadeh, M., McMorris, B. J., Sieving, R. E., Porta, C. M., & Brady, S. S. (2019). Relationships between adolescent stress, depressive symptoms, and sexual risk behavior in young adulthood: A structural equation modeling analysis. *Journal of Pediatric Health Care, 33*(4), 394–403. https://doi.org/10.1016/j.pedhc.2018.11.006

Gilbert, D. T., & Wilson, T. D. (2007). Prospection: Experiencing the future. *Science, 317*(5843), 1351–1354. https://doi.org/10.1126/science.1144161

Gilbert, P. (1995). Biopsychosocial approaches and evolutionary theory as aids to integration in clinical psychology and psychotherapy. *Clinical Psychology & Psychotherapy, 2*(3), 135–156. https://doi.org/10.1002/cpp.5640020302

Gilbert, P. (2000). The relationship of shame, social anxiety and depression: The role of the evaluation of social rank. *Clinical Psychology & Psychotherapy, 7*(3), 174–189. https://doi.org/10.1002/1099-0879(200007)7:3<174::AID-CPP236>3.0.CO;2-U

Gilbert, P. (2005). Social mentalities: A biopsychosocial and evolutionary reflection on social relationships. In M. W. Baldwin (Ed.), *Interpersonal cognition* (pp. 299–335). Guilford Press.

Gilbert, P. (2009). Introducing compassion-focused therapy. *Advances in Psychiatric Treatment, 15*(3), 199–208. https://doi.org/10.1192/apt.bp.107.005264

Gilbert, P., Clarke, M., Hempel, S., Miles, J. N., & Irons, C. (2004). Criticizing and reassuring oneself: An exploration of forms, styles and reasons in female students. *British Journal of Clinical Psychology, 43*(1), 31–50. https://doi.org/10.1348/014466504772812959

Gilboa-Schechtman, E., & Foa, E. B. (2001). Patterns of recovery after trauma: Individual differences and trauma characteristics. *Journal of Abnormal Psychology, 110,* 392–400.

Gilboa-Schechtman, E., & Shahar, G. (2006). The sooner, the better: Temporal patterns in brief treatment of depression and their role in long-term outcome. *Psychotherapy Research, 16*(3), 374–384. https://doi.org/10.1080/10503300500485425

Goldbach, J. T., Sterzing, P. R., & Stuart, M. J. (2018). Challenging conventions of bullying thresholds: Exploring differences between low and high levels of bully-only, victim-only, and bully-victim roles. *Journal of Youth and Adolescence, 47*(3), 586–600. https://doi.org/10.1007/s10964-017-0775-4

Golia, G. M., & McGovern, A. R. (2015). If you save me, I'll save you: The power of peer supervision in clinical training and professional development. *British Journal of Social Work, 45*(2), 634–650. https://doi.org/10.1093/bjsw/bct138

Gonzalez, J. S., Safren, S. A., Cagliero, E., Wexler, D. J., Delahanty, L., Wittenberg, E., Blais, M. A., Meigs, J. B., & Grant, R. W. (2007). Depression, self-care, and medication adherence in Type 2 diabetes: Relationships across the full range of symptom severity. *Diabetes Care, 30*(9), 2222–2227. https://doi.org/10.2337/dc07-0158

Goodyer, I. M., Tsancheva, S., Byford, S., Dubicka, B., Hill, J., Kelvin, R., Reynolds, S., Roberts, C., Senior, R., Suckling, J., Wilkinson, P., Target, M., & Fonagy, P. (2011). Improving mood with psychoanalytic and cognitive therapies (IMPACT): A pragmatic effectiveness superiority trial to investigate whether specialised psychological treatment reduces the risk for relapse in adolescents with moderate to severe unipolar depression: Study protocol for a randomised controlled trial. *Trials, 12*(1), 175. https://doi.org/10.1186/1745-6215-12-175

Gozansky, E., Moscona, G., & Okon-Singer, H. (2021). Identifying variables that predict depression following the general lockdown during the COVID-19 pandemic. *Frontiers in Psychology, 12*, 680768. https://doi.org/10.3389/fpsyg.2021.680768

Graham, J. E., Robles, T. F., Kiecolt-Glaser, J. K., Malarkey, W. B., Bissell, M. G., & Glaser, R. (2006). Hostility and pain are related to inflammation in older adults. *Brain, Behavior, and Immunity, 20*(4), 389–400. https://doi.org/10.1016/j.bbi.2005.11.002

Granger, S., Pavlis, A., Collett, J., & Hallam, K. T. (2021). Revisiting the "manic defence hypothesis": Assessing explicit and implicit cognitive biases in euthymic bipolar disorder. *Clinical Psychologist, 25*(2), 212–222. https://doi.org/10.1080/13284207.2021.1948303

Gray, J. A. (1981). Anxiety as a paradigm case of emotion. *British Medical Bulletin, 37*(2), 193–197. https://doi.org/10.1093/oxfordjournals.bmb.a071700

Gray, J. A. (1987). *The neuropsychology of fear and stress* (2nd ed.). Cambridge University Press.

Green, J. D., Sedikides, C., Pinter, B., & Van Tongeren, D. R. (2009). Two sides to self-protection: Self-improvement strivings and feedback from close relationships eliminate mnemic neglect. *Self and Identity, 8*(2–3), 233–250. https://doi.org/10.1080/15298860802505145

Greenberg, J. R., & Mitchell, S. A. (1983). *Object relations in psychoanalytic theory*. Harvard University Press. https://doi.org/10.2307/j.ctvjk2xv6

Greenberg, L. S. (2011). *Emotion-focused therapy*. American Psychological Association.

Guideline Development Panel for the Treatment of Depressive Disorders. (2022). Summary of the clinical practice guideline for the treatment of depression across three age cohorts. *American Psychologist, 77*(6), 770–780. https://doi.org/10.1037/amp0000904

Guo, J. (2022). Deep learning approach to text analysis for human emotion detection from big data. *Journal of Intelligent Systems, 31*(1), 113–126. https://doi.org/10.1515/jisys-2022-0001

Guthrie, R. M., & Bryant, R. A. (2006). Extinction learning before trauma and subsequent posttraumatic stress. *Psychosomatic Medicine, 68*(2), 307–311. https://doi.org/10.1097/01.psy.0000208629.67653.cc

Haan, N. (1977). *Coping and defending.* Academic Press.

Hagenaars, J. A., & McCutcheon, A. L. (2009). Latent class analysis: The empirical study of latent types, latent variables, and latent structures. In *Applied latent class analysis* (pp. 3–55). Cambridge University Press.

Halamová, J., Kanovský, M., Strnádelová, B., Moró, R., & Bieliková, M. (2022). Face in the crowd and level of self-criticism. *Advances in Cognitive Psychology, 18*(1), 76–84. https://doi.org/10.5709/acp-0348-6

Hamilton, M. (1967). Development of a rating scale for primary depressive illness. *British Journal of Social and Clinical Psychology, 6*(4), 278–296. https://doi.org/10.1111/j.2044-8260.1967.tb00530.x

Hammen, C. (1991). Generation of stress in the course of unipolar depression. *Journal of Abnormal Psychology, 100*(4), 555–561. https://doi.org/10.1037/0021-843X.100.4.555

Hammen, C. (2006, September). Stress generation in depression: Reflections on origins, research, and future directions. *Journal of Clinical Psychology, 62*(9), 1065–1082. https://doi.org/10.1002/jclp.20293

Hammen, C. (2009, August 1). Adolescent depression: Stressful interpersonal contexts and risk for recurrence. *Current Directions in Psychological Science, 18*(4), 200–204. https://doi.org/10.1111/j.1467-8721.2009.01636.x

Hammen, C. C. (1980). *The UCLA Stress Interview.* University of California, Los Angeles.

Hammen, C., Marks, T., Mayol, A., & DeMayo, R. (1985). Depressive self-schemas, life stress, and vulnerability to depression. *Journal of Abnormal Psychology, 94*(3), 308–319. https://doi.org/10.1037//0021-843x.94.3.308

Hanwella, R., & de Silva, V. (2012). Mental health of Special Forces personnel deployed in battle. *Social Psychiatry and Psychiatric Epidemiology, 47*(8), 1343–1351. https://doi.org/10.1007/s00127-011-0442-0

Hao, F., Tan, W., Jiang, L., Zhang, L., Zhao, X., Zou, Y., Hu, Y., Luo, X., Jiang, X., McIntyre, R. S., Tran, B., Sun, J., Zhang, Z., Ho, R., Ho, C., & Tam, W. (2020). Do psychiatric patients experience more psychiatric symptoms during COVID-19 pandemic and lockdown? A case-control study with service and research implications for immunopsychiatry. *Brain, Behavior, and Immunity, 87,* 100–106. https://doi.org/10.1016/j.bbi.2020.04.069

Hardin, C. D., & Higgins, E. T. (1996). Shared reality: How social verification makes the subjective objective. In R. M. Sorrentino & E. T. Higgins (Eds.), *Handbook of motivation and cognition* (Vol. 3, pp. 28–84). Guilford Press.

Hare, D. L., Toukhsati, S. R., Johansson, P., & Jaarsma, T. (2014). Depression and cardiovascular disease: A clinical review. *European Heart Journal, 35*(21), 1365–1372. https://doi.org/10.1093/eurheartj/eht462

Harris, G. M. (2021). Hypnotherapy for agoraphobia: A case study. In *Case studies in mental health treatment* (pp. 193–197). Routledge.

Harshfield, E. L., Pennells, L., Schwartz, J. E., Willeit, P., Kaptoge, S., Bell, S., Shaffer, J. A., Bolton, T., Spackman, S., Wassertheil-Smoller, S., Kee, F., Amouyel, P., Shea, S. J., Kuller, L. H., Kauhanen, J., van Zutphen, E. M., Blazer, D. G., Krumholz, H., Nietert, P. J., . . . Davidson, K. W. (2020). Association between depressive symptoms and incident cardiovascular diseases. *JAMA, 324*(23), 2396–2405. https://doi.org/10.1001/jama.2020.23068

Harter, S. (1990). Self and identity development. In S. S. Feldman & G. R. Elliott (Eds.), *At the threshold: The developing adolescent* (pp. 352–387). Harvard University Press.

Hartmann, H. (1957). *Ego psychology and the problem of adaptation* (D. Rapaport, Trans.). International Universities Press. (Original work published 1939)

Hawton, K., Casañas i Comabella, C., Haw, C., & Saunders, K. (2013). Risk factors for suicide in individuals with depression: A systematic review. *Journal of Affective Disorders, 147*(1–3), 17–28. https://doi.org/10.1016/j.jad.2013.01.004

Hayes, S. C., Strosahl, K. D., & Wilson, K. G. (2012). *Acceptance and commitment therapy: The process and practice of mindful change* (2nd ed.). Guilford Press.

Heindel, J. J., & Vandenberg, L. N. (2015). Developmental origins of health and disease: A paradigm for understanding disease cause and prevention. *Current Opinion in Pediatrics, 27*(2), 248–253. https://doi.org/10.1097/MOP.0000000000000191

Hendler, N. (1984). Depression caused by chronic pain. *Journal of Clinical Psychiatry, 45*(3 Sect. 2), 30–38.

Henrich, C. C., & Shahar, G. (2008). Social support buffers the effects of terrorism on adolescent depression: Findings from Sderot, Israel. *Journal of the American Academy of Child & Adolescent Psychiatry, 47*(9), 1073–1076. https://doi.org/10.1097/CHI.0b013e31817eed08

Henrich, C. C., & Shahar, G. (2014). Moderators of the effect of peer victimization during fifth grade on subsequent symptoms of (anxious) depression: The roles of engagement in bullying and baseline symptomatology. *Prevention Science, 15*, 888–896. https://doi.org/10.1007/s11121-013-0456-9

Herrman, H., Kieling, C., McGorry, P., Horton, R., Sargent, J., & Patel, V. (2019). Reducing the global burden of depression: A Lancet–World Psychiatric Association Commission. *Lancet, 393*(10189), e42–e43. https://doi.org/10.1016/S0140-6736(18)32408-5

Herzog, J. (1982). On father hunger: The father's role in the modulation of aggressive drive and fantasy. In S. H. Cath, A. R. Gurwitt, & J. M. Ross (Eds.),

Father and child, developmental and clinical perspectives (pp. 163–174). Little, Brown and Company.

Hilt, L. M., Sander, L. C., Nolen-Hoeksema, S., & Simen, A. A. (2007). The BDNF Val66Met polymorphism predicts rumination and depression differently in young adolescent girls and their mothers. *Neuroscience Letters*, *429*(1), 12–16. https://doi.org/10.1016/j.neulet.2007.09.053

Hing, M., Cabrera, J., Barstow, C., & Forsten, R. (2012). Special operations forces and incidence of post-traumatic stress disorder symptoms. *Journal of Special Operations Medicine*, *12*(3), 23–35.

Hobfoll, S. E. (1989). Conservation of resources: A new attempt at conceptualizing stress. *American Psychologist*, *44*(3), 513–524. https://doi.org/10.1037/0003-066X.44.3.513

Hobfoll, S. E. (2009). Social support: The movie. *Journal of Social and Personal Relationships*, *26*(1), 93–101. https://doi.org/10.1177/0265407509105524

Hochschild, A. R., & Machung, A. (2003). *The second shift*. Penguin.

Hoge, C. W., Castro, C. A., Messer, S. C., McGurk, D., Cotting, D. I., & Koffman, R. L. (2004). Combat duty in Iraq and Afghanistan, mental health problems, and barriers to care. *The New England Journal of Medicine*, *351*(1), 13–22. https://doi.org/10.1056/NEJMoa040603

Holder, A. (2005). *Anna Freud, Melanie Klein, and the psychoanalysis of children and adolescents*. Routledge.

Hong, J., Novick, D., Moneta, M. V., El-Shafei, A., Dueñas, H., & Haro, J. M. (2017). Functional impairment and painful physical symptoms in patients with major depressive disorder treated with antidepressants: Real-world evidence from the Middle East. *Clinical Practice and Epidemiology in Mental Health*, *13*(1), 145–155. https://doi.org/10.2174/1745017901713010145

Hooley, J. M., Gruber, S. A., Parker, H. A., Guillaumot, J., Rogowska, J., & Yurgelun-Todd, D. A. (2009). Cortico-limbic response to personally challenging emotional stimuli after complete recovery from depression. *Psychiatry Research*, *172*(1), 83–91. https://doi.org/10.1016/j.pscychresns.2009.02.001

Hooley, J. M., Gruber, S. A., Scott, L. A., Hiller, J. B., & Yurgelun-Todd, D. A. (2005). Activation in dorsolateral prefrontal cortex in response to maternal criticism and praise in recovered depressed and healthy control participants. *Biological Psychiatry*, *57*(7), 809–812. https://doi.org/10.1016/j.biopsych.2005.01.012

Horney, K. (1937). *The neurotic personality of our time*. Norton.

Horney, K. (1950). *Neurosis and human growth: The struggle toward self realization*. Norton.

Horowitz, M. J. (1998). *Cognitive psychodynamics: From conflict to character*. Wiley.

Horowitz, M. J. (2014). *Identity and the new psychoanalytic explorations of self-organization*. Routledge. https://doi.org/10.4324/9781315779744

Horwitz, A. V., Wakefield, J. C., & Lorenzo-Luaces, L. (2016). History of depression. In *The Oxford handbook of mood disorders* (pp. 11–23). Oxford University Press.

Høstmælingen, A., Ulvenes, P., Nissen-Lie, H. A., Eielsen, M., & Wampold, B. E. (2022). Trajectories of change in chronic depression: Differences in self-criticism and somatic symptoms between users of antidepressants and nonmedicated patients. *Journal of Counseling Psychology, 69*(1), 85–99. https://doi.org/10.1037/cou0000572

Howard, F. (2020). Social matching systems, intimate personal data, and romantic compatibility on internet dating sites and apps. *Journal of Research in Gender Studies, 10*(1), 80–86. https://doi.org/10.22381/JRGS10120208

Hung, C. I., Liu, C. Y., & Yang, C. H. (2019). Persistent depressive disorder has long-term negative impacts on depression, anxiety, and somatic symptoms at 10-year follow-up among patients with major depressive disorder. *Journal of Affective Disorders, 243*, 255–261. https://doi.org/10.1016/j.jad.2018.09.068

Huprich, S. K. (2012). Considering the evidence and making the most empirically informed decision about depressive personality disorder in *DSM-5*. *Personality Disorders, 3*(4), 470–482. https://doi.org/10.1037/a0027765

Huprich, S. K., Auerbach, J. S., Porcerelli, J. H., & Bupp, L. L. (2016). Sidney Blatt's object relations inventory: Contributions and future directions. *Journal of Personality Assessment, 98*(1), 30–43. https://doi.org/10.1080/00223891.2015.1099539

Hussong, A. M., Midgette, A. J., Richards, A. N., Petrie, R. C., Coffman, J. L., & Thomas, T. E. (2022). COVID-19 life events spill-over on family functioning and adolescent adjustment. *The Journal of Early Adolescence, 42*(3), 359–388. https://doi.org/10.1177/02724316211036744

Iancu, S. C., Wong, Y. M., Rhebergen, D., van Balkom, A. J. L. M., & Batelaan, N. M. (2020). Long-term disability in major depressive disorder: A 6-year follow-up study. *Psychological Medicine, 50*(10), 1644–1652. https://doi.org/10.1017/S0033291719001612

Iqbal, N., & Dar, K. A. (2015). Negative affectivity, depression, and anxiety: Does rumination mediate the links? *Journal of Affective Disorders, 181*(181), 18–23. https://doi.org/10.1016/j.jad.2015.04.002

Islam, M. S., Tasnim, R., Sujan, M. S. H., Ferdous, M. Z., Sikder, M. T., Masud, J. H. B., Kundu, S., Tahsin, P., Mosaddek, A. S. M., & Griffiths, M. D. (2021). Depressive symptoms associated with COVID-19 preventive practice measures, daily activities in home quarantine and suicidal behaviors: Findings from a large-scale online survey in Bangladesh. *BMC Psychiatry, 21*(1), 273. https://doi.org/10.1186/s12888-021-03246-7

Israeli, H., Itamar, S., & Shahar, G. (2018). The heroic self under stress: Prospective effects on anxious mood in Israeli adults exposed to missile attacks. *Journal of Research in Personality, 75*, 17–25. https://doi.org/10.1016/j.jrp.2018.05.003

Itamar, S., & Shahar, G. (2014). Narcissism and heroism: A rendezvous? In A. Besser (Ed.), *Handbook of the psychology of narcissism: Diverse perspectives* (pp. 67–77). Nova Science Publishing.

Johnson, S. M. (2015). Emotionally focused couple therapy. In A. S. Gurman, J. L. Lebow, & D. K. Snyder (Eds.), *Clinical handbook of couple therapy* (pp. 97–128). Guilford Press.

Joiner, T. (2005). *Why people die by suicide*. Harvard University Press.

Joiner, T. E. (1994). Contagious depression: Existence, specificity to depressed symptoms, and the role of reassurance seeking. *Journal of Personality and Social Psychology, 67*(2), 287–296. https://doi.org/10.1037/0022-3514.67.2.287

Joiner, T. E. (2000a). Depression's vicious scree: Self-propagating and erosive processes in depression chronicity. *Clinical Psychology: Science and Practice, 7*(2), 203–218. https://doi.org/10.1093/clipsy.7.2.203

Joiner, T. E. (2000b). Thomas E. Joiner. Award for distinguished scientific early career contributions to psychology. *American Psychologist, 55*(11), 1271–1274. https://doi.org/10.1037/0003-066X.55.11.1271

Joiner, T. E. (2011). *Lonely at the top: The high cost of men's success*. St. Martin's Publishing Group.

Joiner, T. E., Alfano, M. S., & Metalsky, G. I. (1992). When depression breeds contempt: Reassurance seeking, self-esteem, and rejection of depressed college students by their roommates. *Journal of Abnormal Psychology, 101*(1), 165–173. https://doi.org/10.1037/0021-843X.101.1.165

Joiner, T. E., & Coyne, J. C. (Eds.). (1999). *The interactional nature of depression: Advances in interpersonal approaches*. American Psychological Association. https://doi.org/10.1037/10311-000

Joiner, T. E., Hom, M. A., Rogers, M. L., Chu, C., Stanley, I. H., Wynn, G. H., & Gutierrez, P. M. (2016). Staring down death: Is abnormally slow blink rate a clinically useful indicator of acute suicide risk? *Crisis: The Journal of Crisis Intervention and Suicide Prevention, 37*(3), 212–217. https://doi.org/10.1027/0227-5910/a000367

Joiner, T. E., Simpson, S., Rogers, M. L., Stanley, I. H., & Galynker, I. I. (2018). Whether called acute suicidal affective disturbance or suicide crisis syndrome, a suicide-specific diagnosis would enhance clinical care, increase patient safety, and mitigate clinician liability. *Journal of Psychiatric Practice, 24*(4), 274–278. https://doi.org/10.1097/PRA.0000000000000315

Joiner, T. E., Jr., Walker, R. L., Pettit, J. W., Perez, M., & Cukrowicz, K. C. (2005). Evidence-based assessment of depression in adults. *Psychological Assessment, 17*(3), 267–277. https://doi.org/10.1037/1040-3590.17.3.267

Joiner, T. E., Jr., Walker, R. L., Rudd, M. D., & Jobs, D. A. (1999). Scientizing and routinizing the assessment of suicidality in outpatient practice. *Professional Psychology, Research and Practice, 30*(5), 447–453. https://doi.org/10.1037/0735-7028.30.5.447

Jones, H. E., Yoon, D. B., Theiss, J. A., Austin, J. T., & Lee, L. E. (2021). Assessing the effects of COVID-19 on romantic relationships and the coping strategies partners use to manage the stress of a pandemic. *Journal of Family Communication, 21*(3), 152–166. https://doi.org/10.1080/15267431.2021.1927040

Joseph, B. (1983). On understanding and not understanding: Some technical issues. *The International Journal of Psycho-Analysis, 64*(Pt. 3), 291–298.

Judd, L. L., Akiskal, H. S., & Paulus, M. P. (1997). The role and clinical significance of subsyndromal depressive symptoms (SSD) in unipolar major depressive disorder. *Journal of Affective Disorders, 45*(1–2), 5–18. https://doi.org/10.1016/S0165-0327(97)00055-4

Kadushin, C. (2011). *Understanding social network: Theories, concepts, and findings.* Oxford University Press.

Kahneman, D., & Tversky, A. (1979). Prospect theory: An analysis of decision under risk. *Econometrica, 47*(2), 263–293. https://doi.org/10.2307/1914185

Kahneman, D., & Tversky, A. (2000). *Choices, values, and frames.* Cambridge University Press. https://doi.org/10.1017/CBO9780511803475

Kammrath, L. K., Mendoza-Denton, R., & Mischel, W. (2005). Incorporating if . . . then . . . personality signatures in person perception: Beyond the person-situation dichotomy. *Journal of Personality and Social Psychology, 88*(4), 605–618. https://doi.org/10.1037/0022-3514.88.4.605

Kanovský, M., Halamová, J., Strnádelová, B., Moro, R., & Bielikova, M. (2022). Pupil size variation in primary facial expressions–testing potential biomarker of self-criticism. *Artificial Intelligence Review, 55*(3), 2001–2022. https://doi.org/10.1007/s10462-021-10057-5

Kaplan, G. A., Roberts, R. E., Camacho, T. C., & Coyne, J. C. (1987). Psychosocial predictors of depression. Prospective evidence from the human population laboratory studies. *American Journal of Epidemiology, 125*(2), 206–220. https://doi.org/10.1093/oxfordjournals.aje.a114521

Karatzias, T., Shevlin, M., Murphy, J., McBride, O., Ben-Ezra, M., Bentall, R. P., Vallières, F., & Hyland, P. (2020). Posttraumatic stress symptoms and associated comorbidity during the COVID-19 pandemic in Ireland: A population-based study. *Journal of Traumatic Stress, 33*(4), 365–370. https://doi.org/10.1002/jts.22565

Katon, W., Sullivan, M., & Walker, E. (2001). Medical symptoms without identified pathology: Relationship to psychiatric disorders, childhood and adult trauma, and personality traits. *Annals of Internal Medicine, 134*(9 Pt. 2), 917–925. https://doi.org/10.7326/0003-4819-134-9_Part_2-200105011-00017

Kay, A. (2018). *This is going to hurt: The secret diaries of a junior doctor.* Pidacor.

Kefeli, M. C., Turow, R. G., Yıldırım, A., & Boysan, M. (2018). Childhood maltreatment is associated with attachment insecurities, dissociation and alexithymia in bipolar disorder. *Psychiatry Research, 260*, 391–399. https://doi.org/10.1016/j.psychres.2017.12.026

Keller, M. B., Lavori, P. W., Friedman, B., Nielsen, E., Endicott, J., McDonald-Scott, P., & Andreasen, N. C. (1987). The longitudinal interval follow-up evaluation. A comprehensive method for assessing outcome in prospective longitudinal studies. *Archives of General Psychiatry, 44*(6), 540–548. https://doi.org/10.1001/archpsyc.1987.01800180050009

Kempke, S., Luyten, P., Claes, S., Goossens, L., Bekaert, P., Van Wambeke, P., & Van Houdenhove, B. (2013). Self-critical perfectionism and its relationship to fatigue and pain in the daily flow of life in patients with chronic fatigue syndrome. *Psychological Medicine, 43*(5), 995–1002. https://doi.org/10.1017/S0033291712001936

Kempke, S., Luyten, P., Van Wambeke, P., Coppens, E., & Morlion, B. (2014). Self-critical perfectionism predicts outcome in multidisciplinary treatment for chronic pain. *Pain Practice, 14*(4), 309–314. https://doi.org/10.1111/papr.12071

Kendall-Tackett, K. A. (2007). Inflammation, cardiovascular disease, and metabolic syndrome as sequelae of violence against women: The role of depression, hostility, and sleep disturbance. *Trauma, Violence & Abuse, 8*(2), 117–126. https://doi.org/10.1177/1524838007301161

Kenny, D. K., Kashy, D. A., Cook, W. L., Simpson, J. A., & Cappella, J. N. (2020). *Dyadic data analysis.* Routledge.

Kernberg, O. F. (1995). *Object relations theory and clinical psychoanalysis.* Jason Aronson.

Kernberg, O. F. (1984). *Severe personality disorders: Psychotherapeutic strategies.* Yale University Press.

Kernberg, O. F., Yeomans, F. E., Clarkin, J. F., & Levy, K. N. (2008). Transference focused psychotherapy: Overview and update. *The International Journal of Psycho-Analysis, 89*(3), 601–620. https://doi.org/10.1111/j.1745-8315.2008.00046.x

Kessler, R. C. (2002). The epidemiology of depression. In I. H. Gotlib & C. L. Hammen (Eds.), *Handbook of depression* (pp. 23–42). Guilford Press.

Kim, B. K., Gilman, A. B., Kosterman, R., & Hill, K. G. (2019). Longitudinal associations among depression, substance abuse, and crime: A test of competing hypotheses for driving mechanisms. *Journal of Criminal Justice, 62,* 50–57. https://doi.org/10.1016/j.jcrimjus.2018.08.005

Kim, K., Banquer, A. M., Resnik, S. N., Johnson, J. D., & Fernandez, L. (2022). Self-reference and cognitive effort: Source memory for affectively neutral information is impaired following negative compared to positive self-referential processing. *Journal of Cognitive Psychology, 34*(7), 833–845. https://doi.org/10.1080/20445911.2022.2067553

Klaiber, P., Wen, J. H., DeLongis, A., & Sin, N. L. (2021). The ups and downs of daily life during COVID-19: Age differences in affect, stress, and positive events. *The Journals of Gerontology: Series B, Psychological Sciences and Social Sciences, 76*(2), e30–e37. https://doi.org/10.1093/geronb/gbaa096

Kleiman, E. M., Riskind, J. H., & Schaefer, K. E. (2014). Social support and positive events as suicide resiliency factors: Examination of synergistic buffering effects. *Archives of Suicide Research, 18*(2), 144–155. https://doi.org/10.1080/13811118.2013.826155

Klein, D. N., Kotov, R., & Bufferd, S. J. (2011). Personality and depression: Explanatory models and review of the evidence. *Annual Review of Clinical Psychology, 7*(1), 269–295. https://doi.org/10.1146/annurev-clinpsy-032210-104540

Klein, M. (1928). Early stages of the Oedipus conflict. *The International Journal of Psycho-Analysis, 9,* 167–180.

Klein, M. (1935). A contribution to the psychogenesis of manic-depressive states. *The International Journal of Psycho-Analysis, 16*, 145–174.

Klein, M. (1940). Mourning and its relation to manic-depressive states. *The International Journal of Psycho-Analysis, 21*, 125–153.

Klein, M. (1945). The Oedipus complex in the light of early anxieties. *The International Journal of Psycho-Analysis, 26*, 11–33.

Klein, M. H., Kupfer, D. J., & Shea, M. T. (Eds.). (1993). *Personality and depression: A current view*. Guilford Press.

Klein Tuente, S. K., Bogaerts, S., & Veling, W. (2019). Hostile attribution bias and aggression in adults-a systematic review. *Aggression and Violent Behavior, 46*, 66–81. https://doi.org/10.1016/j.avb.2019.01.009

Klerman, G. L., & Weissman, M. M. (1994). *Interpersonal psychotherapy of depression: A brief, focused, specific strategy*. Jason Aronson.

Klomek, A. B., Catalan, L. H., & Apter, A. (2021). Ultra-brief crisis interpersonal psychotherapy based intervention for suicidal children and adolescents. *World Journal of Psychiatry, 11*(8), 403–411. https://doi.org/10.5498/wjp.v11.i8.403

Kochel, K. P., Ladd, G. W., Bagwell, C. L., & Yabko, B. A. (2015). Bully/victim profiles' differential risk for worsening peer acceptance: The role of friendship. *Journal of Applied Developmental Psychology, 41*, 38–45. https://doi.org/10.1016/j.appdev.2015.05.002

Koestner, R., Zuroff, D. C., & Powers, T. A. (1991). Family origins of adolescent self-criticism and its continuity into adulthood. *Journal of Abnormal Psychology, 100*(2), 191–197. https://doi.org/10.1037/0021-843X.100.2.191

Koh, K. B., Kim, C. H., & Park, J. K. (2002). Predominance of anger in depressive disorders compared with anxiety disorders and somatoform disorders. *The Journal of Clinical Psychiatry, 63*(6), 486–492. https://doi.org/10.4088/JCP.v63n0604

Konttinen, H. (2020). Emotional eating and obesity in adults: The role of depression, sleep and genes. *The Proceedings of the Nutrition Society, 79*(3), 283–289. https://doi.org/10.1017/S0029665120000166

Kopala-Sibley, D. C., Klein, D. N., Perlman, G., & Kotov, R. (2017). Self-criticism and dependency in female adolescents: Prediction of first onsets and disentangling the relationships between personality, stressful life events, and internalizing psychopathology. *Journal of Abnormal Psychology, 126*(8), 1029–1043. https://doi.org/10.1037/abn0000297

Kotov, R., Gamez, W., Schmidt, F., & Watson, D. (2010). Linking "big" personality traits to anxiety, depressive, and substance use disorders: A meta-analysis. *Psychological Bulletin, 136*(5), 768–821. https://doi.org/10.1037/a0020327

Kotov, R., Krueger, R. F., Watson, D., Achenbach, T. M., Althoff, R. R., Bagby, R. M., Brown, T. A., Carpenter, W. T., Caspi, A., Clark, L. A., Eaton, N. R., Forbes, M. K., Forbush, K. T., Goldberg, D., Hasin, D., Hyman, S. E., Ivanova, M. Y., Lynam, D. R., Markon, K., ... Zimmerman, M. (2017). The Hierarchical Taxonomy of Psychopathology (HiTOP): A dimensional alternative to traditional nosologies.

Journal of Abnormal Psychology, 126(4), 454–477. https://doi.org/10.1037/abn0000258

Kramer, U., Grandjean, L., & Beuchat, H. (2021). Emotions in clinical practice. In *Emotion measurement* (pp. 595–612). Woodhead Publishing. https://doi.org/10.1016/B978-0-12-821124-3.00018-1

Krause, N. (1988). Positive life events and depressive symptoms in older adults. *Behavioral Medicine, 14*(3), 101–112. https://doi.org/10.1080/08964289.1988.9935131

Krueger, R. F., Derringer, J., Markon, K. E., Watson, D., & Skodol, A. E. (2012). Initial construction of a maladaptive personality trait model and inventory for DSM-5. *Psychological Medicine, 42*(9), 1879–1890. https://doi.org/10.1017/S0033291711002674

Kushner, S. C. (2015). A review of the direct and interactive effects of life stressors and dispositional traits on youth psychopathology. *Child Psychiatry and Human Development, 46*(5), 810–819. https://doi.org/10.1007/s10578-014-0523-x

Lagdon, S., Ross, J., Robinson, M., Contractor, A. A., Charak, R., & Armour, C. (2021). Assessing the mediating role of social support in childhood maltreatment and psychopathology among college students in Northern Ireland. *Journal of Interpersonal Violence, 36*(3–4). https://doi.org/10.1177/0886260518755489

Lahey, B. B. (2009). Public health significance of neuroticism. *American Psychologist, 64*(4), 241–256. https://doi.org/10.1037/a0015309

Lakey, B., & Orehek, E. (2011). Relational regulation theory: A new approach to explain the link between perceived social support and mental health. *Psychological Review, 118*(3), 482–495. https://doi.org/10.1037/a0023477

Lamb, Y. R. (2022). Social media linked to rise in eating disorders. *WebMD*. https://www.webmd.com/mental-health/eating-disorders/features/social-media-eating-disorders

Landrine, H. (1988). Depression and stereotypes of women: Preliminary empirical analyses of the gender-role hypothesis. *Sex Roles, 19*, 527–541. https://doi.org/10.1007/BF00289722

Lassri, D., Luyten, P., Cohen, G., & Shahar, G. (2016). The effect of childhood emotional maltreatment on romantic relationships in young adulthood: A double mediation model involving self-criticism and attachment. *Psychological Trauma: Theory, Research, Practice, and Policy, 8*(4), 504–511. https://doi.org/10.1037/tra0000134

Lassri, D., Luyten, P., Fonagy, P., & Shahar, G. (2018). Undetected scars? Self-criticism, attachment, and romantic relationships among otherwise well-functioning childhood sexual abuse survivors. *Psychological Trauma: Theory, Research, Practice, and Policy, 10*(1), 121–129. https://doi.org/10.1037/tra0000271

Lassri, D., & Shahar, G. (2012). Self-criticism mediates the link between childhood emotional maltreatment on young adults' romantic relationships. *Journal of Social and Clinical Psychology, 31*(3), 289–311. https://doi.org/10.1521/jscp.2012.31.3.289

Latoo, J., Haddad, P. M., Mistry, M., Wadoo, O., Islam, S. M. S., Jan, F., Iqbal, Y., Howseman, T., Riley, D., & Alabdulla, M. (2021). The COVID-19 pandemic: An opportunity to make mental health a higher public health priority. *BJPsych Open*, *7*(5), e172. https://doi.org/10.1192/bjo.2021.1002

Lavie, Y. (2022). *Memoir* [Unpublished manuscript].

Law, M., Cooper, B., Strong, S., Stewart, D., Rigby, P., & Letts, L. (1996). The person-environment-occupation model: A transactive approach to occupational performance. *Canadian Journal of Occupational Therapy*, *63*(1), 9–23. https://doi.org/10.1177/000841749606300103

Leadbeater, B. J., Kuperminc, G. P., Blatt, S. J., & Hertzog, C. (1999). A multivariate model of gender differences in adolescents' internalizing and externalizing problems. *Developmental Psychology*, *35*(5), 1268–1282. https://doi.org/10.1037/0012-1649.35.5.1268

Lemma, A., Target, M., & Fonagy, P. (2011). *Brief dynamic interpersonal therapy*. Oxford University Press. https://doi.org/10.1093/acprof:oso/9780199602452.001.0001

Lerman, S. F., Rudich, Z., Brill, S., Shalev, H., & Shahar, G. (2015). Longitudinal associations between depression, anxiety, pain, and pain-related disability in chronic pain patients. *Psychosomatic Medicine*, *77*(3), 333–341. https://doi.org/10.1097/PSY.0000000000000158

Lerman, S. F., Shahar, G., & Rudich, Z. (2012). Self-criticism interacts with the affective component of pain to predict depressive symptoms in female patients. *European Journal of Pain*, *16*(1), 115–122. https://doi.org/10.1016/j.ejpain.2011.05.007

Lewinsohn, P. M., Gotlib, I. H., & Seeley, J. R. (1995). Adolescent psychopathology: IV. Specificity of psychosocial risk factors for depression and substance abuse in older adolescents. *Journal of the American Academy of Child & Adolescent Psychiatry*, *34*(9), 1221–1229. https://doi.org/10.1097/00004583-199509000-00021

Lewinsohn, P. M., Shankman, S. A., Gau, J. M., & Klein, D. N. (2004). The prevalence and co-morbidity of subthreshold psychiatric conditions. *Psychological Medicine*, *34*(4), 613–622. https://doi.org/10.1017/S0033291703001466

Lewinsohn, P. M., Steinmetz, J. L., Larson, D. W., & Franklin, J. (1981). Depression-related cognitions: Antecedent or consequence? *Journal of Abnormal Psychology*, *90*(3), 213–219. https://doi.org/10.1037/0021-843X.90.3.213

Lewis-Fernández, R., & Kleinman, A. (1995). Cultural psychiatry. Theoretical, clinical, and research issues. *The Psychiatric Clinics of North America*, *18*(3), 433–448.

Lewontin, R. (2000). *The triple helix: Gene, organism, and environment*. Harvard University Press.

Li, L., Li, F., Fortunati, F., & Krystal, J. H. (2020). Association of a prior psychiatric diagnosis with mortality among hospitalized patients with coronavirus disease 2019 (COVID-19) infection. *JAMA Network Open*, *3*(9), e2023282. https://doi.org/10.1001/jamanetworkopen.2020.23282

Li, Q., Zhao, L., Xue, Y., & Feng, L. (2021). Stress-buffering pattern of positive events on adolescents: An exploratory study based on social networks. *Computers in Human Behavior, 114*, 106565. https://doi.org/10.1016/j.chb.2020.106565

Lichterman, P. (2017). Interpretive reflexivity in ethnography. *Ethnography, 18*(1), 35–45. https://doi.org/10.1177/1466138115592418

Lindová, J., Průšová, D., & Klapilová, K. (2020). Power distribution and relationship quality in long-term heterosexual couples. *Journal of Sex & Marital Therapy, 46*(6), 528–541. https://doi.org/10.1080/0092623X.2020.1761493

Loas, G. (1996). Vulnerability to depression: A model centered on anhedonia. *Journal of Affective Disorders, 41*(1), 39–53. https://doi.org/10.1016/0165-0327(96)00065-1

Longe, O., Maratos, F. A., Gilbert, P., Evans, G., Volker, F., Rockliff, H., & Rippon, G. (2010). Having a word with yourself: Neural correlates of self-criticism and self-reassurance. *NeuroImage, 49*(2), 1849–1856. https://doi.org/10.1016/j.neuroimage.2009.09.019

Lorenzo-Luaces, L. (2015). Heterogeneity in the prognosis of major depression: From the common cold to a highly debilitating and recurrent illness. *Epidemiology and Psychiatric Sciences, 24*(6), 466–472. https://doi.org/10.1017/S2045796015000542

Löw, C. A., Schauenburg, H., & Dinger, U. (2020). Self-criticism and psychotherapy outcome: A systematic review and meta-analysis. *Clinical Psychology Review, 75*, 101808. https://doi.org/10.1016/j.cpr.2019.101808

Luborsky, L. (1984). *Principles of psychoanalytic psychotherapy: A manual for supportive-expressive (SE) treatment*. Basic Books.

Luby, J. L. (2010). Preschool depression: The importance of identification of depression early in development. *Current Directions in Psychological Science, 19*(2), 91–95. https://doi.org/10.1177/0963721410364493

Lustman, P. J., Penckofer, S. M., & Clouse, R. E. (2007). Recent advances in understanding depression in adults with diabetes. *Current Diabetes Reports, 7*(2), 114–122. https://doi.org/10.1007/s11892-007-0020-8

Luyten, P., & Blatt, S. J. (2011). Integrating theory-driven and empirically-derived models of personality development and psychopathology: A proposal for *DSM V*. *Clinical Psychology Review, 31*(1), 52–68. https://doi.org/10.1016/j.cpr.2010.09.003

Luyten, P., & Blatt, S. J. (2013). Interpersonal relatedness and self-definition in normal and disrupted personality development: Retrospect and prospect. *American Psychologist, 68*(3), 172–183. https://doi.org/10.1037/a0032243

Lv, X., Xu, B., Tang, X., Liu, S., Qian, J.-H., Guo, J., & Luo, J. (2023). The relationship between major depression and migraine: A bidirectional two-sample Mendelian randomization study. *Frontiers in Neurology, 14*, 1143060. https://doi.org/10.3389/fneur.2023.1143060

Lyness, J. M., King, D. A., Cox, C., Yoediono, Z., & Caine, E. D. (1999). The importance of subsyndromal depression in older primary care patients: Prevalence and associated functional disability. *Journal of the American Geriatrics Society*, *47*(6), 647–652. https://doi.org/10.1111/j.1532-5415.1999.tb01584.x

Lyssenko, L., Schmahl, C., Bockhacker, L., Vonderlin, R., Bohus, M., & Kleindienst, N. (2018). Dissociation in psychiatric disorders: A meta-analysis of studies using the dissociative experiences scale. *The American Journal of Psychiatry*, *175*(1), 37–46. https://doi.org/10.1176/appi.ajp.2017.17010025

Lythe, K. E., Moll, J., Gethin, J. A., Workman, C. I., Green, S., Lambon Ralph, M. A., Deakin, J. F. W., & Zahn, R. (2015). Self-blame—Selective hyperconnectivity between anterior temporal and subgenual cortices and prediction of recurrent depressive episodes. *JAMA Psychiatry*, *72*(11), 1119–1126. https://doi.org/10.1001/jamapsychiatry.2015.1813

Magni, G., Moreschi, C., Rigatti-Luchini, S., & Merskey, H. (1994). Prospective study on the relationship between depressive symptoms and chronic musculoskeletal pain. *Pain*, *56*(3), 289–297. https://doi.org/10.1016/0304-3959(94)90167-8

Main, M., Kaplan, N., & Cassidy, J. (1985). Security in infancy, childhood, and adulthood: A move to the level of representation. *Monographs of the Society for Research in Child Development*, *50*(1/2), 66–104. https://doi.org/10.2307/3333827

Mandel, T., Dunkley, D. M., & Starrs, C. J. (2018). Self-critical perfectionism, daily interpersonal sensitivity, and stress generation: A four-year longitudinal study. *Journal of Psychopathology and Behavioral Assessment*, *40*(4), 701–713. https://doi.org/10.1007/s10862-018-9673-7

Marcus, G. (1995). Ethnography in/of the world system: The emergence of multi-sited fieldwork. *Annual Review of Anthropology*, *24*(1), 95–117. https://doi.org/10.1146/annurev.an.24.100195.000523

Markowitz, J. C. (1998). *Interpersonal psychotherapy of dysthymic disorder*. American Psychiatric Press.

Markus, H., & Wurf, E. (1987). The dynamic self-concept: A social psychological perspective. *Annual Review of Psychology*, *38*(1), 299–337. https://doi.org/10.1146/annurev.ps.38.020187.001503

Markus, H. R., & Kitayama, S. (1991). Culture and the self: Implications for cognition, emotion, and motivation. *Psychological Review*, *98*(2), 224–253. https://doi.org/10.1037/0033-295X.98.2.224

Martland, N., Martland, R., Cullen, A. E., & Bhattacharyya, S. (2020). Are adult stressful life events associated with psychotic relapse? A systematic review of 23 studies. *Psychological Medicine*, *50*(14), 2302–2316. https://doi.org/10.1017/S0033291720003554

Mason, M., Mennis, J., Russell, M., Moore, M., & Brown, A. (2019). Adolescent depression and substance use: The protective role of prosocial peer behavior. *Journal of Abnormal Child Psychology*, *47*(6), 1065–1074. https://doi.org/10.1007/s10802-018-0501-z

Max, M. B., Wu, T., Atlas, S. J., Edwards, R. R., Haythornthwaite, J. A., Bollettino, A. F., Hipp, H. S., McKnight, C. D., Osman, I. A., Crawford, E. N., Pao, M.,

Nejim, J., Kingman, A., Aisen, D. C., Scully, M. A., Keller, R. B., Goldman, D., & Belfer, I. (2006). A clinical genetic method to identify mechanisms by which pain causes depression and anxiety. *Molecular Pain*, *2*, 14. https://doi.org/10.1186/1744-8069-2-14

May, R. (1958). Contributions of existential psychotherapy. In R. May, E. Angel, & E. Ellenberger (Eds.), *Existence: A new dimension in psychiatry and psychology*. Basic Books. https://doi.org/10.1037/11321-002

McAdams, D. P. (1992). The five-factor model in personality: A critical appraisal. *Journal of Personality*, *60*(2), 329–361. https://doi.org/10.1111/j.1467-6494.1992.tb00976.x

McAdams, D. P. (1995). What do we know when we know a person? *Journal of Personality*, *63*(3), 365–396. https://doi.org/10.1111/j.1467-6494.1995.tb00500.x

McAdams, D. P. (2013). The psychological self as actor, agent, and author. *Perspectives on Psychological Science*, *8*(3), 272–295. https://doi.org/10.1177/1745691612464657

McAdams, D. P. (2015). *The art and science of personality development*. Guilford Press.

McAdams, D. P., Anyidoho, N. A., Brown, C., Huang, Y. T., Kaplan, B., & Machado, M. A. (2004). Traits and stories: Links between dispositional and narrative features of personality. *Journal of Personality*, *72*(4), 761–784. https://doi.org/10.1111/j.0022-3506.2004.00279.x

McAdams, D. P., & Ochberg, R. L. (Eds.). (1988). *Psychobiography and life narratives*. Duke University Press.

McAdams, D. P., Reynolds, J., Lewis, M., Patten, A., & Bowman, P. J. (2001). When bad things turn good and good things turn bad: Sequences of redemption and contamination in life narrative, and their relation to psychosocial adaptation in midlife and in students. *Personality and Social Psychology Bulletin*, *27*(4), 474–485. https://doi.org/10.1177/0146167201274008

McCranie, E. W., & Bass, J. D. (1984). Childhood family antecedents of dependency and self-criticism: Implications for depression. *Journal of Abnormal Psychology*, *93*(1), 3–8. https://doi.org/10.1037/0021-843X.93.1.3

McCullough, J. P. (2000). *Treatment for chronic depression: Cognitive behavioral analysis system of psychotherapy (CBASP)*. Guilford Press.

McCullough, J. P. (2006). *Treating chronic depression with disciplined personal involvement: CBASP*. Springer-Verlag. https://doi.org/10.1007/978-0-387-31066-4

McDaniel, M. A., & Einstein, G. O. (2007). *Cognitive psychology program. Prospective memory: An overview and synthesis of an emerging field*. Sage. https://doi.org/10.4135/9781452225913

McDermut, W., Zimmerman, M., & Chelminski, I. (2003). The construct validity of depressive personality disorder. *Journal of Abnormal Psychology*, *112*(1), 49–60. https://doi.org/10.1037/0021-843X.112.1.49

McDonough-Caplan, H., Klein, D. N., & Beauchaine, T. P. (2018). Comorbidity and continuity of depression and conduct problems from elementary school to adolescence. *Journal of Abnormal Psychology, 127*(3), 326–337. https://doi.org/10.1037/abn0000339

McKay, K. A., Tremlett, H., Fisk, J. D., Zhang, T., Patten, S. B., Kastrukoff, L., Campbell, T., Marrie, R. A., & the CIHR Team in the Epidemiology and Impact of Comorbidity on Multiple Sclerosis. (2018). Psychiatric comorbidity is associated with disability progression in multiple sclerosis. *Neurology, 90*(15), e1316–e1323. https://doi.org/10.1212/WNL.0000000000005302

McLaughlin, K. A., Colich, N. L., Rodman, A. M., & Weissman, D. G. (2020). Mechanisms linking childhood trauma exposure and psychopathology: A transdiagnostic model of risk and resilience. *BMC Medicine, 18*(1), 96. https://doi.org/10.1186/s12916-020-01561-6

Measelle, J. R., Stice, E., & Hogansen, J. M. (2006). Developmental trajectories of co-occurring depressive, eating, antisocial, and substance abuse problems in female adolescents. *Journal of Abnormal Psychology, 115*(3), 524–538. https://doi.org/10.1037/0021-843X.115.3.524

Meier, S. M., Petersen, L., Mattheisen, M., Mors, O., Mortensen, P. B., & Laursen, T. M. (2015). Secondary depression in severe anxiety disorders: A population-based cohort study in Denmark. *The Lancet Psychiatry, 2*(6), 515–523. https://doi.org/10.1016/S2215-0366(15)00092-9

Menghini, D., Armando, M., Calcagni, M., Napolitano, C., Pasqualetti, P., Sergeant, J. A., Pani, P., & Vicari, S. (2018). The influence of generalized anxiety disorder on executive functions in children with ADHD. *European Archives of Psychiatry and Clinical Neuroscience, 268*(4), 349–357. https://doi.org/10.1007/s00406-017-0831-9

Mento, C., Silvestri, M. C., Muscatello, M. R. A., Rizzo, A., Celebre, L., Praticò, M., Zoccali, R. A., & Bruno, A. (2021). Psychological impact of pro-anorexia and pro-eating disorder websites on adolescent females: A systematic review. *International Journal of Environmental Research and Public Health, 18*(4), 2186. https://doi.org/10.3390/ijerph18042186

Menzies, I. (1960). *The functioning of social systems as a defence against anxiety* (Pamphlet No. 3). Tavistock Publications.

Mikulincer, M., & Shaver, P. (2016). *Attachment in adulthood: Structure, dynamics, and change*. Guilford Press.

Minuchin, S., & Nichols, M. P. (1998). Structural family therapy. In F. M. Dattilio (Ed.), *Case studies in couple and family therapy: Systemic and cognitive perspectives* (pp. 108–131). Guilford Press.

Miret, M., Ayuso-Mateos, J. L., Sanchez-Moreno, J., & Vieta, E. (2013). Depressive disorders and suicide: Epidemiology, risk factors, and burden. *Neuroscience and Biobehavioral Reviews, 37*(10 Pt. 1), 2372–2374. https://doi.org/10.1016/j.neubiorev.2013.01.008

Mischel, W., & Shoda, Y. (1995). A cognitive-affective system theory of personality: Reconceptualizing situations, dispositions, dynamics, and invariance in personality structure. *Psychological Review, 102*(2), 246–268. https://doi.org/10.1037/0033-295X.102.2.246

Mishna, F., Van Wert, M., & Asakura, K. (2013). The best kept secret in social work: Empirical support for contemporary psychodynamic social work practice. *Journal of Social Work Practice, 27*(3), 289–303. https://doi.org/10.1080/02650533.2013.818944

Mitchell, S. A. (1995a). Interactions in the Kleinian and interpersonal traditions. *Contemporary Psychoanalysis, 31*(1), 65–91. https://doi.org/10.1080/00107530.1995.10746896

Mitchell, S. A. (1995b). *Hope and dread in psychoanalysis*. Basic Books.

Miyauchi, C. M., Takeuchi, H., Taki, Y., Nakagawa, S., Hanawa, S., Sekiguchi, A., Nouchi, R., Sassa, Y., & Kawashima, R. (2022). Shame proneness is associated with individual differences in temporal pole white matter structure. *Social Neuroscience, 17*(2), 117–126. https://doi.org/10.1080/17470919.2022.2039287

Moè, A. (2016). Does displayed enthusiasm favour recall, intrinsic motivation and time estimation? *Cognition and Emotion, 30*(7), 1361–1369. https://doi.org/10.1080/02699931.2015.1061480

Moitra, M., Santomauro, D., Degenhardt, L., Collins, P. Y., Whiteford, H., Vos, T., & Ferrari, A. (2021). Estimating the risk of suicide associated with mental disorders: A systematic review and meta-regression analysis. *Journal of Psychiatric Research, 137*, 242–249. https://doi.org/10.1016/j.jpsychires.2021.02.053

Mongrain, M. (1998). Parental representations and support-seeking behaviors related to dependency and self-criticism. *Journal of Personality, 66*(2), 151–173. https://doi.org/10.1111/1467-6494.00007

Mongrain, M., Lubbers, R., & Struthers, W. (2004). The power of love: Mediation of rejection in roommate relationships of dependents and self-critics. *Personality and Social Psychology Bulletin, 30*(1), 94–105. https://doi.org/10.1177/0146167203258861

Monroe, S. M. (2008). Modern approaches to conceptualizing and measuring human life stress. *Annual Review of Clinical Psychology, 4*(1), 33–52. https://doi.org/10.1146/annurev.clinpsy.4.022007.141207

Monroe, S. M., & Anderson, S. F. (2015). Depression: The shroud of heterogeneity. *Current Directions in Psychological Science, 24*(3), 227–231. https://doi.org/10.1177/0963721414568342

Monroe, S. M., & Harkness, K. L. (2005). Life stress, the "kindling" hypothesis, and the recurrence of depression: Considerations from a life stress perspective. *Psychological Review, 112*(2), 417–445. https://doi.org/10.1037/0033-295X.112.2.417

Monroe, S. M., & Simons, A. D. (1991). Diathesis-stress theories in the context of life stress research: Implications for the depressive disorders. *Psychological Bulletin, 110*(3), 406–425. https://doi.org/10.1037/0033-2909.110.3.406

Moos, R. H. (1994/2003). *Social Climate Scales: A user's guide*. Mind Garden.

Moreira, D. N., & Pinto da Costa, M. (2020). The impact of the Covid-19 pandemic in the precipitation of intimate partner violence. *International Journal of Law and Psychiatry, 71*(1016062), 101606. https://doi.org/10.1016/j.ijlp.2020.101606

Moreno-Agostino, D., Wu, Y. T., Daskalopoulou, C., Hasan, M. T., Huisman, M., & Prina, M. (2021). Global trends in the prevalence and incidence of depression: A systematic review and meta-analysis. *Journal of Affective Disorders, 281*, 235–243. https://doi.org/10.1016/j.jad.2020.12.035

Morita, A., Takahashi, Y., Takahashi, K., & Fujiwara, T. (2022). Depressive symptoms homophily among community-dwelling older adults in Japan: A social networks analysis. *Frontiers in Public Health, 10*, 965026. https://doi.org/10.3389/fpubh.2022.965026

Moroz, M., & Dunkley, D. M. (2019). Self-critical perfectionism, experiential avoidance, and depressive and anxious symptoms over two years: A three-wave longitudinal study. *Behaviour Research and Therapy, 112*(8), 18–27. https://doi.org/10.1016/j.brat.2018.11.006

Morrison, C. M., & Gore, H. (2010). The relationship between excessive Internet use and depression: A questionnaire-based study of 1,319 young people and adults. *Psychopathology, 43*(2), 121–126. https://doi.org/10.1159/000277001

Murayama, K., Nakao, T., Ohno, A., Tsuruta, S., Tomiyama, H., Hasuzawa, S., Mizobe, T., Kato, K., & Kanba, S. (2020). Impacts of stressful life events and traumatic experiences on onset of obsessive-compulsive disorder. *Frontiers in Psychiatry, 11*, 561266. https://doi.org/10.3389/fpsyt.2020.561266

Murphy, J. A., & Byrne, G. J. (2012). Prevalence and correlates of the proposed DSM-5 diagnosis of chronic depressive disorder. *Journal of Affective Disorders, 139*(2), 172–180. https://doi.org/10.1016/j.jad.2012.01.033

Murray, H. A. (1943). *Thematic Apperception Test manual.* Harvard University Press.

Nansel, T. R., Overpeck, M., Pilla, R. S., Ruan, W. J., Simons-Morton, B., & Scheidt, P. (2001). Bullying behaviors among US youth: Prevalence and association with psychosocial adjustment. *JAMA, 285*(16), 2094–2100. https://doi.org/10.1001/jama.285.16.2094

Nasir, M., Baucom, B. R., Georgiou, P., & Narayanan, S. (2017). Predicting couple therapy outcomes based on speech acoustic features. *PLOS ONE, 12*(9), e0185123. https://doi.org/10.1371/journal.pone.0185123

Nation, M., Chapman, D. A., Edmonds, T., Cosey-Gay, F. N., Jackson, T., Marshall, K. J., Gorman-Smith, D., Sullivan, T., & Trudeau, A. T. (2021). Social and structural determinants of health and youth violence: Shifting the paradigm of youth violence prevention. *American Journal of Public Health, 111*(S1), S28–S31. https://doi.org/10.2105/AJPH.2021.306234

National Institute for Health and Care Excellence. (2009a). *Depression: The treatment and management of depression in adults (update).* National Clinical Practice Guideline 90. https://www.nice.org.uk/guidance/cg90

National Institute for Health and Care Excellence. (2009b). *Depression in adults with a chronic physical health problem: Treatment and management,* CG91. https://www.nice.org.uk/guidance/CG91

National Institute of Mental Health. (n.d.). About RDoC. https://www.nimh.nih.gov/research/research-funded-by-nimh/rdoc/about-rdoc

National Institute of Mental Health. (2008). *The National Institute of Mental Health strategic plan.* https://www.nimh.nih.gov/about/strategic-planning-reports

Needles, D. J., & Abramson, L. Y. (1990). Positive life events, attributional style, and hopefulness: Testing a model of recovery from depression. *Journal of Abnormal Psychology, 99*(2), 156–165. https://doi.org/10.1037/0021-843X.99.2.156

Netanyahu, B., & Netanyahu, I. (1977). מכתבי יוני [*Yoni's letters*]. Maariv Press.

Netanyahu, B., & Netanyahu, I. (2001). *The letters of Jonathan Netanyahu: The commander of the Entebbe rescue force* (Kindle ed., M. Yoni, Trans.). Gefen.

Nock, M. K., Joiner, T. E., Jr., Gordon, K. H., Lloyd-Richardson, E., & Prinstein, M. J. (2006). Non-suicidal self-injury among adolescents: Diagnostic correlates and relation to suicide attempts. *Psychiatry Research, 144*(1), 65–72. https://doi.org/10.1016/j.psychres.2006.05.010

Norris, F. H., & Kaniasty, K. (1996). Received and perceived social support in times of stress: A test of the social support deterioration deterrence model. *Journal of Personality and Social Psychology, 71*(3), 498–511. https://doi.org/10.1037/0022-3514.71.3.498

Northoff, G. (2007). Psychopathology and pathophysiology of the self in depression—Neuropsychiatric hypothesis. *Journal of Affective Disorders, 104*(1–3), 1–14. https://doi.org/10.1016/j.jad.2007.02.012

Northoff, G. (2011). Self and brain: What is self-related processing? *Trends in Cognitive Sciences, 15*(5), 186–187. https://doi.org/10.1016/j.tics.2011.03.001

Noyman-Veksler, G., Lerman, S. F., Joiner, T. E., Brill, S., Rudich, Z., Shalev, H., & Shahar, G. (2017). Role of pain-based catastrophizing in pain, disability, distress, and suicidal ideation. *Psychiatry, 80*(2), 155–170. https://doi.org/10.1080/00332747.2016.1230984

O'Connor, L. E., Berry, J. W., Weiss, J., & Gilbert, P. (2002). Guilt, fear, submission, and empathy in depression. *Journal of Affective Disorders, 71*(1–3), 19–27. https://doi.org/10.1016/s0165-0327(01)00408-6

O'Connor, R. C. (2007). The relations between perfectionism and suicidality: A systematic review. *Suicide & Life-Threatening Behavior, 37*(6), 698–714. https://doi.org/10.1521/suli.2007.37.6.698

O'Connor, R. C., & Noyce, R. (2008). Personality and cognitive processes: Self-criticism and different types of rumination as predictors of suicidal ideation. *Behaviour Research and Therapy, 46*(3), 392–401. https://doi.org/10.1016/j.brat.2008.01.007

O'Neill, C., Pratt, D., Kilshaw, M., Ward, K., Kelly, J., & Haddock, G. (2021). The relationship between self-criticism and suicide probability. *Clinical Psychology & Psychotherapy, 28*(6), 1445–1456. https://doi.org/10.1002/cpp.2593

Odgers, C. L., & Jensen, M. R. (2020). Annual Research Review: Adolescent mental health in the digital age: Facts, fears, and future directions. *Journal of Child Psychology and Psychiatry, and Allied Disciplines, 61*(3), 336–348. https://doi.org/10.1111/jcpp.13190

Ogden, T. (1982). *Projective identification and psychotherapeutic technique.* Jason Aronson.
Ogden, T. H. (1992). *The matrix of the mind: Object relations and the psychoanalytic dialogue.* Karnac.
Ogrodniczuk, J. S., & Oliffe, J. L. (2011). Men and depression. *Canadian Family Physician Medecin de Famille Canadien, 57*(2), 153–155.
Orbach, I., Mikulincer, M., King, R., Cohen, D., & Stein, D. (1997). Thresholds and tolerance of physical pain in suicidal and nonsuicidal adolescents. *Journal of Consulting and Clinical Psychology, 65*(4), 646–652. https://doi.org/10.1037/0022-006X.65.4.646
Orhurhu, V., Olusunmade, M., Akinola, Y., Urits, I., Orhurhu, M. S., Viswanath, O., Hirji, S., Kaye, A. D., Simopoulos, T., & Gill, J. S. (2019). Depression trends in patients with chronic pain: An analysis of the nationwide inpatient sample. *Pain Physician, 22*(5), E487–E494. https://doi.org/10.36076/ppj/2019.22.E487
Ormel, J., Rosmalen, J., & Farmer, A. (2004). Neuroticism: A non-informative marker of vulnerability to psychopathology. *Social Psychiatry and Psychiatric Epidemiology, 39*(11), 906–912. https://doi.org/10.1007/s00127-004-0873-y
Ormel, J., & Wohlfarth, T. (1991). How neuroticism, long-term difficulties, and life situation change influence psychological distress: A longitudinal model. *Journal of Personality and Social Psychology, 60*(5), 744–755. https://doi.org/10.1037/0022-3514.60.5.744
Orth, U., Clark, D. A., Donnellan, M. B., & Robins, R. W. (2021). Testing prospective effects in longitudinal research: Comparing seven competing cross-lagged models. *Journal of Personality and Social Psychology, 120*(4), 1013–1034. https://doi.org/10.1037/pspp0000358
Ösby, U., Brandt, L., Correia, N., Ekbom, A., & Sparén, P. (2001). Excess mortality in bipolar and unipolar disorder in Sweden. *Archives of General Psychiatry, 58*(9), 844–850. https://doi.org/10.1001/archpsyc.58.9.844
Osório, C., Greenberg, N., Jones, N., Goodwin, M., Fertout, M., & Maia, A. (2013). Combat exposure and posttraumatic stress disorder among Portuguese special operation forces deployed in Afghanistan. *Military Psychology, 25*(1), 70–81. https://doi.org/10.1037/h0094758
Ozkan, T., Rocque, M., & Posick, C. (2019). Reconsidering the link between depression and crime: A longitudinal assessment. *Criminal Justice and Behavior, 46*(7), 961–979. https://doi.org/10.1177/0093854818799811
Pagura, J., Cox, B. J., Sareen, J., & Enns, M. W. (2006). Childhood adversities associated with self-criticism in a nationally representative sample. *Personality and Individual Differences, 41*(7), 1287–1298. https://doi.org/10.1016/j.paid.2006.05.003
Park, I. H., Lee, B. C., Kim, J. J., Kim, J. I., & Koo, M. S. (2017). Effort-based reinforcement processing and functional connectivity underlying amotivation in medicated patients with depression and schizophrenia. *The Journal of Neuroscience, 37*(16), 4370–4380. https://doi.org/10.1523/JNEUROSCI.2524-16.2017

Parker, G. (2014). Is major depression that major? *Acta Psychiatrica Scandinavica*, *129*(6), 458–459. https://doi.org/10.1111/acps.12189

Pascoe, M. C., Hetrick, S. E., & Parker, A. G. (2020). The impact of stress on students in secondary school and higher education. *International Journal of Adolescence and Youth*, *25*(1), 104–112. https://doi.org/10.1080/02673843.2019.1596823

Patton, M., Racine, N., Afzal, A. R., Russell, K. B., Forbes, C., Trépanier, L., Khu, M., Neville, A., Noel, M., Reynolds, K., & Schulte, F. (2021). The pain of survival: Prevalence, patterns, and predictors of pain in survivors of childhood cancer. *Health Psychology*, *40*(11), 784–792. https://doi.org/10.1037/hea0001116

Paykel, E. S. (2003). Life events and affective disorders. *Acta Psychiatrica Scandinavica. Supplementum*, *418*(Suppl.), 61–66. https://doi.org/10.1034/j.1600-0447.108.s418.13.x

Paykel, E. S. (2008). Basic concepts of depression. *Dialogues in Clinical Neuroscience*, *10*(3), 279–289. https://doi.org/10.31887/DCNS.2008.10.3/espaykel

Pe, M. L., Kircanski, K., Thompson, R. J., Bringmann, L. F., Tuerlinckx, F., Mestdagh, M., Mata, J., Jaeggi, S. M., Buschkuehl, M., Jonides, J., Kuppens, P., & Gotlib, I. H. (2015). Emotion-network density in major depressive disorder. *Clinical Psychological Science*, *3*(2), 292–300. https://doi.org/10.1177/2167702614540645

Pearson, V., & Liu, M. (2002). Ling's death: An ethnography of a Chinese woman's suicide. *Suicide & Life-Threatening Behavior*, *32*(4), 347–358. https://doi.org/10.1521/suli.32.4.347.22338

Pedrini, L., Ferrari, C., Lanfredi, M., Bellani, M., Porcelli, S., Caletti, E., Sala, M., Rossetti, M. G., Piccin, S., Dusi, N., Balestrieri, M., Perlini, C., Lazzaretti, M., Mandolini, G. M., Pigoni, A., Boscutti, A., Bonivento, C., Serretti, A., Rossi, R., Brambilla, P., & the GECO-BIP Group. (2021). The association of childhood trauma, lifetime stressful events and general psychopathological symptoms in euthymic bipolar patients and healthy subjects. *Journal of Affective Disorders*, *289*, 66–73. https://doi.org/10.1016/j.jad.2021.04.014

Perini, G., Cotta Ramusino, M., Sinforiani, E., Bernini, S., Petrachi, R., & Costa, A. (2019). Cognitive impairment in depression: Recent advances and novel treatments. *Neuropsychiatric Disease and Treatment*, *15*, 1249–1258. https://doi.org/10.2147/NDT.S199746

Peters, B. J., Reis, H. T., & Gables, S. L. (2018). Making the good even better: A review and theoretical model of interpersonal capitalization. *Social and Personality Psychology Compass*, *12*(7), e12407. https://doi.org/10.1111/spc3.12407

Pettit, J. W., & Joiner, T. E. (2006). *Chronic depression: Interpersonal sources, therapeutic solutions*. American Psychological Association. https://doi.org/10.1037/11291-000

Pincus, A. L., & Ansell, E. B. (2013). Interpersonal theory of personality. In J. Suls & H. Tennen (Eds.), *Handbook of psychology* (Vol. 5, 2nd ed., pp. 141–159). Wiley.

Piquero, A. R., Jennings, W. G., Jemison, E., Kaukinen, C., & Knaul, F. M. (2021). Domestic violence during the COVID-19 pandemic: Evidence from a systematic review and meta-analysis. *Journal of Criminal Justice, 74*, 101806. https://doi.org/10.1016/j.jcrimjus.2021.101806

Piquero, N. L., & Sealock, M. D. (2004). Gender and general strain theory: A preliminary test of Broidy and Agnew's gender/GST hypotheses. *Justice Quarterly, 21*(1), 125–158. https://doi.org/10.1080/07418820400095761

Plana-Ripoll, O., Pedersen, C. B., Holtz, Y., Benros, M. E., Dalsgaard, S., de Jonge, P., Fan, C. C., Degenhardt, L., Ganna, A., Greve, A. N., Gunn, J., Iburg, K. M., Kessing, L. V., Lee, B. K., Lim, C. C. W., Mors, O., Nordentoft, M., Prior, A., Roest, A. M., . . . McGrath, J. J. (2019). Exploring comorbidity within mental disorders among a Danish national population. *JAMA Psychiatry, 76*(3), 259–270. https://doi.org/10.1001/jamapsychiatry.2018.3658

Post, R. M. (1992). Transduction of psychosocial stress into the neurobiology of recurrent affective disorder. *The American Journal of Psychiatry, 149*(8), 999–1010. https://doi.org/10.1176/ajp.149.8.999

Priel, B., & Shahar, G. (2000). Dependency, self-criticism, social context and distress: Comparing moderating and mediating models. *Personality and Individual Differences, 28*(3), 515–525. https://doi.org/10.1016/S0191-8869(99)00116-6

Radloff, L. S. (1977). The CES-D Scale: A self-report depression scale for research in the general population. *Applied Psychological Measurement, 1*(3), 385–401. https://doi.org/10.1177/014662167700100306

Rafaeli, A., Ashtar, S., & Altman, D. (2019). Digital traces: New data, resources, and tools for psychological science research. *Current Directions in Psychological Science, 28*(6), 560–566. https://doi.org/10.1177/0963721419861410

Rafaeli, E., Bernstein, D. P., & Young, J. (2011). *Schema therapy: Distinctive features*. Routledge.

Raine, A. (2002). Biosocial studies of antisocial and violent behavior in children and adults: A review. *Journal of Abnormal Child Psychology, 30*(4), 311–326. https://doi.org/10.1023/A:1015754122318

Ran, L., Wang, W., Ai, M., Kong, Y., Chen, J., & Kuang, L. (2020). Psychological resilience, depression, anxiety, and somatization symptoms in response to COVID-19: A study of the general population in China at the peak of its epidemic. *Social Science & Medicine, 262*, 113261. https://doi.org/10.1016/j.socscimed.2020.113261

Rand, A. (1969). *The romantic manifesto: A philosophy of literature*. World Pub.

Rapaport, D., Gill, M., & Schafer, R. (1946). *Diagnostic psychological testing: The theory, statistical evaluation, and diagnostic application of a battery of tests* (Vol. 2). Year Book Publishers.

Reiff, C. M., Richman, E. E., Nemeroff, C. B., Carpenter, L. L., Widge, A. S., Rodriguez, C. I., Kalin, N. H., McDonald, W. M., & the Work Group on Biomarkers and Novel Treatments, a Division of the American Psychiatric Association Council of Research. (2020). Psychedelics and psychedelic-assisted psychotherapy. *The American Journal of Psychiatry, 177*(5), 391–410. https://doi.org/10.1176/appi.ajp.2019.19010035

Reuven-Krispin, H., Lassri, D., Luyten, P., & Shahar, G. (2021). Consequences of divorce-based father absence during childhood for young adult well-being and romantic relationships. *Family Relations, 70*(2), 452–466. https://doi.org/10.1111/fare.12516

Ricoeur, P. (1970). *Freud and philosophy: An essay on interpretation*. Yale University Press.

Rieger, S., Göllner, R., Trautwein, U., & Roberts, B. W. (2016). Low self-esteem prospectively predicts depression in the transition to young adulthood: A replication of Orth, Robins, and Roberts (2008). *Journal of Personality and Social Psychology, 110*(1), e16–e22. https://doi.org/10.1037/pspp0000037

Robins, C. J., Ladd, J. S., Welkowitz, J., Blaney, P. H., Diaz, R., & Kutcher, G. (1994). The Personal Style Inventory: Preliminary validation studies of a new measure of sociotropy and autonomy. *Journal of Psychopathology and Behavioral Assessment, 16*(4), 277–300. https://doi.org/10.1007/BF02239408

Robins, C. J., Zerubavel, N., Ivanoff, A. M., & Linehan, M. M. (2018). Dialectical behavior therapy. In W. J. Livesley & R. Larstone (Eds.), *Handbook of personality disorders: Theory, research, and treatment* (pp. 527–540). Guilford Press.

Robins, L. N., Helzer, J. E., Croughan, J., & Ratcliff, K. S. (1981). National Institute of Mental Health Diagnostic Interview Schedule. Its history, characteristics, and validity. *Archives of General Psychiatry, 38*(4), 381–389. https://doi.org/10.1001/archpsyc.1981.01780290015001

Robinson, A., Moscardini, E., Tucker, R., & Calamia, M. (2022). Perfectionistic self-presentation, socially prescribed perfectionism, self-oriented perfectionism, interpersonal hopelessness, and suicidal ideation in U.S. adults: Reexamining the social disconnection model. *Archives of Suicide Research, 26*(3), 1447–1461. https://doi.org/10.1080/13811118.2021.1922108

Rochlen, A. B., McKelley, R. A., & Pituch, K. A. (2006). A preliminary examination of the "Real Men. Real Depression" campaign. *Psychology of Men & Masculinity, 7*(1), 1–13. https://doi.org/10.1037/1524-9220.7.1.1

Rogers, C. R. (1963a). Actualizing tendency in relation to "motives" and to consciousness. In M. R. Jones (Ed.), *Nebraska symposium on motivation* (pp. 1–24). University of Nebraska Press.

Rogers, C. R. (1963b). The concept of the fully functioning person. *Psychotherapy: Theory, Research, & Practice, 1*(1), 17–26. https://doi.org/10.1037/h0088567

Rogers, M. L., Chu, C., & Joiner, T. (2019). The necessity, validity, and clinical utility of a new diagnostic entity: Acute suicidal affective disturbance. *Journal of Clinical Psychology, 75*(6), 999–1010. https://doi.org/10.1002/jclp.22743

Rogers, M. L., Joiner, T. E., & Shahar, G. (2021). Suicidality in chronic illness: An overview of cognitive–affective and interpersonal factors. *Journal of Clinical Psychology in Medical Settings, 28*(1), 137–148. https://doi.org/10.1007/s10880-020-09749-x

Rohde, P., Lewinsohn, P. M., & Seeley, J. R. (1990). Are people changed by the experience of having an episode of depression? A further test of the scar hypothesis. *Journal of Abnormal Psychology, 99*(3), 264–271. https://doi.org/10.1037/0021-843X.99.3.264

Roseman, I. J. (2018). Rejecting the unworthy: The causes, components, and consequences of contempt. In M. Mason (Ed.), *The moral psychology of contempt* (pp. 107–130). Rowman & Littlefield.

Rosenthal, N. E. (1987). *Seasonal Pattern Assessment Questionnaire (SPAQ)* [Database record]. APA PsycTests. https://doi.org/10.1037/t26640-000

Rossi, R., Jannini, T. B., Socci, V., Pacitti, F., & Lorenzo, G. D. (2021). Stressful life events and resilience during the COVID-19 lockdown measures in Italy: Association with mental health outcomes and age. *Frontiers in Psychiatry, 12*, 635832. https://doi.org/10.3389/fpsyt.2021.635832

Rost, F., Luyten, P., Fearon, P., & Fonagy, P. (2019). Personality and outcome in individuals with treatment-resistant depression: Exploring differential treatment effects in the Tavistock Adult Depression Study (TADS). *Journal of Consulting and Clinical Psychology, 87*(5), 433–445. https://doi.org/10.1037/ccp0000391

Roth, W.-M. (2013). *What more in/for science education: An ethnomethodological perspective*. Springer. https://doi.org/10.1007/978-94-6209-254-9

Rottenberg, J. (2014). *The depths: The evolutionary basis of the depression epidemic*. Basic Books.

Rudich, Z., Lerman, S. F., Gurevich, B., & Shahar, G. (2010). Pain specialists' evaluation of patient's prognosis during the first visit predicts subsequent depression and the affective dimension of pain. *Pain Medicine, 11*(3), 446–452. https://doi.org/10.1111/j.1526-4637.2009.00795.x

Rudich, Z., Lerman, S. F., Gurevich, B., Weksler, N., & Shahar, G. (2008). Patients' self-criticism is a stronger predictor of physician's evaluation of prognosis than pain diagnosis or severity in chronic pain patients. *The Journal of Pain, 9*(3), 210–216. https://doi.org/10.1016/j.jpain.2007.10.013

Russell, D. W., Booth, B., Reed, D., & Laughlin, P. R. (1997). Personality, social networks, and perceived social support among alcoholics: A structural equation analysis. *Journal of Personality, 65*(3), 649–692. https://doi.org/10.1111/j.1467-6494.1997.tb00330.x

Rutter, M., Dunn, J., Plomin, R., Simonoff, E., Pickles, A., Maughan, B., Ormel, J., Meyer, J., & Eaves, L. (1997). Integrating nature and nurture: Implications of person-environment correlations and interactions for developmental psychopathology. *Development and Psychopathology, 9*(2), 335–364. https://doi.org/10.1017/S0954579497002083

Ryan, R. M., & Deci, E. L. (2000). Self-determination theory and the facilitation of intrinsic motivation, social development, and well-being. *American Psychologist, 55*(1), 68–78. https://doi.org/10.1037/0003-066X.55.1.68

Sachs-Ericsson, N. J., Sheffler, J. L., Stanley, I. H., Piazza, J. R., & Preacher, K. J. (2017). When emotional pain becomes physical: Adverse childhood experiences, pain, and the role of mood and anxiety disorders. *Journal of Clinical Psychology, 73*(10), 1403–1428. https://doi.org/10.1002/jclp.22444

Sadek, N., & Bona, J. (2000). Subsyndromal symptomatic depression: A new concept. *Depression and Anxiety, 12*(1), 30–39. https://doi.org/10.1002/1520-6394(2000)12:1<30::AID-DA4>3.0.CO;2-P

Sagiv, L., & Schwartz, S. H. (2022). Personal values across cultures. *Annual Review of Psychology, 73*(1), 517–546. https://doi.org/10.1146/annurev-psych-020821-125100

Sameroff, A. J. (Ed.). (2009). *The transactional model of development: How children and contexts shape each other*. American Psychological Association. https://doi.org/10.1037/11877-000

Samuel, D. B., Simms, L. J., Clark, L. A., Livesley, W. J., & Widiger, T. A. (2010). An item response theory integration of normal and abnormal personality scales. *Personality Disorders, 1*(1), 5–21. https://doi.org/10.1037/a0018136

Samuelson, K. W., Bartel, A., Valadez, R., & Jordan, J. T. (2017, September). PTSD symptoms and perception of cognitive problems: The roles of posttraumatic cognitions and trauma coping self-efficacy. *Psychological Trauma: Theory, Research, Practice, and Policy, 9*(5), 537–544. https://doi.org/10.1037/tra0000210

Sander, L., Gerhardinger, K., Bailey, E., Robinson, J., Lin, J., Cuijpers, P., & Mühlmann, C. (2020). Suicide risk management in research on internet-based interventions for depression: A synthesis of the current state and recommendations for future research. *Journal of Affective Disorders, 263*, 676–683. https://doi.org/10.1016/j.jad.2019.11.045

Sandler, J. (1976). Countertransference and role responsiveness. *The International Review of Psycho-Analysis, 3*(1), 43–47.

Sarason, I. G., Pierce, G. R., & Sarason, B. R. (1994). General and specific perceptions of social support. In W. R. Avison & I. H. Gotlib (Eds.), *Stress and mental health*. Springer. https://doi.org/10.1007/978-1-4899-1106-3_6

Sayeed, A., Kundu, S., Al Banna, M. H., Christopher, E., Hasan, M. T., Begum, M. R., Chowdhury, S., & Khan, M. S. I. (2020). Mental health outcomes of adults with comorbidity and chronic diseases during the COVID-19 pandemic: A matched case-control study. *Psychiatria Danubina, 32*(3–4), 491–498. https://doi.org/10.24869/psyd.2020.491

Schafer, R. (1954). *Psychoanalytic interpretation in Rorschach testing*. Grune & Stratton.

Schafer, R. (1968). *Aspects of internalization*. International Universities Press.

Scheff, T. J. (2001). Shame and community: Social components in depression. *Psychiatry, 64*(3), 212–224. https://doi.org/10.1521/psyc.64.3.212.18457

Schiller, M., Hammen, C. C., & Shahar, G. (2016). Comparing three theoretical models of the links between self, stress, and psychopathological Distress during emerging adulthood. *Self and Identity, 15*(3), 302–326. https://doi.org/10.1080/15298868.2015.1131736

Schiller, M., Pinus, M., Hammen, C., & Shahar, G. (2019). Effects of psychological distress and terror stress on young adults' self-concept. *International Journal of Cognitive Psychotherapy, 12*(4), 242–259. https://doi.org/10.1007/s41811-019-00053-7

Schiller, M., & Shahar, G. (2013). Self-esteem instability moderates psychopathological scarring: Support for a malleable self hypothesis. *International Journal of Cognitive Therapy, 6*(1), 17–23. https://doi.org/10.1521/ijct.2013.6.1.17

Schindel-Allon, I., Aderka, I. M., Shahar, G., Stein, M., & Gilboa-Schechtman, E. (2010). Longitudinal associations between post-traumatic distress and depressive symptoms following a traumatic event: A test of three models. *Psychological Medicine, 40*(10), 1669–1678. https://doi.org/10.1017/S0033291709992248

Schmidt, N. B., Kotov, R., & Joiner, T. E. (2004). *Taxometrics: Toward a new diagnostic scheme for psychopathology.* American Psychological Association. https://doi.org/10.1037/10810-000

Schramm, E., Klein, D. N., Elsaesser, M., Furukawa, T. A., & Domschke, K. (2020). Review of dysthymia and persistent depressive disorder: History, correlates, and clinical implications. *The Lancet Psychiatry, 7*(9), 801–812. https://doi.org/10.1016/S2215-0366(20)30099-7

Schramm, E., Zobel, I., Dykierek, P., Kech, S., Brakemeier, E. L., Külz, A., & Berger, M. (2011). Cognitive behavioral analysis system of psychotherapy versus interpersonal psychotherapy for early-onset chronic depression: A randomized pilot study. *Journal of Affective Disorders, 129*(1–3), 109–116. https://doi.org/10.1016/j.jad.2010.08.003

Scott, J., & Carrington, P. J. (2014). *The SAGE handbook of social network analysis.* Sage. https://doi.org/10.4135/9781446294413

Sedikides, C., & Green, J. D. (2004). What I don't recall can't hurt me: Negativity versus information inconsistency as determinants of memorial self-defense. *Social Cognition, 22*(1), 4–29. https://doi.org/10.1521/soco.22.1.4.30987

Sedikides, C., & Green, J. D. (2009). Memory as a self-protective mechanism. *Social and Personality Psychology Compass, 3*(6), 1055–1068. https://doi.org/10.1111/j.1751-9004.2009.00220.x

Sedlinská, T., Mühle, C., Richter-Schmidinger, T., Weinland, C., Kornhuber, J., & Lenz, B. (2021). Male depression syndrome is characterized by pronounced Cluster B personality traits. *Journal of Affective Disorders, 292*, 725–732. https://doi.org/10.1016/j.jad.2021.05.114

Seligman, M. E. (1995). The effectiveness of psychotherapy. The Consumer Reports study. *American Psychologist, 50*(12), 965–974. https://doi.org/10.1037/0003-066X.50.12.965

Seligman, M. E., Railton, P., Baumeister, R. F., & Sripada, C. (2013). Navigating into the future or driven by the past. *Perspectives on Psychological Science, 8*(2), 119–141. https://doi.org/10.1177/1745691612474317

Seyerle, A. A., & Avery, C. L. (2013). Genetic epidemiology: The potential benefits and challenges of using genetic information to improve human health. *North*

Carolina Medical Journal, 74(6), 505–508. https://doi.org/10.18043/ncm. 74.6.505

Shahar, G. (2001). Personality, shame, and the breakdown of social bonds: The voice of quantitative depression research. *Psychiatry, 64*(3), 228–239. https://doi.org/10.1521/psyc.64.3.228.18463

Shahar, G. (2004). Transference-countertransference: Where the (political) action is. *Journal of Psychotherapy Integration, 14*(4), 371–396. https://doi.org/10.1037/1053-0479.14.4.371

Shahar, G. (2006a). Clinical action: Introduction to the special section on the action perspective in clinical psychology. *Journal of Clinical Psychology, 62*(9), 1053–1064. https://doi.org/10.1002/jclp.20290

Shahar, G. (2006b). An investigation of the perfectionism/self-criticism domain of the Personal Style Inventory. *Cognitive Therapy and Research, 30*(2), 185–200. https://doi.org/10.1007/s10608-006-9032-y

Shahar, G. (2008). What measure of interpersonal dependency predicts changes in social support? *Journal of Personality Assessment, 90*(1), 61–65. https://doi.org/10.1080/00223890701693751

Shahar, G. (2010). Poetics, pragmatics, schematics, and the psychoanalysis-research dialogue (rift). *Psychoanalytic Psychotherapy, 24*(4), 315–328. https://doi.org/10.1080/02668734.2010.513544

Shahar, G. (2011). Projectuality vs. eventuality: Sullivan, the ambivalent intentionalist. *Journal of Psychotherapy Integration, 21*(2), 211–220. https://doi.org/10.1037/a0022909

Shahar, G. (2012). "I don't want to be here": Projectuality and eventuality in Ms. T's case. *Journal of Psychotherapy Integration, 22*, 27–32. https://doi.org/10.1037/a0027321

Shahar, G. (2013a). The heroic self: Conceptualization, measurement, and role in distress. *International Journal of Cognitive Therapy, 6*(3), 248–264. https://doi.org/10.1521/ijct.2013.6.3.248

Shahar, G. (2013b). An integrative psychotherapist's account of his focus when treating self-critical patients. *Psychotherapy, 50*(3), 322–325. https://doi.org/10.1037/a0032033

Shahar, G. (2015a). *Erosion: The psychopathology of self-criticism*. Oxford University Press. https://doi.org/10.1093/med:psych/9780199929368.001.0001

Shahar, G. (2015b). Object relations theory. In R. Cautin & S. Lillinfeld (Eds.), *The encyclopedia of clinical psychology*. Wiley. https://doi.org/10.1002/9781118625392.wbecp297

Shahar, G. (2016). Criticism in the self, brain, social relations and social structure: Implications for psychodynamic psychiatry. *Psychodynamic Psychiatry, 44*(3), 395–421. https://doi.org/10.1521/pdps.2016.44.3.395

Shahar, G. (2018). The (suicidal-) depressive position: A scientifically informed reformulation. *Psychodynamic Psychiatry, 46*(2), 265–293. https://doi.org/10.1521/pdps.2018.46.2.265

Shahar, G. (2019). The nature of the beast: Commentary on "Can there be a recovery-oriented diagnostic practice?" *Journal of Humanistic Psychology*, *59*(3), 346–355. https://doi.org/10.1177/0022167818777653

Shahar, G. (2020). The subjective-agentic personality sector (SAPS): Introduction to the special issue on self, identity, and psychopathology. *Journal of Personality*, *88*(1), 5–13. https://doi.org/10.1111/jopy.12497

Shahar, G. (2021a). Integrative psychotherapy with physicians in the trenches: Convergence of cognitive, existential, and psychodynamic processes. *Journal of Humanistic Psychology*. Advance online publication. https://doi.org/10.1177/00221678211065580

Shahar, G. (2021b). Reformulated object relations theory: A bridge between clinical psychoanalysis, psychotherapy integration, and the understanding and treatment of suicidal depression. *Frontiers in Psychology*, *12*, 721746. https://doi.org/10.3389/fpsyg.2021.721746

Shahar, G., Aharonson-Daniel, L., Greenberg, D., Shalev, H., Malone, P. S., Tendler, A., Grotto, I., & Davidovitch, N. (2022). Changes in general and virus-specific anxiety during the spread of COVID-19 in Israel: A 7-wave longitudinal study. *American Journal of Epidemiology*, *191*(1), 49–62. https://doi.org/10.1093/aje/kwab214

Shahar, G., Ahronson-Daniel, L., Greenberg, D., Shalev, H., Tendler, A., Grotto, I., Malone, P., & Davidovitch, N. (2023). Anxiety in the face of the first wave of the spread of COVID-19 in Israel: Psychosocial determinants of a "panic-to-complacency-continuum." *Social Science & Medicine*, *317*, 115585. https://doi.org/10.1016/j.socscimed.2022.115585

Shahar, G., Bauminger, R., & Itamar, S. (2020). A lion's blues: Heroism, heroic self-representations, and emotional distress in the life and character of Yonatan (Yoni) Netanyahu. *Heroism Science*, *5*(2). Advance online publication. https://doi.org/10.26736/hs.2020.02.05

Shahar, G., Blatt, S. J., Zuroff, D. C., Krupnick, J., & Sotsky, S. M. (2004). Perfectionism impedes social relations and response to brief treatment for depression. *Journal of Social and Clinical Psychology*, *23*(2), 140–154. https://doi.org/10.1521/jscp.23.2.140.31017

Shahar, G., Blatt, S. J., Zuroff, D. C., Kuperminck, G. P., & Leadbeater, B. J. (2004). Reciprocal relations between depressive symptoms and self-criticism (but not dependency) among early adolescent girls (but not boys). *Cognitive Therapy and Research*, *28*(1), 85–103. https://doi.org/10.1023/B:COTR.0000016932.82038.d0

Shahar, G., Cohen, G., Grogan, K. E., Barile, J. P., & Henrich, C. C. (2009). Terrorism-related perceived stress, adolescent depression, and social support from friends. *Pediatrics*, *124*(2), e235–e240. https://doi.org/10.1542/peds.2008-2971

Shahar, G., Cross, L. W., & Henrich, C. C. (2004). Representations in action (Or: Action models of development meet psychoanalytic conceptualizations of mental representations). *The Psychoanalytic Study of the Child*, 59(1), 261–293. https://doi.org/10.1080/00797308.2004.11800741

Shahar, G., & Davidson, L. (2003). Depressive symptoms erode self-esteem in severe mental illness: A three-wave, cross-lagged study. *Journal of Consulting and Clinical Psychology*, 71(5), 890–900. https://doi.org/10.1037/0022-006X.71.5.890

Shahar, G., & Davidson, L. (2009). Participation-engagement: A philosophically based heuristic for prioritizing clinical interventions in the treatment of comorbid, complex, and chronic psychiatric conditions. *Psychiatry*, 72(2), 154–176. https://doi.org/10.1521/psyc.2009.72.2.154

Shahar, G., Gallagher, E. F., Blatt, S. J., Kuperminc, G. P., & Leadbeater, B. J. (2004). An interactive-synergetic approach to the assessment of personality vulnerability to depression: Illustration using the adolescent version of the Depressive Experiences Questionnaire. *Journal of Clinical Psychology*, 60(6), 605–625. https://doi.org/10.1002/jclp.10237

Shahar, G., & Govrin, A. (2017). Psychodynamizing and existentializing cognitive-behavioral interventions: The case of behavioral activation (BA). *Psychotherapy*, 54(3), 267–272. https://doi.org/10.1037/pst0000115

Shahar, G., & Henrich, C. C. (2010). Do depressive symptoms erode self-esteem in early adolescence? *Self and Identity*, 9(4), 403–415. https://doi.org/10.1080/15298860903286090

Shahar, G., & Henrich, C. C. (2013). Axis of Criticism Model (ACRIM): An integrative conceptualization of person-context exchanges in vulnerability to adolescent psychopathology. *Journal of Psychotherapy Integration*, 23(3), 236–249. https://doi.org/10.1037/a0031418

Shahar, G., & Henrich, C. C. (2016). Perceived family social support buffers against the effects of exposure to rocket attacks on adolescent depression, aggression, and severe violence. *Journal of Family Psychology*, 30(1), 163–168. https://doi.org/10.1037/fam0000179

Shahar, G., & Henrich, C. C. (2019). Role of adolescent exposure to rockets in the links between personality vulnerability and psychopathology. *Development and Psychopathology*, 31(4), 1367–1380. https://doi.org/10.1017/S0954579418000792

Shahar, G., Henrich, C. C., Blatt, S. J., Ryan, R., & Little, T. D. (2003). Interpersonal relatedness, self-definition, and their motivational orientation during adolescence: A theoretical and empirical integration. *Developmental Psychology*, 39(3), 470–483. https://doi.org/10.1037/0012-1649.39.3.470

Shahar, G., Henrich, C. C., Reiner, I. C., & Little, T. D. (2003). Development and initial validation of the brief adolescent life event scale (BALES). *Anxiety, Stress, and Coping*, 16(1), 119–128. https://doi.org/10.1080/1061580021000057077

Shahar, G., Herishanu-Gilutz, S., Holcberg, G., & Kofman, O. (2015). In first-time mothers, post-partum depressive symptom prospectively predict symptoms of post-traumatic stress. *Journal of Affective Disorders*, 186, 168–170. https://doi.org/10.1016/j.jad.2015.07.021

Shahar, G., Joiner, T. E., Jr., Zuroff, D. C., & Blatt, S. J. (2004). Personality, interpersonal behavior, and depression: Co-existence of stress-specific moderating and mediating effects. *Personality and Individual Differences, 36*(7), 1583–1596. https://doi.org/10.1016/j.paid.2003.06.006

Shahar, G., Lassri, D., & Luyten, P. (2014). Depression in chronic illness: A behavioral medicine approach. In D. Mostofsky (Ed.), *Handbook of behavioral medicine* (pp. 3–22). Wiley. https://doi.org/10.1002/9781118453940.ch1

Shahar, G., Lerman, S. F., Topaz, M., Brill, S., Shalev, H., & Rudich, Z. (2018). Depressive personality vulnerability in chronic physical pain: Centrality of sociotropy. *Journal of Personality, 86*(6), 907–918. https://doi.org/10.1111/jopy.12365

Shahar, G., & Mayes, L. (2017). Cognitive-humanistic psychodynamics: Sidney Blatt's theoretical-philosophical legacy. *Journal of the American Psychoanalytic Association, 65*(3), 457–472. https://doi.org/10.1177/0003065117709013

Shahar, G., & Mayes, L. C. (in press). Development as a multi-systemic endeavor: Personal and professional reflections on S. J. Blatt's philosophy of development. *Psychoanalytic Inquiry*.

Shahar, G., Noyman, G., Schnidel-Allon, I., & Gilboa-Schechtman, E. (2013). Do PTSD symptoms and trauma-related cognitions about the self constitute a vicious cycle? Evidence for both cognitive vulnerability and scarring models. *Psychiatry Research, 205*(1–2), 79–84. https://doi.org/10.1016/j.psychres.2012.07.053

Shahar, G., Porcerelli, J. H., Kamoo, R., Epperson, C. N., Czarkowski, K. A., Magriples, U., & Mayes, L. C. (2010). Defensive projection, superimposed on simplistic object relations, erodes patient-provider relationships in high-risk pregnancy: An empirical investigation. *Journal of the American Psychoanalytic Association, 58*(5), 953–974. https://doi.org/10.1177/0003065110392228

Shahar, G., & Priel, B. (2002). Positive life events and adolescent emotional distress: In search for protective-interactive processes. *Journal of Social and Clinical Psychology, 21*(6), 645–668. https://doi.org/10.1521/jscp.21.6.645.22798

Shahar, G., & Priel, B. (2003). Active vulnerability, adolescent distress, and the mediating/suppressing role of life events. *Personality and Individual Differences, 35*(1), 199–218. https://doi.org/10.1016/S0191-8869(02)00185-X

Shahar, G., Rogers, M. L., Shalev, H., & Joiner, T. E. (2020). Self-criticism, interpersonal conditions, and biosystemic inflammation in suicidal thoughts and behaviors within mood disorders: A bio-cognitive-interpersonal hypothesis. *Journal of Personality, 88*(1), 133–145. https://doi.org/10.1111/jopy.12446

Shahar, G., & Schiller, M. (2016a). A conqueror by stealth: Introduction to the special issue on humanism, existentialism, and psychotherapy integration. *Journal of Psychotherapy Integration, 26*(1), 1–4. https://doi.org/10.1037/int0000024

Shahar, G., & Schiller, M. (2016b). Treating the depressive self: A psychodynamic-integrative approach. In K. Kyrios, S. Bhar, G. Doron, M. Mikulincer, R. Roulding,

& M. Nedeljkovic (Eds.), *The self in understanding and treating psychological disorders* (pp. 29–39). Cambridge University Press. https://doi.org/10.1017/CBO9781139941297.005

Shahar, G., Scotti, M. A., Rudd, M. D., & Joiner, T. E. (2008). Hypomanic symptoms predict an increase in narcissistic and histrionic personality disorder features in suicidal young adults. *Depression and Anxiety, 25*(10), 892–898. https://doi.org/10.1002/da.20363

Shahar, G., & Ziv-Beiman, S. (2020). Using termination as an intervention (UTAI): A view from an integrative, cognitive-existential psychodynamics perspective. *Psychotherapy* (Chicago, Ill.), *57*(4), 515–520. https://doi.org/10.1037/pst0000337

Shedler, J. (2022). Integrating clinical and empirical approaches to personality: The Shedler-Westen Assessment Procedure (SWAP). In R. E. Feinstein (Ed.), *Personality disorders* (pp. 87–108). Oxford University Press.

Sheehan, D. V., Lecrubier, Y., Sheehan, K. H., Amorim, P., Janavs, J., Weiller, E., Hergueta, T., Baker, R., & Dunbar, G. C. (1998). The Mini-International Neuropsychiatric Interview (M.I.N.I.): The development and validation of a structured diagnostic psychiatric interview for *DSM-IV* and *ICD-10*. *The Journal of Clinical Psychiatry, 59*(Suppl. 20), 22–33.

Sheerin, C. M., Lind, M. J., Brown, E. A., Gardner, C. O., Kendler, K. S., & Amstadter, A. B. (2018). The impact of resilience and subsequent stressful life events on MDD and GAD. *Depression and Anxiety, 35*(2), 140–147. https://doi.org/10.1002/da.22700

Shem, S. (1978). *The house of God* (1st ed.). Richard Marek Publishers.

Sheridan, C. L., & Smith, L. K. (1987). Toward a comprehensive scale of stress assessment: Development, norms and reliability. *International Journal of Psychosomatics, 34*(4), 48–54.

Shevlin, M., Hyland, P., Nolan, E., Owczarek, M., Ben-Ezra, M., & Karatzias, T. (2022). *ICD-11* 'mixed depressive and anxiety disorder' is clinical rather than sub-clinical and more common than anxiety and depression in the general population. *British Journal of Clinical Psychology, 61*(1), 18–36. https://doi.org/10.1111/bjc.12321

Shulman, S., Kalnizki, E., & Shahar, G. (2009). Meeting developmental challenges during emerging adulthood: The role of personality and social resources. *Journal of Adolescent Research, 24*(2), 242–267. https://doi.org/10.1177/0743558408329303

Siegrist, J., Tough, H., Brinkhof, M. W. G., Fekete, C., & the SwiSCI study group. (2020). Failed reciprocity in social exchange and wellbeing: Evidence from a longitudinal dyadic study in the disability setting. *Psychology & Health, 35*(9), 1134–1150. https://doi.org/10.1080/08870446.2019.1707826

Simonton, D. K. (1998). Mad King George: The impact of personal and political stress on mental and physical health. *Journal of Personality, 66*(3), 443–466. https://doi.org/10.1111/1467-6494.00018

Skodol, A. E., Stout, R. L., McGlashan, T. H., Grilo, C. M., Gunderson, J. G., Shea, M. T., Morey, L. C., Zanarini, M. C., Dyck, I. R., & Oldham, J. M. (1999). Co-occurrence of mood and personality disorders: A report from the Collaborative Longitudinal Personality Disorders Study (CLPS). *Depression and Anxiety*, *10*(4), 175–182. https://doi.org/10.1002/(SICI)1520-6394(1999)10:4<175::AID-DA6>3.0.CO;2-2

Smith, M. M., Sherry, S. B., Ray, C., Hewitt, P. L., & Flett, G. L. (2021). Is perfectionism a vulnerability factor for depressive symptoms, a complication of depressive symptoms, or both? A meta-analytic test of 67 longitudinal studies. *Clinical Psychology Review*, *84*, 101982. https://doi.org/10.1016/j.cpr.2021.101982

Smith, M. M., Sherry, S. B., Rnic, K., Saklofske, D. H., Enns, M., & Gralnick, T. (2016). Are perfectionism dimensions vulnerability factors for depressive symptoms after controlling for neuroticism? A meta-analysis of 10 longitudinal studies. *European Journal of Personality*, *30*(2), 201–212. https://doi.org/10.1002/per.2053

Smith, R. C. (2020). It's time to view severe medically unexplained symptoms as red-flag symptoms of depression and anxiety. *JAMA Network Open*, *3*(7), e2011520. https://doi.org/10.1001/jamanetworkopen.2020.11520

Smith, T. W. (1992). Hostility and health: Current status of a psychosomatic hypothesis. *Health Psychology*, *11*(3), 139–150. https://doi.org/10.1037/0278-6133.11.3.139

Snow, C. P. (1959). *The two cultures and the scientific revolution*. Cambridge University Press.

Society for the Exploration of Psychotherapy Integration. (2023). SEPI website. https://www.sepiweb.org/

Soenens, B., Vansteenkiste, M., & Luyten, P. (2010). Towards a domain-specific approach to the study of parental psychological control: Distinguishing between dependency-oriented and achievement-oriented psychological control. *Journal of Personality*, *78*(1), 217–256. https://doi.org/10.1111/j.1467-6494.2009.00614.x

Soffer, N., Gilboa-Shechtman, E., & Shahar, G. (2008). The relationships of childhood emotional abuse and neglect to depressive vulnerability and low self-efficacy. *International Journal of Cognitive Therapy*, *1*(2), 151–162. https://doi.org/10.1521/ijct.2008.1.2.151

Soffer-Dudek, N., & Shahar, G. (2009). What are sleep-related experiences? Associations with transliminality, psychological distress, and life stress. *Consciousness and Cognition*, *18*(4), 891–904. https://doi.org/10.1016/j.concog.2008.07.007

Solomon, A. (2015). *The noonday demon: An atlas of depression*. Scribner.

Solomon, D. A., Keller, M. B., Leon, A. C., Mueller, T. I., Lavori, P. W., Shea, M. T., Coryell, W., Warshaw, M., Turvey, C., Maser, J. D., & Endicott, J. (2000). Multiple recurrences of major depressive disorder. *The American Journal of Psychiatry*, *157*(2), 229–233. https://doi.org/10.1176/appi.ajp.157.2.229

Spence, D. P. (1982). *Narrative truth and historical truth: Meaning and interpretation in psychoanalysis*. Norton.
Spiranovic, C., Hudson, N., Winter, R., Stanford, S., Norris, K., Bartkowiak-Theron, I., & Cashman, K. (2021). Navigating risk and protective factors for family violence during and after the COVID-19 'perfect storm.' *Current Issues in Criminal Justice, 33*(1), 5–18. https://doi.org/10.1080/10345329.2020.1849933
Stallings, M. C., Dunham, C. C., Gats, M., Baker, L., & Bengtson, V. L. (1997). Relationships among life events and psychological well-being: More evidence for a two-factor theory of well-being. *Journal of Applied Gerontology, 16*(1), 104–119. https://doi.org/10.1177/073346489701600106
Stein, M. B., Slavin-Mulford, J., Siefert, C. J., Sinclair, S. J., Smith, M., Chung, W.-J., Liebman, R., & Blais, M. A. (2015). External validity of SCORS-G ratings of Thematic Apperception Test narratives in a sample of outpatients and inpatients. *Rorschachiana, 36*(1), 58–81. https://doi.org/10.1027/1192-5604/a000057
Stensland, M. (2021). "If you don't keep going, you're gonna die": Helplessness and perseverance among older adults living with chronic low back pain. *The Gerontologist, 61*(6), 907–916. https://doi.org/10.1093/geront/gnaa150
Sterzing, P. R., Auslander, W. F., & Goldbach, J. T. (2014). An exploratory study of bullying involvement for sexual minority youth: Bully-only, victim-only, and bully-victim roles. *Journal of the Society for Social Work and Research, 5*(3), 321–337. https://doi.org/10.1086/677903
Stolorow, R. D., Brandshaft, B., & Atwood, G. E. (1987). *Psychoanalytic treatment: An intersubjective approach*. Analytic.
Strenger, C. (1989). The classic and the romantic vision in psychoanalysis. *The International Journal of Psycho-Analysis, 70*(Pt. 4), 593–610.
Styron, W. (1992). *Darkness visible: A memoir of madness*. Vintage.
Sullivan, H. S. (1953). *The interpersonal theory of psychiatry*. Norton.
Sullivan, H. S. (1954). *The psychiatric interview*. Norton.
Summers, F. (2003). The future as intrinsic to the psyche and psychoanalytic theory. *Contemporary Psychoanalysis, 39*(1), 135–153. https://doi.org/10.1080/00107530.2003.10747206
Swann, W. B., Jr., Stein-Seroussi, A., & Giesler, R. B. (1992). Why people self-verify. *Journal of Personality and Social Psychology, 62*(3), 392–401. https://doi.org/10.1037/0022-3514.62.3.392
Szkody, E., Stearns, M., Stanhope, L., & McKinney, C. (2021). Stress-buffering role of social support during COVID-19. *Family Process, 60*(3), 1002–1015. https://doi.org/10.1111/famp.12618
Tang, T. C., Jou, S. H., Ko, C. H., Huang, S. Y., & Yen, C. F. (2009). Randomized study of school-based intensive interpersonal psychotherapy for depressed adolescents with suicidal risk and parasuicide behaviors. *Psychiatry and Clinical Neurosciences, 63*(4), 463–470. https://doi.org/10.1111/j.1440-1819.2009.01991.x

Taylor, D. (2015). Treatment manuals and the advancement of psychoanalytic knowledge: The treatment manual of the Tavistock Adult Depression Study. *The International Journal of Psycho-Analysis, 96*(3), 845–875. https://doi.org/10.1111/1745-8315.12360

Taylor, N. L., Su, J., Dick, D. M., & the Spit for Science Working Group. (2022). Depressive symptoms and drinking to cope in relation to alcohol use outcomes among White and Black/African American college students. *Substance Use & Misuse, 57*(5), 708–718. https://doi.org/10.1080/10826084.2022.2034871

Teo, T. (2017). From psychological science to the psychological humanities: Building a general theory of subjectivity. *Review of General Psychology, 21*(4), 281–291. https://doi.org/10.1037/gpr0000132

ter Meulen, W. G., Draisma, S., van Hemert, A. M., Schoevers, R. A., Kupka, R. W., Beekman, A. T. F., & Penninx, B. W. J. H. (2021). Depressive and anxiety disorders in concert: A synthesis of findings on comorbidity in the NESDA study. *Journal of Affective Disorders, 284*, 85–97. https://doi.org/10.1016/j.jad.2021.02.004

Thieberger, J. (1991). The concept of reparation in Melanie Klein's writing. *Melanie Klein & Object Relations, 9*(1), 32–46.

Tibi, L., van Oppen, P., van Balkom, A. J. L. M., Eikelenboom, M., Rickelt, J., Schruers, K. R. J., & Anholt, G. E. (2017). The long-term association of OCD and depression and its moderators: A four-year follow up study in a large clinical sample. *European Psychiatry, 44*, 76–82. https://doi.org/10.1016/j.eurpsy.2017.03.009

Tolin, D. F., Gilliam, C., Wootton, B. M., Bowe, W., Bragdon, L. B., Davis, E., Hannan, S. E., Steinman, S. A., Worden, B., & Hallion, L. S. (2018). Psychometric properties of a structured diagnostic interview for *DSM-5* anxiety, mood, and obsessive-compulsive and related disorders. *Assessment, 25*(1), 3–13. https://doi.org/10.1177/1073191116638410

Treynor, W., Gonzales, R., & Nolen-Hoeksema, S. (2003). Rumination reconsidered: A psychometric analysis. *Cognitive Therapy and Research, 27*(3), 247–259. https://doi.org/10.1023/A:1023910315561

Trull, T. J., & Widiger, T. A. (2013). Dimensional models of personality: The five-factor model and the *DSM-5*. *Dialogues in Clinical Neuroscience, 15*(2), 135–146. https://doi.org/10.31887/DCNS.2013.15.2/ttrull

Tuccitto, D. E., Giacobbi, P. R., Jr., & Leite, W. L. (2010). The internal structure of positive and negative affect: A confirmatory factor analysis of the PANAS. *Educational & Psychological Measurement, 70*(1), 125–141. https://doi.org/10.1177/0013164409344522

Twito-Weingarten, L., & Knafo-Noam, A. (2022). The development of values and their relation to morality. In M. Killen & J. G. Semanta (Eds.), *Handbook of moral development* (pp. 339–356). Routledge. https://doi.org/10.4324/9781003047247-27

Tzelgov, J. (1997). Automatic but conscious: That is how I act most of the time. In R. S. Wyer, Jr. (Ed.), *The automaticity of everyday life* (pp. 217–230). Erlbaum.

Uchino, B. N., Bowen, K., Carlisle, M., & Birmingham, W. (2012). Psychological pathways linking social support to health outcomes: A visit with the "ghosts" of research past, present, and future. *Social Science & Medicine, 74*(7), 949–957. https://doi.org/10.1016/j.socscimed.2011.11.023

Vaillant, G. E. (2011). Involuntary coping mechanisms: A psychodynamic perspective. *Dialogues in Clinical Neuroscience, 13*(3), 366–370. https://doi.org/10.31887/DCNS.2011.13.2/gvaillant

Van Orden, K. A., Lynam, M. E., Hollar, D., & Joiner, T. E., Jr. (2006). Perceived burdensomeness as an indicator of suicidal symptoms. *Cognitive Therapy and Research, 30*(4), 457–467. https://doi.org/10.1007/s10608-006-9057-2

Van Orden, K. A., Witte, T. K., Cukrowicz, K. C., Braithwaite, S. R., Selby, E. A., & Joiner, T. E., Jr. (2010). The interpersonal theory of suicide. *Psychological Review, 117*(2), 575–600. https://doi.org/10.1037/a0018697

Van Orden, K. A., Witte, T. K., Gordon, K. H., Bender, T. W., & Joiner, T. E., Jr. (2008). Suicidal desire and the capability for suicide: Tests of the interpersonal-psychological theory of suicidal behavior among adults. *Journal of Consulting and Clinical Psychology, 76*(1), 72–83. https://doi.org/10.1037/0022-006X.76.1.72

Vandervoort, D. J. (2006). Hostility and health: Mediating effects of belief systems and coping styles. *Current Psychological Research & Reviews, 25*(1), 50–66. https://doi.org/10.1007/s12144-006-1016-2

Viner, R. (1996). Melanie Klein and Anna Freud: The discourse of the early dispute. *Journal of the History of the Behavioral Sciences, 32*(1), 4–15. https://doi.org/10.1002/(SICI)1520-6696(199601)32:1<4::AID-JHBS1>3.0.CO;2-Y

Vitriol, V., Cancino, A., Serrano, C., Ballesteros, S., Ormazábal, M., Leiva-Bianchi, M., Salgado, C., Cáceres, C., Potthoff, S., Orellana, F., & Asenjo, A. (2021). Latent class analysis in depression, including clinical and functional variables: Evidence of a complex depressive subtype in primary care in Chile. *Depression Research and Treatment, 2021*, 6629403. https://doi.org/10.1155/2021/6629403

Wachtel, P. L. (1994). Cyclical processes in personality and psychopathology. *Journal of Abnormal Psychology, 103*(1), 51–54. https://doi.org/10.1037/0021-843X.103.1.51

Wachtel, P. L. (1997). *Psychoanalysis, behavior therapy, and the relational world*. American Psychological Association. https://doi.org/10.1037/10383-000

Wachtel, P. L. (2009). Knowing oneself from the inside out, knowing oneself from the outside in: The "inner" and "outer" worlds and their link through action. *Psychoanalytic Psychology, 26*(2), 158–170. https://doi.org/10.1037/a0015502

Wachtel, P. L. (2014). *Cyclical psychodynamics and the contextual self: The inner world, the intimate world, and the world of culture and society*. Routledge. https://doi.org/10.4324/9781315794037

Wachtel, P. L. (2017). Psychoanalysis and the Moebius Strip: Reexamining the relation between the internal world and the world of daily experiences. *Psychoanalytic Psychology, 34*(1), 58–68. https://doi.org/10.1037/pap0000101

Wakefield, J. C. (2015). DSM-5, psychiatric epidemiology and the false positives problem. *Epidemiology and Psychiatric Sciences, 24*(3), 188–196. https://doi.org/10.1017/S2045796015000116

Wakefield, J. C. (2016). Diagnostic issues and controversies in *DSM-5*: Return of the false positives problem. *Annual Review of Clinical Psychology, 12*(1), 105–132. https://doi.org/10.1146/annurev-clinpsy-032814-112800

Wakefield, J. C., & Schmitz, M. F. (2014). Predictive validation of single-episode uncomplicated depression as a benign subtype of unipolar major depression. *Acta Psychiatrica Scandinavica, 129*(6), 445–457. https://doi.org/10.1111/acps.12184

Walker, J., Holloway, I., & Sofaer, B. (1999). In the system: The lived experience of chronic back pain from the perspectives of those seeking help from pain clinics. *Pain, 80*(3), 621–628. https://doi.org/10.1016/S0304-3959(98)00254-1

Wallis, D., Coatsworth, J. D., Mennis, J., Riggs, N. R., Zaharakis, N., Russell, M. A., Brown, A. R., Rayburn, S., Radford, A., Hale, C., & Mason, M. J. (2022). Predicting self-medication with Cannabis in young adults with hazardous Cannabis use. *International Journal of Environmental Research and Public Health, 19*(3), 1850. https://doi.org/10.3390/ijerph19031850

Watson, D. (2001). Dissociations of the night: Individual differences in sleep-related experiences and their relation to dissociation and schizotypy. *Journal of Abnormal Psychology, 110*(4), 526–535. https://doi.org/10.1037/0021-843X.110.4.526

Watson, D., & Clark, L. A. (1994). *Manuel for the positive and negative affect schedule—Expanded form*. University of Iowa.

Watson, D., Clark, L. A., & Tellegen, A. (1988). Development and validation of brief measures of positive and negative affect: The PANAS scales. *Journal of Personality and Social Psychology, 54*(6), 1063–1070. https://doi.org/10.1037/0022-3514.54.6.1063

Watzlawick, P., Beavin Bavelas, J., & Jackson, D. D. (1967). *Pragmatic of human communication: A study of interactional patterns, pathologies, and paradoxes*. W. W. Norton.

Weinberg, D., Shahar, G., Noyman, G., Davidson, L., McGlashan, T. H., & Fennig, S. (2012). Role of the self in schizophrenia: A multidimensional examination of short-term outcomes. *Psychiatry, 75*(3), 285–297. https://doi.org/10.1521/psyc.2012.75.3.285

Werner, A. M., Tibubos, A. N., Rohrmann, S., & Reiss, N. (2019). The clinical trait self-criticism and its relation to psychopathology: A systematic review—Update. *Journal of Affective Disorders, 246*(1), 530–547. https://doi.org/10.1016/j.jad.2018.12.069

Westen, D. (1991). Social cognition and object relations. *Psychological Bulletin, 109*(3), 429–455. https://doi.org/10.1037/0033-2909.109.3.429

Westen, D. (1995). A clinical-empirical model of personality: Life after the Mischelian ice age and the NEO-lithic era. *Journal of Personality, 63*(3), 495–524. https://doi.org/10.1111/j.1467-6494.1995.tb00504.x

Westen, D. (1996). A model and method for uncovering the nomothethic from the idiographic: An alternative to the five-factor model? *Journal of Research in Personality, 30*(3), 400–413. https://doi.org/10.1006/jrpe.1996.0028

Westen, D. (1998). The scientific legacy of Sigmund Freud: Toward a psychodynamically informed psychological science. *Psychological Bulletin, 124*(3), 333–371. https://doi.org/10.1037/0033-2909.124.3.333

Westen, D., Gabbard, G. O., & Ortigo, K. M. (2008). Psychoanalytic approaches to personality. In J. P. Oliver, R. W. Robins, & L. A. Pervin (Eds.), *Handbook of personality psychology: Theory and research* (3rd ed., pp. 61–113). Guilford Press.

Westen, D., Lohr, N., Silk, K., & Kerber, K. (1985). *Measuring object relations and social cognition using the TAT: Scoring manual.* University of Michigan.

Westen, D., Shedler, J., Bradley, B., & DeFife, J. A. (2012). An empirically derived taxonomy for personality diagnosis: Bridging science and practice in conceptualizing personality. *The American Journal of Psychiatry, 169*(3), 273–284. https://doi.org/10.1176/appi.ajp.2011.11020274

Whelton, W. J., & Greenberg, L. S. (2005). Emotion in self-criticism. *Personality and Individual Differences, 38*(7), 1583–1595. https://doi.org/10.1016/j.paid.2004.09.024

Whiffen, V. E., & Sasseville, T. M. (1991). Dependency, self-criticism, and recollections of parenting: Sex differences and the role of depressive affect. *Journal of Social and Clinical Psychology, 10*(2), 121–133. https://doi.org/10.1521/jscp.1991.10.2.121

Widiger, T. A., Sellbom, M., Chmielewski, M., Clark, L. A., DeYoung, C. G., Kotov, R., Krueger, R. F., Lynam, D. R., Miller, J. D., Mullins-Sweatt, S., Samuel, D. B., South, S. C., Tackett, J. L., Thomas, K. M., Watson, D., & Wright, A. G. C. (2019). Personality in a hierarchical model of psychopathology. *Clinical Psychological Science, 7*(1), 77–92. https://doi.org/10.1177/2167702618797105

Wills, T. A., Resko, J. A., Ainette, M. G., & Mendoza, D. (2004). Role of parent support and peer support in adolescent substance use: A test of mediated effects. *Psychology of Addictive Behaviors, 18*(2), 122–134. https://doi.org/10.1037/0893-164X.18.2.122

Wilson, S., & Olino, T. M. (2021). A developmental perspective on personality and psychopathology across the life span. *Journal of Personality, 89*(5), 915–932. https://doi.org/10.1111/jopy.12623

Winnicott, D. W. (1958). *Through pediatrics to psychoanalysis: Collected papers, 1958.* Basic Books.

Winnicott, D. W. (1960). The theory of the parent-infant relationship. *The International Journal of Psycho-Analysis, 41*, 585–595.

Winnicott, D. W. (1965). Ego distortions in terms of true and false self. In *The maturational process and the facilitating environment* (pp. 140–152). Hogarth.

Winnicott, D. W. (1971). *Playing and reality*. Routledge.
Winnicott, D. W. (1973). *The child, the family, and the outside world*. Penguin.
Wiseman, H., & Barber, J. P. (2004). The core conflictual relationship theme approach to relational narratives: Interpersonal themes in the context of intergenerational communication of trauma. In A. Lieblich, D. P. McAdams, & R. Josselson (Eds.), *Healing plots: The narrative basis of psychotherapy* (pp. 151–170). American Psychological Association. https://doi.org/10.1037/10682-008
Woo, A. K. (2010). Depression and anxiety in pain. *Reviews in Pain, 4*(1), 8–12. https://doi.org/10.1177/204946371000400103
Woody, M. L., & Gibb, B. E. (2015). Integrating NIMH research domain criteria (RDoC) into depression research. *Current Opinion in Psychology, 4*, 6–12. https://doi.org/10.1016/j.copsyc.2015.01.004
World Health Organization. (2012, October 10). *Depression: A global crisis*. https://www.wfmh.org/2012DOCS/WMHDay%202012%20SMALL%20FILE%20FINAL.pdf
World Health Organization. (2018). *International classification of diseases* (11th ed.). https://icd.who.int
Wright, A. G. C., Pincus, A. L., & Hopwood, C. J. (2023). Contemporary integrative interpersonal theory: Integrating structure, dynamics, temporal scale, and levels of analysis. *Journal of Psychopathology and Clinical Science, 132*(3), 263–276. https://doi.org/10.1037/abn0000741
Yalom, I. D. (1980). *Existential psychotherapy*. Basic Books.
Young, G. (2022). *Causality and neu-stages of development: Toward a unified psychology*. Springe Nature. https://doi.org/10.1007/978-3-030-82540-9
Zahra, S. T., Saleem, S., & Khurshid, H. (2021). Mediation analysis of social deficits between self-criticism and aggression in adolescents. *Clinical Child Psychology and Psychiatry, 26*(3), 870–881. https://doi.org/10.1177/13591045211005823
Zeiss, A. M., & Lewinsohn, P. M. (1988). Enduring deficits after remissions of depression: A test of the scar hypothesis. *Behaviour Research and Therapy, 26*(2), 151–158. https://doi.org/10.1016/0005-7967(88)90114-3
Zetsche, U., Bürkner, P. C., & Schulze, L. (2018). Shedding light on the association between repetitive negative thinking and deficits in cognitive control: A meta-analysis. *Clinical Psychology Review, 63*, 56–65. https://doi.org/10.1016/j.cpr.2018.06.001
Zetzel, E. R. (1970). *The capacity for emotional growth*. International Universities Press.
Zigmond, A. S., & Snaith, R. P. (1983). The hospital anxiety and depression scale. *Acta Psychiatrica Scandinavica, 67*(6), 361–370. https://doi.org/10.1111/j.1600-0447.1983.tb09716.x
Zonder, M. (2006). *Sayeret Matkal: The elite unit of Israel*. Keter.
Zuroff, D. C. (1992). New directions for cognitive models of depression. *Psychological Inquiry, 3*(3), 274–277. https://doi.org/10.1207/s15327965pli0303_19

Zuroff, D. C., & Mongrain, M. (1987). Dependency and self-criticism: Vulnerability factors for depressive affective states. *Journal of Abnormal Psychology*, *96*(1), 14–22. https://doi.org/10.1037/0021-843X.96.1.14

Zuroff, D. C., Mongrain, M., & Santor, D. A. (2004a). Conceptualizing and measuring personality vulnerability to depression: Comment on Coyne and Whiffen (1995). *Psychological Bulletin*, *130*(3), 489–511. https://doi.org/10.1037/0033-2909.130.3.489

Zuroff, D. C., Mongrain, M., & Santor, D. A. (2004b). Investing in the Personality Vulnerability Research Program—Current dividends and future growth: Rejoinder to Coyne, Thompson, and Whiffen (2004). *Psychological Bulletin*, *130*(3), 518–522. https://doi.org/10.1037/0033-2909.130.3.518

Index

A

ACRIM (axis of social criticism), 164
Action (ecodynamic pattern), 93, 101–102, 164, 177
Action, interpersonal, 79
Action/transactional theories, 40
Active vulnerability model, 37, 40, 51
Adaptive interpersonal schemas and scripts, 159
Adaptive positions, 159
Adaptive projective identification, 159
Adaptive structures, 159
Adelphi University, 168
Adjustment disorder, 17–18
Adorno, T. W., 95
Affect
  criticism-based, 100, 125, 133, 142–143
  object relations theory and, 75–76
  regulation, 69, 76–77, 88, 125, 133, 143
Affective spectrum, 87–88
Affective tone, 143
Affleck, Ben, 119
Agency, human, 46
Agents in relations (AIR), 78
Agitation, 131
Agreeableness, 41
Alexander, F., 159
Ali, Z., 123
Alteration of reformulated depressive position, 166–171
American Psychological Association. *See* APA
Amotivation, 16, 29
Anaclitic/dependent constellation, 48
Anderson, S. F., 16
Anhedonia, 16, 29

Antidepressant medications, 168
Anxiety, 108
  comorbid, 27
  disorders, 51
  as position, 61–62
Anxiety and depressive disorder, mixed, 17–18
APA (American Psychological Association), 13, 17–20, 23, 32, 36–37
Appetite, 16
Assessment, 137–149
  case formulation, 149
  future directions for practice, 178–179
  of reformulated depressive position, 142–149
  of symptoms and complexity of depression, 138–142
Attachment theory, 46, 47
Atypical features, of complex unipolar depression, 23
Auerbach, John, 159
Authenticity, downregulation of, 76, 88, 143, 144
Autonomous constellation, 48
Autonomous motivation, 77, 144
Avolition, 16
Awareness, 68–69
Awareness, existential, 160
Axis of social criticism (ACRIM), 164

B

BAI (Beck Anxiety Inventory), 140
BALES (Brief Adolescent Life Event Scale), 147

Balint, Michael, 55, 68
Bandura, Albert, 34, 46
Barber, Jacques, 168
BDI-II (Beck Depression Inventory–II), 138, 140
Beck, A. T., 14, 47–48, 67
Beck Anxiety Inventory (BAI), 140
Beck Depression Inventory–II (BDI-II), 138, 140
Behavioral activation, 160
Behavioral inhibition/activation syndrome (BIS/BAS), 42, 44
Belongingness, thwarted, 124–125
Ben Gurion University of the Negev, 53
Big Five personality traits, 41–42
Bipolar spectrum disorders, 51, 131, 140
BIS/BAS (behavioral inhibition/activation syndrome), 42, 44
Blatt, Sidney
 on adaptive structures, 151, 159, 161, 171
 and A. T. Beck, 47–48
 influence on Shahar, 5–6, 13–14, 34, 50n1
 Object Relations Inventory, 144
Borg, M. B., 162
Bowen, Murray, 163
Bowen family theory, 163
Bowlby, John, 55
Brain areas, 69
Brief Adolescent Life Event Scale (BALES), 145, 147
Brief Symptom Inventory (BSI), 140
Bromberg, Phillip, 166
Bronfenbrenner, Urie, 86, 96, 108, 162
BSI (Brief Symptom Inventory), 140
Burdensomeness, perceived, 124–125

C

Cardiovascular disease, 30
Caregiving mentality, 48
Catatonia, 24
CBASP (cognitive behavioral analysis system of psychotherapy), 167
Center for Epidemiologic Studies Depression Scale (CES-D), 138, 140
Chronicity, 141
Chronic MDD, 18–19, 26
Chronosystems, 87
Chu, C., 25
Cloninger, C. R., 42

Cognition, negative, 16
Cognitive behavioral analysis system of psychotherapy (CBASP), 167
Cognitive cluster, 16
Cognitive-evolutionary model, 48
Cohesion, of networks, 177
Collision (ecodynamic pattern), 93, 95
Community character, 162
Comorbidities, depressive, 27–29
Comorbidity (type C), 29, 106, 112–114, 141–142
Comprehensive Scale of Stress Assessment, 147
Compulsive purposefulness, 77
Conduct disorders, comorbid, 27
Congruency hypothesis, 49
Conscientiousness, 41
Constructs, in RDOC, 33
Contempt, 133
Corrective emotional experiences, 120
Counteracting deficiency, 76, 120
COVID-19 pandemic, 3, 14–15
 and dyadic relationships, 86
 and ecodynamics, 84
 and higher-order social systems, 92
 and object relations theory, 79–80
Coyne, James C., 14, 34, 37–39, 81–82
Critical expressed emotion, 164
Criticism, theme of, 7
Criticism-based affect, 143
Cults, 134–135
Curiosity, 41, 81, 171, 195
Cyclical psychodynamics, 54

D

Damon, Matt, 119
Davidson, Larry, 158
DCS (Depression Complexity Scale), 138, 141–142, 149, 176, 178
Defense mechanisms, 62–64, 101
Deficiency, counteraction of, 143
Demoralization, 27, 115, 158. *See also* Remoralization
Density, of networks, 177
Dependency/sociotropy, 49
Dependent interpersonal stress, 107
Depression. *See also* Depression, suicidal; Depression complications
 avoidance of, 144
 brief recurrent, 26
 chronic, 26–27

comorbidities of, 27–29, 31
double, 26
as epiphenomenon, 28
forensic, 31
gradations of complexity of, 175–176
manifestations of, 23–24, 141
in men, 24–25, 107–108
prevalence of, 14
research, future directions in, 175–181
role of self-criticism in, 48–52, 73, 75, 77
secondary, 28–29
sequelae of, 29–31
subsyndromal, 17, 19, 21
treatment-resistant, 27
uncomplicated, 22
unipolar, 15–18, 22–24
Depression, suicidal, 25–26, 123–135
  interpersonal-psychological theory of suicide, 124–127
  Zvika's complex depression, 131–135
  Zvika's suicide, 127–131
Depression Complexity Scale (DCS), 138, 141–142, 149, 176, 178
Depression complications, 13–34
  features of, 22–31
  mechanisms of, 31–34
  unipolar depression, manifestations of, 15–21
Depressive and anxiety disorder, mixed, 17–18
Depressive anxiety, 62
Depressive Experiences Questionnaire (DEQ), 37, 49n1, 53
Depressive personality disorder, 17, 19
Depressive positions, 65–66, 71–72, 176–177. *See also* Reformulated depressive position
Depue, R. A., 34
DEQ (Depressive Experiences Questionnaire), 37, 49n1, 53
Detachment (ecodynamic pattern), 93, 96
Determinism, reciprocal, 34
Diagnostic and Statistical Manual of Mental Disorders, Fifth Edition, Text Revision (DSM-5-TR; APA), 17–20, 23
Diagnostic Interview for DSM-5 Anxiety, Mood, and Obsessive-Compulsive and Related Disorders (DIAMOND), 139–140
Diagnostic Interview Schedule, 139
Diffusion of toxic patient-context exchanges, 162–166

Displacement, 62–63
Dissociative disorders, comorbid, 27
Domains, in RDOC, 33
Domestic violence, 15
Double depression, 26
Downey, G., 82
Downregulation of authenticity, 76, 88, 143
Dread of recurrence, 18–19
Drinking to cope, 29
DSM-5-TR (*Diagnostic and Statistical Manual of Mental Disorders, Fifth Edition, Text Revision;* APA), 17–20, 23, 32, 36–37
Dual/rival vulnerability model, 37, 39–40, 51
Dunbar, R., 34
Dunkley, David, 50
Durkheim, Émile, 125
Dynamic interpersonal psychotherapy, 167
Dysthymic disorder, 17–18, 26

E

Eagle, M. N., 68
Eating disorders, comorbid, 27
Ecodynamics and ecodynamic analysis, 7, 81–121
  and chronicity, 106–107
  and chronic physical pain, 114–118
  and comorbidity (type C), 106, 112–114
  and heterogeneity, 106–112
  and interpersonal relationships, 84–86
  key variables in depression, 82–84
  parent-child dyad examples, 89–91
  patterns complicating depression, 101–105
  and personality and social ecology, 92–96
  and self-criticism, 101–102, 174
  and suicidality, 106, 121. *See also* depression, suicidal
  and systems, 86–89
  and youth violence, 118–121
  of Zvika's depression, 131–135
Ecodynamics Questionnaire (EDQ), 138, 147–149, 177, 178
El-Mallakh, R. S., 123
Emerging Risk Factors Collaboration, 30
Emotional cluster, 15–16
Emotional instability. *See* Neuroticism
Emotions, nuanced, 67–68

Entebbe, Uganda, 109
Enthusiasm, 171
Erickson, Milton, 159
Erikson, E. H., 47
Erosion (Shahar), 6, 53–54, 87, 107, 174, 180
Exciting object, 78, 134
Exclusion (ecodynamic pattern), 93, 95
Existential awareness, 160
Exosystems, 87
Experimental avoidance, 77
Explicating the future, 161
Externalization, 79
Extraction (ecodynamic pattern), 93, 94, 104, 111, 134, 165, 177
Extroversion, 41

F

Fairbairn, Ronald, 55, 78, 134
Farmer, Ann, 44
Father hunger, 134
Fear extinction, 29
Ferenczi, S., 68
Fighting for the future, 161
Five-factor personality models (FFPM), 41–44
Fonagy, Peter, 47, 168
Forensic outcomes, 31
Forms of Self-Criticizing/Attacking and Self-Reassuring Scale (FSCRS), 53
Fourth Way (philosophy), 129–130
The Fourth Way (book), 130
Frank, Jerome D., 27
Frankl, Victor, 160
French, T. M., 159
Freud, Anna, 61–64
Freud, Sigmund, 61–64
FSCRS (Forms of Self-Criticizing/Attacking and Self-Reassuring Scale), 53
Future, work with, 160–162
"The Future as Intrinsic to the Psyche and Psychoanalytic Theory" (Summers), 70
Future self, 69

G

Gadassi, Avner, 107, 109
Gaza, 53
Genetic polymorphisms, 178
Gilbert, Paul, 47, 48

Going-on-being, 76
Good Will Hunting (film), 119–120
Granger, S., 144
Grey's Anatomy (TV series), 103
Guntrip, Harry, 55, 68
Gurdjieff, George, 129

H

Hamilton Rating Scale for Depression (HRSD), 139
Hammen, Constance, 13–14, 34, 107, 147
Harshfield, E. L., 30
Hated-Self subscale, of FSCRS, 53
Health problems, 29–31, 106, 114–118, 141–142
Heidegger, Martin, 158–160
Henrich, Chris, 40, 52
Hermeneutics of suspicion, 68
Heroic self-representations, 108
Hierarchical taxonomy of psychopathology (HiTOP), 42
Higher-order social systems, 86, 91–92
Hippocrates, 35
HiTOP (hierarchical taxonomy of psychopathology), 42
Hobfoil, Steven, 84–85
Homophily, of networks, 177
Hope, 77
Horney, Karen, 77, 167
Horowitz, M. J., 67
Hostility, chronic, 121
The House of God (Shem), 103
HRSD (Hamilton Rating Scale for Depression), 139
Humor, 171
Hypnotherapy, 181

I

ICD-11 (*International Classification of Diseases, 11th Revision;* WHO), 17–20, 32, 37
Identity theory, 46–47
IDF (Israeli defense forces), 108–109, 114
Immersion (ecodynamic pattern), 93, 94, 102–104, 111, 164, 177
Infatuation (ecodynamic pattern), 93, 95
Inflammation, multisystemic, 121
Instruments. *See* Measurement instruments

Intellectualization, 77
International Classification of Diseases, 11th Revision (*ICD-11;* WHO), 17–20, 32, 37
Interpersonal actions, 79
Interpersonal-psychological theory of suicide (IPTS), 124–127
Interpersonal psychotherapy (IPT), 166–168
Interpersonal relationships, 84–86
Interpretation of defense, 169
Intersubjectivity, 46
Interventions, in-the-world, 160
Introjective Depression, 187
Introjective/self-critical constellation, 48
Inventories. *See* Measurement instruments
IPT (interpersonal psychotherapy), 166–168
IPTS (interpersonal-psychological theory of suicide), 124–127
Isolation, 63, 144
Israel, 53

J

JAMA, 30
Jewish-Israeli culture, 108–112
Johns Hopkins School of Medicine, 115
Joiner, Thomas
   on acquired capacity, 127, 127n1
   on acute suicidal risk, 126
   on burdensomeness, 25
   on evidence-based assessment of depression, 137
   influence on Shahar, 5, 14, 34
   on IPTS, 124
   review in *Psychological Assessment*, 139–140
Joseph, Betty, 159

K

Kernberg, Otto, 47, 67
Ketamine, 16
Kierkegaard, Søren, 160
Klein, Melanie. *See also* Object relations theory
   on depressive positions, 71–72, 176–177
   on manic defenses, 120
   on projective identification, 158–159
Klerman, G. L., 34

Knafo-Noam, A., 108
Kohut, H., 68

L

Lahey, B. B., 44
Latent class analysis, 32
Legal problems, 31, 106, 118–121
Lerman, Sheera, 115
Lewinsohn, P. M., 41
Lewontin, R., 34
Libidinal ego, 78
LIFE (Longitudinal Interval Follow-Up Evaluation), 139–140
Life events, positive, 84
Loewald, H. W., 70
Longitudinal Interval Follow-Up Evaluation (LIFE), 139–140
Luborsky, Lester, 168

M

Macrosystems, 87, 108
Major depressive disorder (MDD), 18–19, 22, 26
Maladaptive personality traits model, 42
Manic defenses, 76, 120
Manifestations of depression, 141
McAdams, Dan, 43, 46–47
McCullough, James P., 168
MDD (Major depressive disorder), 18–19, 22, 26
Measurement instruments
   Beck Anxiety Inventory (BAI), 140
   Beck Depression Inventory–II (BDI-II), 138, 140
   Brief Adolescent Life Event Scale (BALES), 145, 147
   Brief Symptom Inventory (BSI), 140
   Center for Epidemiologic Studies Depression Scale (CES-D), 138, 140
   Comprehensive Scale of Stress Assessment, 147
   Depression Complexity Scale (DCS), 138, 141–142, 149, 176, 178
   Depressive Experiences Questionnaire (DEQ), 37, 49n1, 53
   Diagnostic Interview for DSM-5 Anxiety, Mood, and Obsessive-Compulsive and Related Disorders (DIAMOND), 139–140
   Diagnostic Interview Schedule, 139

Ecodynamics Questionnaire (EDQ), 138, 147–149, 177, 178
Forms of Self-Criticizing/Attacking and Self-Reassuring Scale (FSCRS), 53
Hamilton Rating Scale for Depression (HRSD), 139
Hated-Self subscale, of FSCRS, 53
Longitudinal Interval Follow-Up Evaluation (LIFE), 139–140
Mini International Neuropsychiatric Interview (MINI), 139–140
Object Relations Inventory (ORI), 144
Personality Inventory *(DSM-5-TR),* 42
Personal Style Inventory (PSI), 49n1
Positive Affect Negative Affect Scale (PANAS), 143
Q-sort, 179
Reformulated Depressive Position Inventory (ReDPI), 138, 145–146, 149, 178
Schedule for Affective Disorders and Schizophrenia (SADS), 139
Seasonal Pattern Assessment Questionnaire, 140
Self-Inadequacy Subscale, of FSCRS, 53
Shedler-Westen Assessment Procedure (SWAP-200), 179
Social Cognition and Object Relations Scale (SCORS), 144
Structured Clinical Interview for the DSM (SCID), 139–140
Tavistock Adult Depression Study (TADS), 168–169
Thematic Appercention Test (TAT), 143
UCLA Life Stress Interview, 53, 147
Mediation, 166
Medications, antidepressant, 168
Melancholic features, of complex depression, 23
Men, depression in, 24–25, 107–108
"Men Cry at Night" (Gadassi), 107
Menninger, Karl A., 123
Mentalistic fallacy, 81
Mesosystems, 87
Microsystems, 87
Mini International Neuropsychiatric Interview (MINI), 139–140
Minuchin, Salvador, 163
Mischel, W., 46, 67
Mitchell, S. A., 60
Mixed depressive and anxiety disorder, 17–18
Mixed features, of complex depression, 24
Mnegic neglect effect, 68
Monroe, S. M., 16, 34
Mood, 16
Moos, Rudolf, 147
Motivational cluster, 16

N

National Institute for Health and Care Excellence (NICE), 30
National Institute of Mental Health (NIMH), 32–33
Netanyahu, Ben-Zion, 109
Netanyahu, Binyamin, 109
Netanyahu, Cela, 109
Netanyahu, Yonatan, 109–112
Network analysis of RORT, 176–177
Neurobiology, 178
Neurotic defenses, 64
Neuroticism, 41, 44–45, 50
"Neuroticism" (Ormel, Rosemalen and Farmer), 44
NICE (National Institute for Health and Care Excellence), 30
NIMH (National Institute of Mental Health), 32–33
Nonchronic MDD, 18–19, 22, 26
Noyce, R., 51

O

Object Relations Inventory (ORI), 144
Object relations theory. *See also* Reformulated object relations theory
and affect, 75–76
and affect regulation, 76–77
COVID-19 example, 79–80
and interpersonal actions, 79
new definitions on Klein's positions, 71–72
overview of, 60–66
perspective on, 66–67
reformulated depressive position, 72–75
and schemas and scripts, 77–78
and the time axis, 78–79
Objects, good, 159
OCEAN acronym, 41–42
O'Connor, R. C., 51
Openness, 41
Operation Thunderbolt, 109

Oppression (ecodynamic pattern), 93, 95–96
Organismic valuing, 87
Organizational dynamics, Tavistock model of, 162–163
ORI (Object Relations Inventory), 144
Ormel, Johan, 44–45, 50
Ouspensky, Paul, 129
Overlap model, 36–39

P

Paiget, Jean, 144
Pain (journal), 117
PANAS (Positive Affect Negative Affect Scale), 143
Paranoid-schizoid anxiety, 62
Paranoid-schizoid position, 65–66
Parental representations, 133–134
Parent-child dyads, 89–91
Part-object relations, 65
Passive vulnerability model, 37, 39–40
Peer supervision, 179–180
Perceived social support, 83–85, 112–113
Perfectionism, 50n1
Personality, 6–7, 35–55
 active vulnerability model of, 40
 critiques of trait models of, 43–45
 disorder clusters, 42
 overlap model of, 36–39
 passive vulnerability model of, 39–40
 pioneering theories of, 47–51
 scarring model of, 41, 52–55
 and self-criticism, 52–55
 subjective-agentic models of, 45–47
 as term, 34
 trait models of, 41–42
Personality Inventory *(DSM-5-TR)*, 42
Personal Style Inventory (PSI), 49n1
Person–environment fit, 95
Physical pain, chronic, 30
Physical/vegetative cluster, 16
Physicians, 103–104
Playing with the future, 161
Poetics, 137
Positions
 anxiety, 61–62
 defense mechanisms, 62–64
 object relations, 65
 pros and cons of, 66–67
Positive Affect Negative Affect Scale (PANAS), 143

Positive life events, 84, 113
Post, R. M., 13
Posttraumatic syndrome disorder (PTSD), 29
Prefrontal cortex, 69
Projected self, 69–71
Projection, 63
Projective identification, 64, 158–159
Prospection, 69
PSI (Personal Style Inventory), 49n1
Psychedelic-assisted psychotherapy, 181
Psychoanalytic object relations theory, 46
Psychodynamic social work theory, 162
Psychoeducation, 154–157
Psychological Assessment (journal), 139
Psychomotor retardation, 16
Psychotherapy, 151–171
 alteration of reformulated depressive position, 166–171
 diffusion of toxic patient-context exchanges, 162–166
 future directions for practice, 179–181
 psychoeducation provision in, 154–157
 remoralization, 158–162
 treating a suicidal patient, 152–154
Psychotherapy, interpersonal (IPT), 166–168
Psychotic features, 24
PTSD (posttraumatic syndrome disorder), 29
Purposefulness, compulsive, 143, 144

Q

Q-sort, 179
Questionnaires. *See* Measurement instruments

R

Rand, Ayn, 67
Rapaport, 143
Rationalization, 77, 144
RDOC (Research Domain Criteria; NIMH), 32–33, 37
Reaction formation, 63
Received social support, 83–85
Recurrence of depression, dread of, 18–19
ReDPI (Reformulated Depressive Position Inventory), 138, 145–146, 149
Reflection, 169

Reformulated depressive position, 72–80
  alteration of, 169–171
  circumvention of, 171
  and IPTS, 125–127
Reformulated Depressive Position Inventory (ReDPI), 138, 145–146, 149, 178
Reformulated object relations theory (RORT), 5–8, 73, 176–177
Relationship features, 91
Relationships, interpersonal, 84–86
Remoralization, 158–162. *See also* Demoralization
Representations of self and others, 143–144
Repression, 62
Repressive line, 68
Research Domain Criteria (RDOC; NIMH), 32–33, 37
Ricoeur, P., 68
Rival vulnerability. *See* Dual/rival vulnerability model
Robins, Clive, 49n1
Rogers, Carl, 100–101
Role responsiveness, 79
RORT (reformulated object relations theory), 5–8, 73
Rosemalen, Judith, 44
Rudich, Zvia, 115, 117

S

SADS (Schedule for Affective Disorders and Schizophrenia), 139
Sandler, J., 79
SAPS (subjective-agentic personality sector), 6–7, 36
Sartre, Jean-Paul, 160
Sayeret Matkal, 111
Scales. *See* Measurement instruments
Scarring, 37, 41, 51–54, 73
Schafer, R., 70
Schedule for Affective Disorders and Schizophrenia (SADS), 139
Schemas, 77–78, 88
Schematics, 137
Schiller, Moran, 13–14, 52, 160
Schmitz, M. F., 31–32, 100
SCID (Structured Clinical Interview for the DSM), 139–140
SCORS (Social Cognition and Object Relations Scale), 144
Scripts, 77–78, 88

Sean Maguire (fictional character), 119–120
Seasonal Pattern Assessment Questionnaire, 140
Self, mental representations of, 125
Self-concept, 45–47
Self-critical cascade, 54–55
Self-criticism
  in chronic pain, 115–116
  and ecodynamics, 101–102, 174
  and models of personality, 36–40
  and perfectionism, 50n1
  role in depression, 48–52, 73, 75, 77
  and scarring, 52–54
  and youth violence, 118–119
Self-efficacy, 29
Self-focused attention, 178
Self-Inadequacy Subscale, of FSCRS, 53
Self-injury, lethal, capacity for, 125
Self-medication, 29
Semistructured interviews, 138–139, 147
Shahar, Golan. *See also* Erosion
  on chronic pain, 115
  on representations of the future, 160
  on scarring, 52–54
Shame, 133
Shedler-Westen Assessment Procedure (SWAP-200), 179
Shoda, Y., 67
Sleep, 16
SNA (social network analysis), 177
Social Climate Scales, 147
Social Cognition and Object Relations Scale (SCORS), 144
Social-cognitive theory, 46, 47
Social contexts, patients', 165
Social-environmental factors, 39
Social-learning theory, 46
Social mentalities, 48
Social network analysis (SNA), 177
Social-rank mentality, 48
Social support, 82–84
"Social Support: The Movie" (Hobfoil), 84–85
Society for the Exploration of Psychotherapy Integration, 9
Sociotropy, 49
Soffer-Dudek, N., 38
Somatic disorders, 51
Somatic disorders, comorbid, 27
Soroka University Hospital, 115
Splitting, 63–64
Stolorow, R. D., 68

Strenger, C., 68
Stress, 82–84
Stress-diathesis model, 37, 39, 49
Stressful life events, 113
Stress/trauma-related disorders, comorbid, 27
Structural family therapy, 163
Structured Clinical Interview for the DSM (SCID), 139–140
Subjective-agentic models, 45–47
Subjective-agentic personality sector (SAPS), 6–7, 36
Subjectivity, 46
Substance use, 29, 51
Suicidality, 16, 25–26, 141–142
Suicidal patients, treating, 152–154
Suicide
    interpersonal-psychological theory of, 124–127
    risk assessment, 5
Sullivan, Harry Stack, 69, 78, 167
Summers, F., 70, 78
Svrakic, D. M., 42
SWAP-200 (Shedler-Westen Assessment Procedure), 179
Symptom measures, 138

T

TAT (Thematic Apperception Test), 143
Tavistock Adult Depression Study (TADS), 168–169
Tavistock model of organizational dynamics, 162–163
Taxometrics, 176
TCM (temperament and character model), 42, 44
Tension, 16
Thematic Apperception Test (TAT), 143
This Is Going to Hurt (Kay), 103
Time axis, 125, 134
Toxic patient-context exchanges, 162–166
Trait models, 41–45
Transference, negative, 27
True self, 171
Twito-Weingarten, L., 108
Tzabar, 108–110

U

UCLA, 13
UCLA Life Stress Interview, 53, 147

Unipolar depression, 15–18, 22–24
Units of analysis, in RDOC, 33
University of Pennsylvania in Philadelphia, 168

V

Van Orden, K. A., 25
Van Sant, Gus, 119
Vardimon, Ofek, 31
Vicious cycles, 88
Virtual reality techniques, 181
Vitriol, V., 32, 100

W

Wachtel, Paul, 34, 54, 79, 100, 105
Wakefield, J. C., 31–32, 100
Walker, J., 117
Watson, D., 38
Weissman, M. M., 34
Westen, Drew, 35, 47, 144
Whiffen, V. E., 37–39
WHO (World Health Organization), 14, 17–20
Widiger, T. A., 42
Will Hunting (fictional character), 119–120
Williams, Robin, 119
Winnicott, Donald, 55, 65, 68, 171
Working with immersion, 164
World Health Organization (WHO), 14, 17–20
World Mental Health Survey, 14

Y

Yale University, 5, 13
Yalom, Irvin D., 160
Yom Kippur War, 129
Young, G., 143
Youth violence, 118–121

Z

Zetzel, Elizabeth, 99, 100
Zuroff, David, 14, 38, 39, 50
Zvika (stepfather), 4–5
    ecodynamics of, 134–135
    psychopathology of, 131–132
    reformulated depressive position of, 132–134
    suicide of, 127–131

About the Author

Golan Shahar, PhD, serves as a professor of clinical-health psychology and the Zlotowski Chair of Neuropsychology at Ben-Gurion University of the Negev (BGU), where he is also head of the Stress, Self & Health (STREALTH) research laboratory. Dr. Shahar also serves as an adjunct professor of public health at BGU and as an adjunct professor of child study and adult psychiatry at Yale University School of Medicine.

Dr. Shahar received a bachelor of arts in behavioral sciences in 1993, a master of arts in clinical psychology in 1997, and a PhD in psychology in 1999 from BGU. He completed postdoctoral training in psychopathology research at the Departments of Psychology and Psychiatry at Yale University. Before Dr. Shahar returned to his alma mater, he served on the faculties of Bar-Ilan University (1999–2000) and Yale University (2002–2004).

Dr. Shahar's research focuses on the links between stress, depression and suicidality, and psychosomatics. His research program has been funded by highly competitive and prestigious research funds in Israel and the United States and has yielded more than 200 publications appearing in top venues in psychology, psychiatry, and pediatrics. His first scientific book, *Erosion: The Psychopathology of Self-Criticism*, was published in 2015 by Oxford University Press. In addition to his empirical research, Prof. Shahar is internationally known as a leading clinical theorist and practitioner, advancing an integrative framework for assessment and psychotherapy in complex psychopathological and psychosomatic conditions.